Citizenship and Conscience

Citizenship and Conscience

A STUDY IN THE THEORY AND PRACTICE
OF RELIGIOUS TOLERATION IN ENGLAND
DURING THE EIGHTEENTH CENTURY

By *Richard Burgess Barlow*

PHILADELPHIA · UNIVERSITY OF PENNSYLVANIA PRESS

© 1962 by the Trustees of the University of Pennsylvania

Published in Great Britain, India, and Pakistan
by the Oxford University Press
London, Bombay, and Karachi

Library of Congress Catalogue Card Number : 62–7197

7395
Printed in the United States of America

FOR

Helen Burgess

AND

James Arthur Barlow

Preface

CAREFUL STUDENTS of the seventeenth century have asserted that by the time Charles II was "restored" to the throne of England the majority of his subjects, whom Professor W. K. Jordan has described as "the centre of gravity of public opinion," had embraced the cause of religious toleration. Professor Jordan has in fact declared that "the case for religious toleration had been won by 1660; there remained only the difficult process of accommodating institutions to the fact of historical change."[1] Professor Gerald Cragg has also defended the same thesis, arguing that by the time of Charles' return, toleration had been "discussed from every possible angle and experience had proved its need."[2] If this is true, one may perhaps not unreasonably wonder how it came to pass that toleration tarried until 1689, that the limited and partial indulgence granted by the "Toleration Act" was not secure for another quarter of a century, that all nonconformity continued to be pronounced a crime in the laws of England until the case of *Harrison* v. *Evans* in 1767, and that even this decision by the Lord Chief Justice continued to be ignored by local magistrates for many years to come.

The attempt to explain these and other problems has led me not only to examine in detail some aspects of what Professor Jordan allowed to be "the difficult process of accommodating institutions to the fact of historical change," but also to investi-

---

[1] W. K. Jordan, *Religious Toleration in England from the Reformation to the Restoration* (London, 1940), IV, 469.
[2] G. R. Cragg, *From Puritanism to the Age of Reason* (Cambridge, 1950), p. 190.

gate matters of opinion. As a result it seems clear that by 1660 the theoretical as well as the constitutional position on toleration was by no means settled. Although it is quite true, as Thomas Lyon has argued in his *Theory of Religious Liberty in England, 1603–1639,* that even by this early period "a belief in toleration was coming to be held by many respectable men as the best solution to the problem of the relationship between Church and State,"[3] and that Locke's *Letters* on the subject— most of the ideas for which were formulated during the early sixteen-sixties—contained the embryo of all subsequent theorizing, these elements were hardly conclusive. Locke's precepts were never sufficiently definitive to prevent both Churchmen and Dissenters from continuing to draw basically different conclusions from his premises throughout the century. Indeed, by the seventeen-eighties the idea of toleration had clearly outgrown the restrictions placed upon it by "the Great Philosopher," although the statute book had not nearly caught up to him by the end of the century.

In pursuit of such inquiries I have found the MS *Minute Books* of both the Protestant Dissenting Deputies and their parent organization, the General Body of Ministers of the Three Denominations in and about the Cities of London and Westminster, an accurate barometer of the changing attitudes of these two most politically conscious nonconformist groups toward the practical functioning of religious toleration in eighteenth-century England. These records nevertheless pale in significance before an extensive selection of pamphlets gleaned from the vast collections in Dr. Williams's Library, London; for from them alone can one begin to appreciate in contemporary terms the various opinions expressed on all sides of the

---

[3] T. Lyon, *The Theory of Religious Liberty in England, 1603–1639* (Cambridge, 1937), p. 146.

toleration issue, not only with relationship to matters of theoretical controversy, but also such very concrete elements as the registration of meeting houses and the legal validity of an occasional conformist's claim to hold office in a municipal corporation. Some of these pamphlets have been used by denominational historians who have made reference to the issue of toleration so far as it involved their own religious groups, but no one has yet tried to form a representative classification of this literature and draw upon it to attempt a picture of non-conformists in general as they were both theoretically and practically affected by problems of religious toleration during the entire century. The one work which comes nearest to answering these specifications is Anthony Lincoln's excellent prize essay, *Some Political and Social Ideas of English Dissent, 1763–1800,* from which I have not only derived the title of my fifth chapter, but whose ideas I have found to be more fully confirmed in the pamphlet literature than those in any other secondary work dealing with the period. I am also under obligation to Dr. N. C. Hunt for permitting me to consult his unpublished Ph.D. thesis in the Cambridge University Library, entitled *Some Religious and Economic Organisations and the Government, 1730–1742.*[4]

The divisions of such a subject must at best be somewhat arbitrary and the seven chapter headings which I have chosen, though rather loose chronologically, seemed most closely related to the pamphlet literature. Since there is a clear break in Dissenting activity between the disbanding of the Dodson Committee in 1796 and the nineteenth-century battle for re-

---
[4] Since this preface was originally written, Dr. Hunt has published an expanded and excellently documented version of the first part of his thesis dealing with the Quakers and the Protestant Dissenting Deputies and their relations with the government down to 1742. The book is entitled *Two Early Political Associations* (London, 1961).

peal, I have not dealt with the familiar story of how the Deputies and their Standing Committee were rejuvinated during the eighteen-twenties and pressed repeal of the Corporation and Test Acts through to victory. These matters have been too thoroughly treated in B. L. Manning's *Protestant Dissenting Deputies* and R. W. Cowherd's *Politics of English Dissent* to need repeating here.

Both in the compilation of my bibliography and in the effort to interpret its contents the help of Miss Gwendoline Woodward of Dr. Williams's Library has been invaluable. To the late Norman Sykes, Dean of Winchester, who as Dixie Professor of Ecclesiastical History in the University of Cambridge, supervised my research on this topic, I am also profoundly indebted. Professors Holden Furber and Crane Brinton have provided considerable encouragement and practical help, and I have profited much from conversations with Dr. G. S. R. Kitson Clark, whose lectures first roused my interest in the subject. That the final product of my research is not more worthy of their kind assistance is entirely my own fault.

R. B. B.

Cambridge, Massachusetts
April 7, 1961

Contents

	Preface	7
I	Toleration and the Rights of Conscience	15
II	The First Attempt at Repeal	57
III	The Quiet Years, 1740–1760	98
IV	Anti-Subscription and the Revival of Dissenting Activity	132
V	The Appeal to Candour	171
VI	The Appeal to Human Rights	221
VII	The Principles of Pitt Triumphant	272
	Bibliography	300
	Acknowledgments	340
	Index	341

*Citizenship
and
Conscience*

CHAPTER I

Toleration and the Rights of Conscience

IT HAS BEEN SAID that only where real toleration exists can politics be non-theological, and *vice versa* only where the idea of theocracy is abandoned can there be real toleration.[1] In other words, while religion and politics are intermingled, the civil magistrate is justified in imposing an established church upon all of his subjects. When the territorial coincidence of Church and State is disrupted and numerous sects appear, the one element essential for introduction of a genuine freedom of religious belief and practice is to recognize the separation of citizenship from churchmanship.[2]

A survey of the striking series of evolutions through which the theory and practice of religious toleration passed in England from the end of the civil wars to the dawn of the nineteenth century gives some substance to these generalizations. Originally depending upon purely theological argu-

---

[1] *Vide* J. N. Figgis in *The Cambridge Modern History* (Cambridge, 1908) II, 740.

[2] With the territorial coincidence of Church and State toleration is impossible except in that very limited sense conveyed in section XVII of Jeremy Taylor's *Liberty of Prophesying* (London, 1646), where the author concludes that laws upheld by "the governors of the Church" must be paramount, but "personal dispensations" may be granted if they are consistent with "the public good." *Vide* H. F. Russell Smith, *Religious Liberty in the Reigns of Charles II and James II* (Cambridge, 1911), chap. III.

ments, as Anthony Lincoln has pointed out, the theory of toleration gradually changed its character, "transforming itself from a Christian liberty into a natural right and as such into a political demand."[3] In Milton's view, freedom of conscience was to be justified solely from "fundamental principles of the Gospel," whereas his younger contemporaries, Thomas Barlow and John Owen, after bowing respectfully in the direction of scripture, were content to argue for toleration on the grounds of practical psychology, insisting that the human conscience was constructed in a manner which rendered completely futile the attempts of either priest or magistrate to control it. In the writings of John Locke, and even in the works of his severe critic Henry Stebbing, such reasoning veered more and more in the direction of political necessity, a trend fully justified by Bishop Warburton's timely discovery that Church and State were allied on the basis of "civil utility." As the century wore on purely theological arguments became increasingly unpopular, and it was as a natural right due in political terms to "all honest men, be they Calvinist, Arminians, Socinians, Papists, Jews, Turks, or Infidels," that the movement for increased toleration found its widest appeal. Indeed, did not the security of the state depend upon the number of its wise, faithful, and active citizens regardless of their "speculative opinions?" Once this question was raised seriously, any pretence at a specifically religious approach to civil government was rendered obsolete; as the basic substrate of society and politics Luthero-Calvinism had reached the end of its tether.[4]

---

[3] Anthony Lincoln, *Some Political and Social Ideas of English Dissent, 1766–1800* (Cambridge, 1938), p. 182.

[4] Both Protestant systems, the Lutheran and the Calvinist, had maintained the territorial unity of Church and State. The major difference was that whereas Lutheran pastors were in theory officers of the State, since disputes in religious matters were settled by the prince and punish-

Although Henry VIII had virtually assumed the position of a Lutheran prince in England and the medieval theory of the coincidence of Church and State had continued to be the supposed basis of government after the Restoration, an awkward situation developed. Charles II, who became head of Church and State in 1661, was known to be a member of the Anglican Communion in name only and died a Roman Catholic, while his brother James openly professed "popery" throughout his reign. Furthermore, leading ministers of state— men like Arlington, Buckingham, Clifford, Coventry, Lauderdale, Shaftesbury, and Halifax—made no attempt to hide the fact that they were not orthodox believers in the established religion of the country which they had a hand in governing. With nothing but empiricism to guide them, politicians were compelled to advocate in practice a religious policy at least liberal enough to permit the larger nonconformist sects, now so deeply rooted in the nation at large, to worship as they pleased. It was evident that the system of a united Church and State had broken down; and, sooner or later, it would have to be modified.

That a toleration of nonconformist sects was not adopted as the basis of a new ecclesiastical settlement at the time of the Restoration nevertheless should cause little surprise. If, as Professor W. K. Jordan contends, the case for it had been won by then, the actual restoration of Charles II was accomplished, as H. M. Gwatkin long ago indicated, "by a coalition of two parties which had always been opposed to toleration" and had

---

ments for all offences were administered by his courts, in the Calvinist system these rôles were reversed. Here the magistrate was in theory an official in the Church whose duty it was to administer punishments for all sorts of crime as sin. In other words, the one system was Erastian, the other theocratic; in the former the Church advised, in the latter it commanded.

followed consistently the old view of a territorial coincidence of Church and State: the Presbyterians and the Episcopalians.[5] It is rather to the failure of the idea of "comprehension" that the practical realization of toleration must be traced, for Presbyterians, finding themselves equally with Baptists and Independents excluded from the re-established Church of England, made common cause with their former rivals. Here indeed adversity created strange associates, but so long as they remained in alliance their numbers guaranteed the ultimate failure of a policy of persecution and presaged an actual modification of the statute law of the realm in favor of toleration.

This coalition of the "Three Denominations" proved to be rather uneasy, because the leading Presbyterians, whom Charles II's Declaration concerning Ecclesiastical Affairs had proclaimed to be "neither enemies . . . to episcopacy or liturgy, but modestly to desire such alterations in either, as without shaking the foundations, might best allay the present disputes,"[6] strove to keep alive not only the ideal but the hope of such a "comprehension" as would readmit them to the national church. Into the complex details of various conferences held between Richard Baxter and other leading Presbyterians on the one side and latitudinarian Anglicans such as John Tillotson and Edward Stillingfleet on the other, it is hardly pertinent to enter.[7] The crux of the matter lay in the fact that Baxter, while ardently desiring comprehension for his fellow Presbyterians, came to insist that it must be accom-

---

[5] Cf. W. K. Jordan, *The Development of Religious Toleration in England* (London, 1940), IV, 467–468 and H. M. Gwatkin, "Religious Toleration in England," *The Cambridge Modern History* (Cambridge, 1908), V, 324 *et seq.*

[6] *Vide* William Cobbett, *Parliamentary History* (London, 1808), IV, 133.

[7] These negotiations are dealt with in some detail by Professor Norman Sykes in an excellent treatment of "comprehension versus toleration," on

panied by an "indulgence" or toleration for other Dissenters.[8] Nevertheless, the reign of Charles II closed without advancing the cause of either comprehension or toleration, despite the king's extra-parliamentary attempts to relax the persecuting laws; nor did the beginning of his brother James' reign promise any relief for Protestant Dissenters. It was only when the failure of James' policy of reliance upon Anglicans to effect his schemes for the promotion of Roman Catholicism was evident that he turned to the expedient of Declarations of Indulgence, and with these measures toleration came within the field of practical politics.[9]

Alarmed that Dissenters might succumb to the temptations held out by the first royal Declaration of Indulgence, the veteran politician George Savile, Marquis of Halifax, hastened into print with his famous *Letter* of warning. With great force he raised the question of how a Roman Catholic sovereign could possibly embrace both the persons and principles of Protestant Dissenters except as a temporary means to the end of suppressing first the Anglicans and then all other religious deviants. "This alliance between infallibility and liberty," he asserted, "is bringing together the two most contrary things that are in the world!"[10]

---

pp. 60–104 of his Ford Lectures, *From Sheldon to Secker* (Cambridge, 1959). My brief remarks on the comprehension issue are simply a summary of Professor Sykes' conclusions.

[8] There was no real distinction drawn between the terms "indulgence" and "toleration". Neither of them, of course, implied that religious freedom was a natural right; but the term indulgence, which Charles II and his brother James were so fond of using, seemed to carry with it more emphatically than toleration the implication that the existing state of things was right and that departures from it would merely be magnanimously connived at.

[9] *Vide* W. C. Costin and J. S. Watson, *The Law and Working of the Constitution: Documents, 1600–1914* (London, 1952), I, 343–345 for a copy of James' First Declaration, 1687.

[10] Halifax, George Savile, First Marquis, *A Letter to a Dissenter upon*

But unless Halifax could point to the probability of toleration from more reliable and creditable quarters, his attack upon the sincerity of James II might be expected to fail, for people in prison hardly pause to examine the credentials of the hand which turns the key in the lock and invites them into freedom. Accordingly, he had to convince the prospective beneficiaries of James II's Declaration that relief was available from the side of an equally determined former enemy, the Church of England. Admittedly, the record of that Church since 1662 had little to justify the hope of sudden conversion; but, argued Halifax, "the common danger hath so laid open that mistake that all the former haughtiness towards you is for ever extinguished." Recent events had "turned the spirit of persecution into a spirit of peace, charity, and condescension," and to suspect the sincerity of the established church at this juncture "would be an uncharitable objection and very much mistimed."[11] The confidence which was to be denied to James' change of heart must be allowed to Anglican prelates, who were showing signs of moderation as welcome as uninvited. "It is not equal dealing to blame our adversaries for doing ill and not commend them when they do well," insisted Halifax, to which Edmund Calamy aptly replied: "Better late than never!"[12]

Events soon confirmed this new attitude on the part of the Established Church which Halifax had predicted and proclaimed. For in the petition of Archbishop William Sancroft and his suffragans against James' order for reading the Declaration of Indulgence of 1688 in all cathedral and parish

---

the Occasion of His Majesty's Late Gracious Declaration of Indulgence (London, 1687), p. 3.
[11] Ibid., pp. 11–12.
[12] Edmund Calamy, An Historical Account of My Own Life (London, 1830), I, 201.

churches, the signers expressly asserted their good will toward Protestant Dissenters.[13] Sancroft himself did not hesitate to implement the friendly phrases of the petition by embarking upon a project which would not only "comprehend" a majority of Dissenters within the establishment but would also grant "some indulgence" to those whose consciences forced them to remain without. William Wake, a careful witness to the events, reported that the Archbishop's basic proposal was a revision of the Prayer Book with a view to eliminating or making optional certain "indifferent" ceremonies which offended the Presbyterians, such as the use of the ring in marriage and the sign of the cross in baptism.[14]

Although the hand of Sancroft was removed from the helm when the ecclesiastical settlement was fashioned after the Glorious Revolution, the chief High Church layman, the Earl of Nottingham, introduced two bills into the House of Lords representing the dual policy of the Archbishop. One aimed at comprehension of Presbyterians within the Established Church and the other at indulgence for the sects. Gilbert Burnet reported that all the bishops who "adhered to King James' interest" and refused to take the oath of allegiance to William and Mary voted their support for the comprehension measure before they left the House of Lords.[15] But this formula of the High Church party for preventing a repetition of James' policy by uniting Episcopalians and moderate Presbyterians against the extremes of the sects failed to materialize. The

---

[13] The bishops affirmed solemnly and publicly that their reluctance to obey the royal command arose not "from any want of tenderness to Dissenters," with whom they were willing to come to such an agreement "as shall be thought fit when the matter shall be considered and settled in Parliament and Convocation." *Ibid.*, pp. 200–201.

[14] Norman Sykes, *William Wake* (Cambridge, 1957), I, 48.

[15] Gilbert Burnet, *Original Memoirs*, ed. H. C. Foxcroft (Oxford, 1902), p. 317.

project miscarried chiefly because of a revulsion of High Church sentiment caused by the incipient Nonjuror schism[16] and because of the fears of the sects about their probable future if it were enacted. It was obvious that if comprehension succeeded, the numbers benefiting from toleration would be narrowed very considerably. With the Church strengthened by a large reinforcement, it seemed plain to most Independents and Baptists that any chance to obtain eventual relaxation of the Corporation and Test Acts would be ruined. Furthermore, it was all too probable that the Toleration Act, if passed, might soon be repealed.

Thus the Toleration Bill became of greater prominence. The High Church Party, having wrecked comprehension at the price of letting toleration through, soon began, as the next chapter will show, to scrutinize and examine carefully the loopholes left by the provisions of that statute, and so to challenge the Dissenting academies and the practice of occasional conformity.

In the vacuum caused by the failure of comprehension, the Toleration Act passed quickly. Introduced into the House of Lords on March 11, 1689, it reached the Commons on April 18, and received the royal assent during the following month. Nevertheless it was a very circumscribed indulgence which was granted. The word "toleration" did not appear in the phrasing

---

[16] A small minority of Anglican clergymen, slightly over four hundred at most, refused the oath of allegiance to William and Mary, but they included the Archbishop of Canterbury and seven other bishops, and it was these high-ranking ecclesiastics who constituted the heart of the problem. In August, 1689, they were suspended from their functions and hence withdrew from the House of Lords, but they were given almost six months in which to become reconciled to the Revolution Settlement. Since all remained adamant, William III deprived them of their positions and appointed others in their places in February, 1690. The Nonjuror schism then became an accomplished fact.

of the Act from beginning to end. Entitled "An Act for Exempting their Majesteyes Subjects dissenting from the Church of England from the Penalties of Certaine Lawes," the measure stated that its object was simply to bring "some ease to scrupulous consciences in the exercise of religion." Several years later, in fact, Henry Sacheverell was to insist at his impeachment trial that after careful study of both the title and the contents of the Act, he was "unable to inform himself that a toleration hath been granted by law."[17]

Certainly no Dissenter, no matter how scrupulous his conscience, was exempted from "paying of tythes or other parochiall duties or any other duties to the Church or Minister."[18] None of the statutes of uniformity or conformity passed under the Tudors or Stuarts was repealed; but the new law did exempt from such penalties all who took the oaths of allegiance and supremacy, signed a declaration against the doctrine of transubstantiation, and subscribed to the doctrinal provisions of the Thirty-Nine Articles, that is, excluding the four articles dealing with the ritual and discipline of the Anglican Church. Baptists were further exempted from the article on infant baptism, and Quakers were not required to subscribe at all. Instead they were allowed to make a declaration of faith in the Holy Trinity and the divine inspiration of the Bible.

Only "orthodox" Protestant Dissenters, then, were granted the right to exist. So far as Roman Catholics, Unitarians, Deists, Atheists, or any "blasphemers of the Trinity" were concerned, this was an act of intolerance, and it assumed without question the authority of the magistrate to prescribe and regu-

---

[17] *The Answer of Henry Sacheverell, D.D. to the Articles of Impeachment Exhibited against him by the Honourable House of Commons* (London, 1710), p. 8.
[18] Costin and Watson, *op. cit.* I, 65.

late the religious opinions of all Englishmen. The Church of England was left unchanged and in possession of all her endowments, rights, and privileges; indeed, the act described the Dissenting ministers whom it was designed to benefit as "persons in pretended Holy Orders, or pretending to Holy Orders,"[19] thus casting marked aspersions on the validity of their office.

Under such narrow conditions and restrictions, Dissenting clergymen were authorized to preach and administer the sacraments, always providing that they did so "with unlocked doors." Burnet reported that an attempt was made in the Commons to attach a time limit of seven years to the indulgence "as a necessary restraint upon the Dissenters, that they might demean themselves so as to merit the continuation of it when the term of years now offered should come to an end . . . ,"[20] but this proposal was rejected; and, meager as it was, the Act of 1689 proved a landmark both in political and ecclesiastical history. Henceforth a man might be a citizen of England without being a member of the English Church. Limitations had been introduced by statute into the medieval idea of the state. Politics were beginning to be separated from theology.

In October of the same year that the Toleration Act was passed the *Epistola de Tolerantia,* written by Locke to Limborch three years before, was translated into English. The appearance of this book signaled a new stage in the history of English thought no less significant than that marked by the passing of the Toleration Act in the history of English politics. In fact, the three decades which elapsed between the publication of John Milton's *Treatise of Civil Power in Ecclesiastical*

---
[19] *Ibid.,* p. 66.
[20] Gilbert Burnet, *A History of My Own Time* (Oxford, 1823), IV, 16.

Causes,[21] and the translation of Locke's *Letter* might almost have been three centuries, so different was the basic approach of the two writers. Both, however, were forced to grapple with similar problems.

The idea of toleration with which Milton, Locke, and those who followed them were struggling has been divided convincingly by Anthony Lincoln into three major aspects. It was, first of all, partly the legal problem of "a religious right which had been transformed into a juridical conception from the union of Christian and citizen in one man."[22] Then, it was partly a proprietary question, since religious belief could be listed among those rights which were a man's property and which it was the duty of the civil magistrate to protect. As Bishop Burnet put it:

> If by the laws of any government, the Christian religion or any form of it become a part of the subjects' property, it then falls under another consideration, not as it is a religion, but as it becomes one of the principal rights of the subject to believe and profess it; and then we must judge of the invasions made on that as we do of any other invasion that is made on our other rights.[23]

In the third place, it was psychological—a recognition that the secular authority had no practical means of controlling an individual's thought, since, in Bishop Barlow's words, "'tis in no man's capacity to believe any positive truth of religion till it be sufficiently revealed to his understanding. . . . When that is the magistrate cannot certainly know, and therefore can compel none to the belief in these or those opinions."[24] Such

---
[21] Published in 1659.
[22] Lincoln, *op. cit.*, p. 184.
[23] Gilbert Burnet, *An Enquiry into the Measures of Submission to the Supream Authority* (London, 1689), p. 3.
[24] Thomas Barlow, *Several Miscellaneous and Weighty Cases of Conscience* (London, 1692), p. 93.

questions of law, property, and psychology found clear illustration not only in the writings of Milton, Locke, and Warburton, but all intermediary thinkers from Thomas Barlow to John Owen and Henry Stebbing were forced to wrestle with them.

At the outset of his *Treatise,* John Milton insisted that his argument for toleration would be "drawn from the scriptures only and therein from true, fundamental principles of the Gospel to all knowing Christians undeniable."[25] Above all he aimed to show not that toleration was a natural right or private property of the individual, but that true Christianity preferred the scripture before the church and acknowledged none but the scripture sole interpreter of itself to the conscience. Consequently, thundered Milton, if the church was insufficient to be implicitly believed, "what can there else be named of more authority but the conscience, than which only God is greater . . . ?" Some would object that such a doctrine overthrew all church discipline, all censure of errors, but:

My answer is that what they hear is plain scripture, which forbids not church sentence or determining but as it ends in violence upon the conscience unconvicted. Let who so will interpret or determine, so it be according to true church discipline, which is exercised on those only who have willingly joined themselves in that covenant of union, and proceeds only to a separation from the rest, proceeds never to any corporal enforcement or forfeiture of monies, which in spiritual things are the two arms of antichrist, not of the true church, the one being an inquisition, the other no better than a temporary indulgence for sin, whether by the church exacted or by the magistrate.[26]

Toleration accordingly was upheld as "the fundamental

---

[25] Milton, *op. cit.,* p. 1.
[26] *Ibid.,* pp. 7–8.

privilege of the Gospel, the new birth-right of every true believer, Christian libertie."[27] The mind must be free from coercion by officials of either Church or State because of the Gospel example that men must be persuaded to belief by reason and revelation. Indeed, if the church governors could not use force in matters of religion, "because they cannot infallibly determine the conscience without convincement," much less had civil magistrates authority to use force where they could much less judge, "unless they mean only to be the civil executioners of them who have no civil power to give them such commission, nor yet ecclesiastical to any force or violence in religion." To sum up in brief: "If we must believe as the magistrate appoints, why not rather as the church? If not as either without convincement, how can force be lawful?"[28] Since therefore no man, no synod, no session of men, although called a church, could judge definitely the sense of scripture for another man's conscience:

> It follows that he who holds in religion that belief or those opinions which to his conscience and utmost understanding appear with most evidence or probability in the scripture, though to others he seem erroneous, can no more be justly censured for a heretic than his censurers, who do but the same thing while they censure him.[29]

What then was the duty of the civil magistrate? Milton replied that it was primarily to protect the consciences of his fellow citizens from being violated. Furthermore, the magistrate must use the power of his office to suppress "poperie and idolatry," but this was incumbent upon him "for just reason of state more than of religion," since the one enslaved the con-

---

[27] *Ibid.*, p. 31.
[28] *Ibid.*, p. 10.
[29] *Ibid.*, p. 11.

science to the will of a foreign prince, while the other was contrary to all scripture, both thereby tending to unhinge any sound basis for civil government.[30] Then, too, unlike Luther and Calvin, Milton held that Church and State were completely separate societies. In other words, he had ceased to hope for a "comprehension," and could not share the hope of many Anglican and Presbyterian divines to have Christian truth established in a national church.[31] Consequently, despite all his emphasis upon scripture, Milton had begun to move in the direction of those who were later to argue for toleration as a legal and political, rather than as primarily a religious right.

"The Church itself," wrote Milton in 1659, "cannot, much less the State, settle or impose one tittle of religion upon our obedience, but can only recommend or propound it to our free and conscientious examination."[32] Six years later, at the behest of Robert Boyle, Thomas Barlow, later Bishop of Lincoln, wrote an elaborate treatise on toleration in which, although attempting to speak for the Established Church, he agreed basically with Milton's view of conscience.[33] As could well be expected, he took a more conservative approach to the problem, setting the pattern for arguments later phrased by Proast, Stebbing, and Warburton. The ruler who tolerated religions different from that legally established, said Barlow, could compel his subjects "to those media and the use of them" by

---

[30] *Ibid.*, pp. 19–20.
[31] *Vide Ibid.*, p. 27.
[32] *Ibid.*, p. 25.
[33] Written in 1664, Barlow's essay on "Toleration in Matters of Religion" was not published until 1692, but it represents the ideas which he was expressing during the 1660's, when Owen, Locke, and Proast were all his contemporaries at Oxford. Robert Boyle, fearing on the one hand that Barlow's position would not be strong enough to restrain the violent measures against nonconformists and, on the other, that it might expose the author to the resentment of his fellow churchmen, advised against its immediate publication. *Vide D.N.B.*

which they might be informed of the reasons and truth of his religion. For example, if a king granted toleration to Papists, and thus in no way compelled them to become Protestants, he might nevertheless compel attendance at sermons and disputations "as parents compel children to go to school for information, though they cannot compel them to an assent and belief of what they are taught." We were bound by scripture to try all things and to hold fast that which is good and so might "by our lawful governors be compelled to an examination and rational trial of several religions, though not to the belief of any."[34]

Bishop Barlow's reasoning, unlike Milton's, was based rather on expediency than principle. He did, of course, give lip service to scriptural arguments,[35] but his major attention was absorbed by the political, legal, and psychological problems involved. When dangerous insurrections and seditions might follow "to the hazard of the publick peace and safety of the commonweal," if toleration were denied, then, he said:

> ... I think the magistrate, in prudence and conscience, may and ought to grant their desires, and rather tolerate a false religion ... than hazard the unsettlement and ruine of the true. For as in the body natural we endure a gangrened member with much pain and patience (tho without hopes of cure) when it cannot be cut off without endangering the whole, so in the body politick or ecclesiastical an

---

[34] Thomas Barlow, *The Case of Toleration in Matters of Religion,* published in *Several Miscellaneous and Weighty Cases of Conscience* (London, 1692), pp. 92–93.

[35] "It is very difficult and dangerous for the civil magistrate to use temporal and compulsory punishments for matters of religion because we find no warrant for it in the Gospel; there is neither any precept or practice of our saviour or his apostles to compel any to be Christians." The only means they used were preaching and "a rational pressing of religious truth to others." Barlow, *op. cit.,* pp. 38–40.

erring part may and ought to be endured and tolerated when the cutting off would hazard the weal of the whole, and, indeed, such a toleration in such a case is rather necessary than voluntary in the magistrate; only he in this case makes a virtue of necessity (by way of favour and kindness) freely, which probably they might have by force. Thus he secures the peace and the religious establishment.[36]

All this was but granting impunity when the magistrate could not punish, but on the basis of such a very practical premise, Barlow urged that toleration was "most consonant to the principles of right reason and the perpetual procedure of all nations." He argued that "in the present condition of this kingdom wherein, by the unhinging of all government and an unhappy civil war, Papists, Schismatics, and Sectaries are multiplied into so great a number that possibly it may be more safe for the publick to pardon than punish; to grant a moderate toleration rather than run the hazard of further divisions and bloodshed."[37]

Barlow made it quite clear that the tolerated sects were by no means ever to be placed on a par with the establishment. Indeed, among several religions in any nation all could not be true, and that which was established by the just authority of a government was thought to be the most correct one. It followed that toleration must necessarily relate to those religions which were at least supposed to be false. Accordingly, those who were tolerated could not expect the rewards and encouragements which a prince distributed to men who cheerfully obeyed and conformed to an established religion; "for as rewards and punishments are the *sepimenta legis,* the great mounds and hedges to keep men to their duty and obedience to

---

[36] *Ibid.,* pp. 12–14.
[37] *Ibid.,* pp. 15–16.

any law of God or man, so they go together and are inseparable and belong only to those who are under the obligation of such a law."[38] Just as he to whom the law was not given needed to fear no punishment for nonconformity, so he could not expect to hope for those rewards which were designated for the encouragement of that obedience which he refused to give.

As to the problem of property: "Pagans and infidels have as good title to their patrimonies and just propriety in their estates real and personal; to become Christian neither gives them a new nor confirms the old title."[39] Consequently, if heretics or infidels did not forfeit their livelihood, they certainly could not be expected to forfeit their liberty or life. The Church could, in fact, take away only what it gave on condition. That is to say, admission to the Church by baptism gave the contracting party communion with the Church and a right to certain spiritual advantages such as hearing the Word preached, the eucharist, absolution, etc. These the Church gave, and these only "for heresie or impietie" could it take away.

Bishop Barlow closed his treatise with an eloquent plea for toleration based not upon the scripture, but on human psychology. Reiterating that to persecute and punish men with loss of livelihood, liberty, or life for religious opinions did not fall within the province of the magistrate, because "he cannot know whether or how they are criminals," he concluded:

> The internal acts of the soul . . . cannot be compelled, nor is there any possibility that they should be capable of compulsion. I confess that the body may be compelled, the feet to go to church, the ears to hear prayers, sermons, disputa-

---

[38] *Ibid.*, p. 8.
[39] *Ibid.*, p. 18.

tions, the hand to subscribe articles and canons, but all this (if the heart and hand do not go together) is so far from true religion and sincerity that it is downright hypocrasie."⁴⁰

John Owen, Barlow's pupil at Oxford, had more extreme views than his master on the subject of toleration; but then, he had broken away from the Establishment and found no difficulty in placing the sects on a par with it. Emphasizing the idea that the magistrate was utterly incapable of enforcing "a practical compliance" with the state religion, he went on to show that "prohibition of men under severe and destructive penalties from the exercise of the worship of God which is suitable to their light, so that in nothing it interferes with the fundamentals of the Christian religion or the publick tranquility, is destitute of all foundation in scripture and reason at all times."⁴¹ Furthermore, like Milton, he held that Church and State were entirely separate spheres. The argument that it was to the interest of England "to stand on the bottom of uniformity" and "to comprehend them only whom the Church compriseth so that the kingdoms of peace should be extended only unto them unto whom the Church's peace is extended" was contrary both to reason and to sound policy of government. "Church and State are not like Hypocrates twins, laughing and crying together!"⁴² The ecclesiastical constitution was based upon mutable and changeable laws of Parliament. Accordingly, the attempt to plant the Kingdom's peace on the foundation of the Church's uniformity, which might on a thousand ocasions in which the peace of the Kingdom was not the least concerned, be narrowed "into a scantling wholly unappropriate to such a superstruction," was without doubt

---
⁴⁰ *Ibid.*, p. 83.
⁴¹ John Owen, *Indulgence and Toleration Considered* (London, 1667), pp. 7–8.
⁴² *Ibid.*, pp. 17–18.

one of the greatest mistakes of government into which man was capable of falling, for :
> All the world knows how full at this day it is of various opinions and practices in things concerning religion, and how unsuccessful the attempts of all sorts have been for their extinguishment. It is no less known how unavoidable unto men, considering the various alotments of their condition in divine Providence, their different apprehension and persuasions about things are. He therefore that will build the interest of a nation on an uniformity of sentiment and practices in these things had need well fix this floating Delos : if he intend not to have his government continually tossed up and down.[43]

Every Englishman, Owen insisted, constituted a part of "the true civil interest of the nation in the polity, government, and laws thereof," simply by virtue of the fact that he "falls into it from the womb," and he was entitled to its protection. Religion, however, had to be a matter of personal choice. Indeed, what possible difference could their religion make to the government "when men are peaceful and useful in the Commonwealth?" When Dissenters were many "and such as in whose peace and industry the welfare of the nation is exceedingly concerned," was it not madness "to put laws in execution against them to their ruine, extirpation, and destruction?"[44]

Both Owen and Locke were acquainted with that aspect of Calvinism which, after experiencing persecution as a minority religion, had in the interest of self-preservation expanded Calvin's view of the English prayer book as containing "toler-

---
[43] *Ibid.,* lvi.
[44] *Ibid.,* pp. 7–8.
[45] These *"tolerabiles ineptias"* Calvin pronounced "some follies, which however, might be easily allowed to pass." *Vide* Mark Pattison, "Calvin at Geneva," *Essays,* Henry Nettleship, ed. (Oxford, 1889),II, 18.

able ineptitudes."[45] As Professor R. H. Bainton has suggested, the bulk of the toleration controversy in late seventeenth-century England had arisen over just such matters. Uniformity was, of course, required where polity and liturgy were concerned; but the great traditional dogmas of the Church were seldom mentioned, for in this area the Establishment was latitudinarian. Prominent Dissenters like Edmund Calamy argued against these "stresses upon a nicety rather than upon the main substance;"[46] but "when they distinguished the essentials from the non-essentials and made the latter more numerous in order to remove them from the area of constraint on the assumption that no one would care to persecute over a matter unessential to salvation, then the argument proved to be a boomerang."[47] The leaders of the Established Church, after hearing the Dissenters' view that the great body of Anglican teaching and practice was not essential to salvation, simply replied in effect: "Very good, then, if your eternal salvation is in no way jeopardized, why in the interest of order will you not obey the edicts of the Christian magistrate so that all Englishmen can worship in dignity and decorum?"

John Owen, as we have seen from his argument against comprehension, had appeared to have the answer. These disputed points could not be settled, and persecution over the uncertain was hardly reasonable.[48] The Established Church, however, was claiming that the uncertain might be regulated, not in the name of an absolute truth, but merely for the sake

---

[46] Edmund Calamy, *A Defense of Moderate Nonconformity* (London, 1703), p. 62.

[47] R. H. Bainton, *The Travail of Religious Liberty* (Philadelphia, 1951), p. 239.

[48] John Owen, *op. cit.*, pp. 5–6: "They who impose them say they are things indifferent . . . . But the differences that have been almost this hundred years about things indifferent is enough to frighten and discourage unbaised men from having anything to do with them. . . ."

of good order. The man who spurned such efforts on the part of the civil magistrate was to be punished not for his faith, but for his stubbornness.

Locke presented a more searching analysis of the situation. He agreed with the Established Church that the magistrate might regulate "indifferent things," but only in so far as such regulation could be proved useful to the commonwealth as a whole, for "the public good is the rule and measure of all lawmaking." Furthermore, he warned that things ever so indifferent in their own nature, when brought into the Church and the worship of God were really out of the magistrate's jurisdiction, because "they have no connexion with civil affairs," but belong to the inner life. "The only business of the church is the salvation of souls, and it in no way concerns the commonwealth or any member of it that this or the other ceremony be made use of."[49]

Neither did the use or ommission of any ceremonies in different religious assemblies "either advantage or prejudice the life, liberty, or estate of any man." For example, the washing of an infant with water was in itself an indifferent thing; but, if the magistrate should understand this to contribute to curing or preventing any disease to which children in general were subject, then he might regulate the matter. Nevertheless, no man could argue that the magistrate had the same right to ordain by law that all children should be baptized by certain priests in a sacred font for the purification of their souls. This became clear once we considered the Christian magistrate's right to impose such a law upon his Jewish subjects, for, "if we acknowledge that such an injury may not be done unto a Jew as to compel him against his own opinion to practice in his religion a thing that is in its nature indifferent,

---

[49] John Locke, *Works* (London, 1823), VI, 30.

how can we maintain that anything of this kind may be done to a Christian?"[50]

Since the magistrate had no power to impose by law the use of rites and ceremonies in any church, so neither had he the right to forbid the use of such ceremonies as were already approved and practiced by a church, because, if he did so, he would destroy the church itself "the end of whose institution is only to worship God after its own manner." This was not to argue that the civil magistrate should permit any cult to practice such enormities as human sacrifice or religious prostitution, for these things were not lawful in the ordinary course of life nor in any private house. But, if any people in a religious assembly wanted to sacrifice a calf, they ought not to be punished by law, for a man who owned a calf might lawfully kill it at home and burn any part of it, because "no injury is thereby done to anyone, no prejudice to another man's goods." For the same reason he might kill his calf also in a religious meeting. Whether this ceremony would be pleasing to God was the responsibility of the members of that particular cult to consider: "The part of the magistrate is only to take care that the commonwealth receive no prejudice and that there can be no injury done to any man."[51]

From this discussion it became apparent that for Locke there could be no mutual association of two societies so different in purpose as Church and State. Indeed, "he jumbles heaven and earth together who mixes these societies which are in their original, end, and business, and everything perfectly distinct and infinitely different from each other."[52] The duty of the civil magistrate was "by the impartial execution of equal

---

[50] *Ibid.*, p. 32.
[51] *Ibid.*, p. 34.
[52] *Ibid.*, p. 21.

laws to secure unto all the people in general and to everyone of his subjects in particular the just possession of those things belonging to this life."[53] Such civil jurisdiction could never extend to the Church's only purpose, the salvation of souls, for three basic reasons : First of all, "no man can if he would conform his faith to the dictates of another," for genuine religion consisted in "the inward and full persuasion of the mind and faith is not faith without believing." Secondly, freedom of conscience from civil control arose not only from Milton's doctrine of "Christian libertie," but from the basic composition of the human understanding. The power of the magistrate consisted only in outward force, but "human nature" was such that it could not be compelled to belief in anything by such means. Consequently, Locke was prepared to uphold freedom of conscience as a psychological prerogative quite apart from its being a religious privilege. Thirdly, "even the most enlightened civil magistrates are prone to error," and if the religion of their territories were to depend upon their individual judgments, a man's eternal salvation could be won or lost by the accident of his birthplace.[54]

What, then, of Milton's assertion that the magistrate must not tolerate idolatry in a church? Locke replied by asking: "What power can be given to the magistrate for the suppression of an idolatrous church which may not in time and place be made use of to the ruin of an orthodox one?" Civil power was basically the same everywhere, and the religion of every prince was, of course, orthodox to himself. If, then, such power was given to the civil magistrate in religious matters as at Geneva under Calvin, he might obliterate with the sword any religion which he deemed idolatrous. By the same rule

---
[53] *Ibid.*, p. 10.
[54] *Ibid.*, pp. 11–12.

another magistrate in a neighboring country might persecute the Calvinist religion, and, in India, Christianity itself, for :
> The civil power can either change everything in religion according to the prince's pleasure, or it can change nothing. If it be once permitted to introduce anything into religion by means of laws and penalties, there can be no bounds put to it; but it will, in the same manner, be lawful to alter everything according to that rule of truth which the magistrate has framed unto himself.[55]

No man, therefore, should be deprived of his possessions on account of religion "not even Americans subject to a Christian prince are to be punished either in body or goods for not embracing our faith or worship." Locke justified his assertion by an account which he insisted was based upon universal principles of "human nature." Suppose, he said, that a small band of Christians destitute of all possessions arrived in a pagan country where the inhabitants took pity on them, provided the necessities of life, and permitted them to settle there. In this way Christianity was introduced, but for a long time remained in the minority while all lived in peace, friendship, and with equal justice. At length, however, the magistrate became a Christian, and then immediately all compacts were broken, all civil rights violated so that idolatry might be extirpated. Unless the original pagan inhabitants, "strict observers of the rules of equity and the law of nature and by no means offending against the laws of society," renounced their old religion, they would be turned out of their lands and possessions, and perhaps even forfeit their lives. From this "it appears what zeal for the church joined with the desire for dominion is capable to produce, and how easily the pretence of religion and of the cure of souls serves a cloke to covetousness, rapine, and ambi-

---

[55] *Ibid.*, p. 35.

tion." Whoever maintained that idolatry should be uprooted by penal statutes, fire, and sword should apply this story to himself, for neither pagans in America nor Dissenting Christians in Europe could "with any right be deprived of their worldly goods by the predominating faction of a court-church; nor are any civil rights to be either changed or violated upon account of religion in one place more than another."[56]

All this was well and good, but how could one ignore the Old Testament insistence that idolators must be rooted out? Locke responded that this provision was designed for members of the Jewish commonwealth and hardly applied to any other people. Those who, after having been initiated according to the rites of Moses and made citizens of the Jewish state, renounced the God of Israel were proceeded against as traitors and rebels because their commonwealth was an absolute theocracy and in it there could be no distinction between Church and State. Laws concerning the worship of God were the civil laws of those people and a part of their political government in which God himself was the legislator. Now, asserted Locke:

> If anyone can show me where there is a commonwealth at this time constructed upon that foundation, I will acknowledge that the ecclesiastical laws do there become a part of the civil and that the subjects of that government both may and ought to be kept in strict conformity with that church by the civil power. *But there is absolutely no such thing under the Gospel as a Christian commonwealth.* There are, indeed, many cities and kingdoms that have embraced the faith of Christ, but they have retained their ancient forms of government, with which the law of Christ hath not at all meddled. He, indeed, hath taught men how by faith and

---

[56] *Ibid.*, p. 36.

good works they may attain eternal life. But he instituted no commonwealth, he prescribed no new and peculiar form of government, nor put he the sword into any magistrate's hand with commission to make use of it in forcing men to forsake their former religion and *receive his*.[57]

Furthermore, foreigners were not compelled by force to observe the rites of Moses' Law, but were permitted to live at peace within Israelite territory.

So much for outward ceremonies and modes of worship; what of the magistrate's function in tolerating creeds and articles of faith? Such "speculative opinions" which were required only to be believed surely could not be imposed upon anyone by the law of the land, for "it is absurd that things should be enjoined by laws which are not in man's power to perform." Also the magistrate should not forbid the preaching or professing of any speculative opinions because again "they have no manner of relation to the civil rights of his subjects." For example, if a Roman Catholic professes faith in transubstantiation, if a Jew denies that the New Testament is the word of God, and if a heathen rejects both Testaments, may not the power of the magistrate and the estates of the people be equally secure whether any man believes these things or not? Locke was prepared to admit that such opinions were false and absurd, "but the business of laws is not to provide for the truth of opinions, but for the safety and security of the commonwealth and of every particular man's goods and person."[58]

With more extreme language than that employed by Milton or Owen, and in flat disagreement with Bishop Barlow, John Locke thus asserted that the state had no concern with the

---

[57] *Ibid.*, p. 38. The italics are mine.
[58] *Ibid.*, p. 39.

establishment of religious truth whether it be in Christian or any other form, for "truth certainly would do well enough if she were once left to shift for herself."[59] The civil magistrate, no matter how high his station, was but a finite human creature and could claim no direct knowledge of truth. Furthermore:
> It is neither declarations of indulgence nor acts of comprehension such as have been practiced or projected amongst us that can work. The first will but palliate, the second increase our evil. Absolute liberty, just and true liberty, equal and impartial liberty is what we stand in need of.[60]

Locke's "absolute liberty" nevertheless had its limitations, for he stated with great vehemence that "no opinions contrary to human society or to those moral rules which are necessary to the preservation of civil society are to be tolerated by the magistrate."[61] Even though the magistrate was not the defender of religious orthodoxy, Locke's very concept of a commonwealth presupposed the profession of some religion. Hence:
> Those are not to be tolerated who deny the being of God. Promises, covenants, and oaths which are the bonds of human society can have no hold upon an atheist. The taking away of God, though but even in thought, dissolves all. Besides, those that by their atheism undermine and destroy all religion can have no pretence of religion whereupon to challenge the privilege of toleration.[62]

In addition, "those that will not own and teach the duty of tolerating all men in matters of religion," and those who "deliver themselves up to the protection and service of another prince" (i.e., Roman Catholics), thus endangering the security

---
[59] *Ibid.*, p. 40.
[60] *Ibid.*, p. 45.
[61] *Ibid.*, p. 4.
[62] *Ibid.*, p. 47.

of the state, were shut out by Locke from any right to toleration by the civil magistrate.

From the outset Locke had asserted that toleration was completely "agreeable to the Gospel of Jesus Christ and to the genuine reason of mankind,"[63] but the basic thrust of all his arguments leaned in the direction of reason rather than revelation. As a matter of fact, the issue had become purely political, emerging from Locke's definition of the state as "a society of men constituted only for procuring and advancing their own civil interests," which he further stipulated were "life, liberty, health . . . and the possession of outward things such as money, lands, houses, furniture, and the like."[64] Toleration, then, was to be defended as a personal property right which the basic nature of every commonwealth gave to its inhabitants. Locke actually went so far as to state that "the natural fellowship we are born into," in addition to the "charity, bounty, and liberality enjoined upon us by the Gospel," required that "no private person has any right in any manner to prejudice another person in his civil enjoyments because he is of another church or religion."[65] In other words, there was a "duty of toleration" as well as a right to it, and this positive concept arose not only from Christian principles but from natural law.

Before such doctrines were to receive their definite interpretation for the Church of England by Bishop Warburton, they were forced to run the gantlet of severe criticism by Archdeacon Jonas Proast and the Reverend Henry Stebbing— criticism which betrayed a vigorous reaction to Locke's departure from old arguments based on the feasibility of establishing a Christian commonwealth. Shocked by the statement that

---
[63] *Ibid.*, p. 9.
[64] *Ibid.*, p. 10.
[65] *Ibid.*, p.17.

"neither Pagan, nor Mohametan, nor Jew ought to be excluded from the civil rights of the commonwealth because of his religion," and that all the religions and sects in the world which were but consistent with civil society and ready to tolerate each other, ought everywhere to be tolerated and protected, or to enjoy an "equal and impartial liberty," Proast saw "no reasons from any experiment that has been made that true religion would be any way a gainer by it."[66] He agreed with Locke that the nature of the human understanding prevented its being compelled to anything by outward force, but, like Bishop Barlow, he argued that force could properly be used to bring men to a consideration of the truths on which the state religion was based: "Who can deny that indirectly and at a distance it does some service toward the bringing men to embrace that truth which otherwise through carelessness and negligence they would never acquaint themselves with or through prejudice they would reject and condemn unheard, under the notion of error?"[67]

Also, Proast went on to ask, what was a more practical method of bringing men to make a wiser and more rational choice than the religious prejudices which they had taken up at birth or by erroneous reasoning, "but that of laying such penalties upon them as may balance the weight of those prejudices which induced them to prefer a false way before the true, and recover them to so much sobriety and reflection to put the question themselves whether it be really worth the while to undergo such inconvenience for adhering to a religion which for anything they know may be false, or for rejecting another which for anything they know may be true, till they

---

[66] Jonas Proast, *The Argument of the Letter concerning Toleration briefly consider'd and answer'd* (Oxford, 1690), p. 2.
[67] *Ibid.*, p. 4.

have brought it to the bar of reason and given it a fair tryal there."[68]

Like Barlow, Proast did not claim for the magistrate authority to compel any man to his religion, but only to procure for all his subjects the means of discovering the way to salvation: "The power I ascribe to the magistrate is given to him to bring men not to his own, but to the true religion."[69] Although, as Locke had pointed out, the religion of every prince was orthodox to himself, yet if this power kept within its bounds, it could serve no interest other than the truth among those who had any concern for their eternal salvation: "Because the penalties which enables him that has it to inflict are not such as may tempt such persons to renounce a religion which they do not believe to be so."[70] If, after an impartial examination of the controversy between the magistrate and them, they found that truth did not lie on his side, "they have gained thus much, however, even by the magistrate's misapplying his power." The only harm was suffering some tolerable inconvenience for following their own reason and conscience.

These arguments were to be developed in more elaborate and forceful terms for the Church of England by Henry Stebbing; but, before this occurred, the Bangorian controversy, which raged during the decade after 1717, absorbed the attention of leading figures in Church and State. The whole matter centered upon a sermon preached before the king by Benjamin Hoadly, in which the good bishop of Bangor attempted to prove that the nature of Christ's kingdom was wholly not of this world, and therefore that its sanctions, rewards, and punishments were entirely spiritual. Conse-

---

[68] *Ibid.*, p. 11.
[69] *Ibid.*, p. 21.
[70] *Ibid.*

quently, clergymen had no right to busy themselves in secular government, nor did civil magistrates have any authority to punish men for matters purely of a religious nature. Hoadly reasoned that Christianity had become so encrusted with secular ceremonies and alien traditions that its original form had been almost completely obscured. Always a good Lockean, like Bishop Joseph Butler, the classical spokesman for the empirical school of ecclesiastics, he never tired of seeking for the facts as opposed to theory:

> The only cure for our evils . . . is to have recourse to the originals of things, to the Law of Reason, in those points which can be traced back thither; and to the declarations of Jesus Christ and his immediate followers, in such matters as took their rise solely from those declarations. For the case is plainly that words and sounds have had such an effect (not upon the nature of things, which is unmovable, but) upon the minds of men in thinking of them; that the very same word remaining (which at first truly represented one certain thing) by having multitudes of new inconsistent ideas, in every age and every year added to it, becomes itself the greatest hinderance to the true understanding of the nature of the thing first intended by it.[71]

In the battle of pamphlets which resulted dozens of writers took part, but perhaps Hoadly's most forceful supporter was John Balguy and his most vigorous opponent Henry Stebbing. Arguing with both Locke and Hoadly that "he only is sincere in my esteem whose ear is always open to information and who continues ever ready and willing to receive new light and fresh evidence,"[72] Balguy held that this unbiased approach could lead only to Hoadly's conclusions about church

---

[71] Benjamin Hoadly, *Sermons* (London, 1754), I, 285.
[72] John Balguy, *Silvanus' Letter to the Reverend Dr. Sherlock* (London, 1720).

authority. Stebbing, however, insisted that men's passions and prejudices being what they were, such a doctrine could only lead to "carelessness and indifference in matters of religion." Furthermore, "his Lordship has given us such a rarified notion of the Church and so volatilized it that people are afraid in time it will quite disappear!"[73]

Having whetted his teeth in the Bangorian controversy, Henry Stebbing turned to launch a full scale attack upon John Locke, the inspirer of Bishop Hoadly's dangerous notions. From the outset he upheld the thesis that "true religion in the nature of the thing is capable of being supported and encouraged by the methods of civil administration."[74] Since it was acknowledged on all sides that one end of the magistrate's office was to secure the public good and that whatever affected the public good thus fell under his care, how could it be questioned that his province extended to the area of religion? He had not only the right but the duty to use all human means at his disposal to exercise this charge; not that they by themselves begot true religion, but, Stebbing insisted, they put men into the fit temper and disposition to receive it:

> ... This, I say is the effect of the inconveniences of this world, they dispose us to sober thought and serious consideration which the hurry of our passions whilst they reign without control will by no means allow. ... That which prejudices men against the faith is commonly some worldly interest or other which presents itself in opposition to it: the proper remedy therefore to this evil will be to place truth and interest in the same view, which, if it doth not end in conviction (as for want of abilities to judge

---

[73] Henry Stebbing, *An Appeal to the Word of God.* ... (London, 1720), pp. xvii–xviii.

[74] Henry Stebbing, *An Essay Concerning Civil Government considered as it stands related to Religion* (London, 1724), pp. 119–128.

sometimes it may not) will at least have this certain good effect that men will neither foolishly neglect nor wantonly depart from it. . . .[75]

On the basic question of how religion might be conveyed to others by the magistrate, Locke, as we have seen, held that this was impossible by its very nature, "for no man can, if he would, conform his faith to the dictates of another."[76] But Stebbing insisted that his argument implied no sort of promise or stipulation blindly to submit to whatever the magistrate should think fit to establish in matters of religion, for "if I consent that the magistrate shall have authority to distribute yearly out of the publick stock so much money as he shall judge to be necessary and convenient for the maintenance of publick teachers, I do not hereby so much as pretend to engage myself not to examine their doctrines and either to embrace or reject them, as I shall see most reasonable."[77] Even if one consented yet further that civil officials should have power to make use of "outward restraint" as a "bridle to wantonness," he would still remain at liberty either to differ from the religion of the magistrate and submit to the "inconveniences" which should be laid upon him, or to conform and avoid them.[78] In short, to vest the magistrate with the care of

[75] *Ibid*, pp. 21, 26.
[76] John Locke, *Works* (London, 1823), VI, 10.
[77] Stebbing, *op. cit.*, p. 71.
[78] Excluding all Dissenters from offices under the supreme magistrate gave a considerable curb to licentiousness, said Stebbing, but it was no violation of conscience for: "it must be a very tender conscience indeed which cannot serve God in peace and quietness unless it be suffered to rest itself upon a cushion of state." Furthermore, it was absurd to talk of a natural right to that which results merely from "civil institution" and had no existence outside of a commonwealth: "It is evident that a capacity to serve one's country in offices of trust implies divers qualifications which are not the objects of *right* either *natural* or *civil*. Thus, for instance, a capacity to serve one's country in the office of a judge implies the qualifications of wisdom, learning, and integrity, but does any one

religion was not to abandon the care of our own salvation, but "to give up a part of our liberty and property in order to promote the salvation of ourselves and of others."[79]

Stebbing declared firmly that his doctrine, unlike Locke's, had been "deduced by way of direct and positive proof from principles plain and evident."[80] He readily admitted that entering into society was not as necessary to secure a man the exercise of his religion as it was to the enjoyment of his "life, liberty, and possession," yet it would never follow from this that religion might not receive very great advantages from society. Who could not see that wholesome laws of society operated upon the human disposition itself and led many to fear God who, if left wholly to themselves, would have trampled his authority under their feet? If it was the will of God for us to serve and obey him, Stebbing insisted that "the means which he proposeth for this end must be adapted to the circumstances under which he hath created us . . . whereas . . . obedience to himself by purely rational motives is not enough because of man's passion and wilfulness."[81]

After all, human institutions suffered from the same frailties as the finite creatures who established them, and the case was clear that through ignorance of the true means to secure the public good on the one hand and through ambition and avarice on the other, there might be a misapplication of power, and then all those evils would follow with respect to the civil concerns of men which by virtue of a like misapplication would follow with regard to their religion. Indeed, "if Mr. Locke had well considered this he would have found less cause

---

understand so little language as to say that a man has a *right* to be either learned or upright?" *Ibid.*, p. 85.
[79] *Ibid.*, p. 72.
[80] *Ibid.*, p. 129.
[81] *Ibid.*, p. 69.

to make himself merry with those who 'because all men are promiscuously apt to be misled by passion and lust' are for putting the care of religion into the hands of those [meaning the magistrates] who are as apt to be misled by passion and lust as themselves."[82] But, asked Stebbing, was not the very reason for civil government founded on the fact that men were apt to be misled by passions and lusts? Locke and his followers would apparently have magistrates who were not men, but creatures above them. So long as we were men, however, we had to be contented to be governed, if governed at all, by mere humans.

The reason, then, was still wanting why those evils which arose from the misapplication of power were an objection in one case and no objection in another, "although the evils which may be apprehended are according to their respective natures the same in both."[83] If Locke could give instances of false opinions supported by human laws under the notion of true religion, it was quite easy to present as many instances of false claims supported by force of arms under the notion of civil right, and for one war justly begun there had been ten undertaken through avarice and lust for power. The evil was great in both cases, no doubt; but did anyone think this was a good reason against the use of war? Must one nation sit down and tamely submit to be ravaged by another because magistrates might be wicked and ambitious, or because mistakes might be committed in judging right and property? "The rule," concluded Stebbing, "I conceive to be this, that when the consequences which may in reason ordinarily be apprehended from the misapplication of any power are *as bad as* or

---

[82] Stebbing, *op. cit.*, p. 136. The quotation from Locke is to be found on p. 31 of his *Third Letter concerning Toleration* (London, 1692).
[83] *Ibid.*, p. 139.

worse than those which may be apprehended from the *want* of such *power,* that no such power ought to be given. On the contrary, it must be reasonable to put any power into the magistrate's hand which being rightly used will produce greater good than the misapplication of it will produce evil."[84] This was the case of civil government in general. Without it there would be worse consequences than could ordinarily arise from maladministration. The same might be said of war "without which no government can possibly subsist." In these cases the rule proceeded upon the maxim that of two evils the lesser was always to be chosen.

Accordingly, to give Locke's objection any weight, it had to be stated as follows: The consequences which would ordinarily happen from magistrates making use of an authority given them to support true religion toward encouraging *false* religion are such that, on the whole, it would be better if they had no such power. Certainly, if this were the argument, the conclusion was just; but the premises contained far more than could proved true. For how did Lockeans attempt to prove it? By having us look at Popish, Pagan, and Islamic countries. Stebbing admitted that he saw here "enough to move the pity and indignation of every serious and good man":

... But I am not certain (nor do I think it is possible for them to show me) that if there had never been any publick provision made for support of religion by civil magistrates the state of religion throughout the world would not have been in a far more deplorable condition. For by these provisions a general sense of religion and of morality, an awe for a supreme invisible power, which is the foundation of all religion, are, amidst all the corruptions so much com-

---

[84] *Ibid.,* pp. 140–141.

plain'd of, tolerably preserved. If any man think otherwise, let him compare the state of religion in Turkey, China, or any civilized country with the religion of the Hottentots, who are as free from all restraints of civil power as they are from all sense of religion. The same thing may be said of Christianity, which, if left destitute of all support from human laws, might (for ought that appears, at least, to the contrary) have by this time been everywhere degenerated into a superstition worse than that of Popery.[85]
Far better to have religion, though blended with some false notions, than to have no religion at all.

Stebbing concluded by attacking Locke's effort to expose the absurdity of punishing Dissenters "to make them consider" the reasons for their religious peculiarities. The substance of Locke's argument in his *Second Letter* was that Dissenters were actually punished *because they were* Dissenters and not to make them consider. He insisted that it was unjust because some might have considered already, and it was quite impossible to distinguish between those who had and those who had not done so. Stebbing answered that they were "punished" neither because they were Dissenters nor to make them consider:

> . . . They are not punished merely because they are Dissenters, because it is supposed that if it could certainly be known beforehand that they are sincere Dissenters, they would not be punished. Nor are they punished to make them consider, because these penalties being intended as a test whereby to distinguish the sincere from the insincere, it is presumed that those who submit to the penalties are sincere, i.e., have considered already. . . . The proper immediate reason why these penalties are laid upon them is because they are men capable of *imposing* upon the magis-

---

[85] *Ibid.*, p. 144.

trate by pretending scruples of conscience where there are none, or where under a true care there would be none, and because their submitting to these penalties hath the nature of an evidence to show that they do not impose upon him.[86] He insisted that his method did not propose to bring over all Dissenters to the national religion. On the contrary, it granted "a liberty for all those to separate who separate honestly" and the moderate penalties which he proposed served only to provide a remedy against "licentiousness."

A milder and more systematic thinker who, like Stebbing, defended civil disabilities for all Dissenters, yet spoke out strongly for toleration was William Warburton, Bishop of Gloucester. In his *Alliance between Church and State,* which first appeared in 1736, the right to freedom of conscience was again explicitly upheld; and after that date, such a right was widely defended by Dissenters and Churchmen alike. Although he argued for the necessity of an established church and a test law to protect it, Warburton insisted that he was in no way casting aspersions on "the divine doctrine of toleration." Indeed:

> . . . This discourse is so far from giving any entry . . . to the infringement of religious liberty that it lays the foundation of it on the only solid and impregnable ground. For on these two cardinal principles, on which, as on two hinges, our theory is raised and turns, namely—that the State hath only the care of bodies, and the Church only the care of souls—and that each society is sovereign and independent of the other, is demonstrably deduced the indefeasible right of religious liberty. He who would see the several parts of this demonstration at large may read the *Letters concerning Toleration.*[87]

---

[86] *Ibid.,* p. 211.
[87] William Warburton, *The Alliance Between Church and State* (Lon-

Warburton then proceeded to drive home with what he considered irrefutable logic the necessity for an established church and a test law. Church and State, each being independent organizations with different jurisdictions—the one over bodies, the other over souls—could not exist apart from each other in this life. This was so because the Church alone could "supply the sanction of rewards which society wants and has not,"[88] for "no society can ever find a fund sufficient for that purpose, without raising it on the people as a tax, to pay it back to them as a reward."[89] But as religion was absolutely necessary to civil government so civil government was necessary to religion. Since the Church had care only over souls, it must seek the protection of the institution which had care over bodies.

Because an established religion was necessary to society, the refusal of those who held different opinions to pay taxes for its support was unjust, declared Warburton, adding that "this maintenance is not assigned by the public for the support of opinions, but for the use and necessities of the State."[90] These different religious opinions, however, made necessary a test law for the security of the established church and the order of society :

> . . . For when there are diversities of religions in a state each of which thinks itself the only true, or, at least, the most pure, every one aims at advancing itself on the ruins of the rest : which it calls bringing into conformity with itself; and, when reason fails, will attempt to do it by civil aid, which can be brought about only by the attempter's getting into the public administration. But when it happens

---

don, 1741 ed.), p. 137. This is only one of several references to Locke's *Letters. Vide* especially pp. 144 and 146.
[88] *Ibid.*, p. 16.
[89] *Ibid.*, p.14.
[90] *Ibid.*, p. 76.

that one of these religions is the established, and all the rest under toleration, then it is that these latter, still more inflamed, as stimulated with envy at the advantages the Established Church enjoys, act in concert, and proceed with joint attacks to disturb its quiet. In this imminent danger, the Established Church demands the promised aid of the State, which gives her a test law for her security. Whereby the entrance into the administration, (the only way that mischief to the Established Church is effected) is shut to all but the members of that Church. . . .[91]

Such was the flavor of Warburton's argument. Aiming to erect for the Church of England a solid defense against "the old battery of *imperium in imperio*," he had reached the glorious conclusion not only that "by the Law of Nature every man has a right of worshipping God according to his own conscience," but that an established church and an attendant test law were also based "on the great and unerring maxims of the Law of Nature and of Nations." He was able to achieve this great intellectual feat only upon the basis of "civil utility"; but for Warburton truth and utility had met together in a union as happy as unexpected: "We have proved, and it cannot be too oft repeated that public Utility and Truth do coincide"; and, if this was so, "then to provide for that Utility, Truth must also be provided for."[92]

All phases of Church and State relations were thus measured by Warburton according to the yardstick of social usefulness rather than by any supernatural or divine sanction. He fully agreed with Locke's concept of natural law and the right to freedom of thought which the very structure of man's conscience rendered necessary. This right, together with the prin-

---

[91] *Ibid.*, pp. 114–115.
[92] *Ibid.*, pp. 68–69.

ciple that "an established religion is . . . the universal voice of nature and not confined to certain ages, people, or religions,"[93] constituted the two great pillars upon which the structure of human society must rest. Test legislation was justified because it was socially useful; indeed, it was socially imperative. Liberties which might exist without danger in a state of nature could be most injurious after men had organized themselves into a civil commonwealth; and, as Locke had held, to put under restraint opinions which flatly denied the basis of all ordered society, could never be regarded as exercising tyranny over the conscience. With Stebbing, Warburton held that test legislation was no more than a restraint exercised by the state as a part of her inherent right of self-defense. Whereas all men who held opinions, no matter how heterodox, which were harmless to the state, possessed a natural right to them without molestation, they had no such right to occupy political offices. It was the civil magistrate's primary function to guard these positions carefully in accordance with the basic right of the State to self-preservation.

By the use of such casuistry, Warburton was able to emerge triumphant with full justification both for tolerating the sects and preserving inviolate the privileged position of the Establishment, claiming to have metamorphosed these two elements into a pattern "formed solely from the contemplation of Nature and the unvariable Reason of Things." And his efforts were not in vain, for these principles of "alliance" between Church and State were to be voiced over and over again throughout the eighteenth century by those Anglican divines who sought to maintain the delicate balance of religious forces established by the ecclesiastical provisions of the Revolution Settlement, but not to tread one inch beyond.

---

[93] *Ibid.*, p. 70.

So it was that by the seventeen-thirties, the cumulative heritage of Milton, Barlow, Owen, Proast, Stebbing—and especially Locke—had effected on all sides a belief in the freedom of conscience in matters of religion. Nevertheless, the issue had not been settled conclusively by Locke, for the "great philosopher" continued to be quoted in support both of those who favored expanding the toleration by repeal of the Test and Corporation Acts, and by those, like Warburton, who opposed such action. It was certain, however, that none of the parties in these disputes was at all inclined to rest his case upon arguments grounded in Christian truth or scriptural purity. Rather, accepted as a natural right, freedom of conscience was considered in its legal and political aspects, and the question of how far the individual could safely be allowed to assert his possession of this right against that other inherent natural right of self-preservation on the part of the State was continually raised by members of the Establishment in defense of their exclusive title to political office. All further arguments for or against an increase in toleration were thus so firmly enmeshed in subsequent political and constitutional problems that, if they are to be understood, some attention must be directed to the major Dissenting groups and their struggle with Parliament over the issue of civil rights.

CHAPTER II

The First Attempts at Repeal

BETWEEN LOCKE'S STATEMENT of the principle of toleration as "the chief characteristical mark of the true church" and the provisions of the Toleration Act of 1689 there was a great gulf fixed. The Act had granted orthodox Protestant Dissenters freedom of public worship, but they did not feel secure in the enjoyment of this liberty. Although they registered more than two thousand chapels during the next twenty years, most title deeds to these buildings provided for disposal of the property in case worship should again be suppressed.[1] So long as King William lived they could count on protection; but, even under his "benevolent reign," events soon conspired to prove that they were by no means yet in full possession of the meager protection granted in 1689.

The difficulties surrounding the ordination of Edmund Calamy to the Presbyterian ministry in 1694 furnish an illustration of the uncertainty with which, like Plato's men in a cave, Dissenters emerged into the full daylight of legal protection. Calamy with two friends, Thomas Reynolds and Joseph Bennett, asked for a public ordination—although there had been nothing of the kind since the Act of Uniformity in 1662 —in order, as the applicants put it, to bring the rights of the

---

[1] *Vide* Duncan Coomer, *English Dissent under the Early Hanoverians* (London, 1946), p. 61, and "The Early Meeting Houses and their Trusts" in A. H. Drysdale, *History of the Presbyterians in England* (London, 1889), p. 441–7.

"Dissenting Interest out of private corners into the light."[2] But before they could act upon such a request, the veteran ministers John Howe and William Bates felt obliged to consult with Sir John Somers, the attorney-general, to "inquire whether such a proceeding on our part might not be ill taken and draw ill consequences after it"; and after the interview they refused to "have any concern in the matter if there were any present besides the ordainers and the ordained."[3] In the end Calamy had his way, but the older generation of ministers clearly felt that such a public proclamation of the meaning of toleration was inadvisable.

It was not the ordination of ministers, but their training which proved to be a major testing-point of the scope and meaning of the Toleration Act. Did the allowance of public worship to Dissenters and the requirement from their ministers of subscription to tests of theological orthodoxy imply even tacit recognition of the training of such ministers outside the two universities? Indeed, since the Act of Uniformity of 1662, Oxford and Cambridge had become the exclusive preserve of the Church of England, the former requiring subscription to all of the Thirty-Nine Articles on matriculation and the latter at graduation, both thereby excluding conscientious Dissenters from membership.

To meet this educational need the Dissenting academies had come into existence, in which ministers ejected from the Church of England by the Act of 1662 provided higher education for the sons of Dissenters entering the learned professions as well as theological training for the ministry and thus also earned their own living. These academies depended for their

---

[2] Edmund Calamy, *An Historical Account of My Own Life* (London, 1830), I, 130.
[3] *Ibid.*, pp. 344–345.

prosperity on the abilities of their teachers and often migrated from place to place as persecution threatened. By 1689 they numbered several dozen. After the Toleration Act they multiplied rapidly and began to receive concerted financial support from denominational fund boards.[4] With this increase in numbers and the provision of busaries, High Church opinion became alarmed, and several attacks were launched upon them.

Richard Frankland, who trained "upwards of three hundred" young nonconformists for the ministry, had set up the first Dissenting academy in the North of England at Rathmell in 1670.[5] After many migrations occasioned by enforcement of the "Five Mile Act," which forbade any of the clergy driven to resign by the Act of Uniformity to come within five miles of a borough town or any place where they had formerly ministered, Frankland re-established his academy at Rathmell in 1689. Still he found no peace, for until his death in 1698 hardly a year passed during which he failed to experience "much vexation from ecclesiastical courts." In 1690 he suffered a sentence of excommunication from the Archiepiscopal Court at York; and, although this was revoked by William III, further indictments for keeping an improperly licenced school were brought against Frankland in 1692, 1695, and 1697.

Similarly, Dr. Joshua Oldfield, a member of Christ's College, Cambridge, unable to graduate because of his refusal to subscribe, had become head of Coventry Academy in 1693

---

[4] *Vide* W. D. Jeremy, *The Presbyterian Fund and Dr. Daniel Williams's Trust* (London, 1885) and Herbert McLachlan, *English Education under the Test Acts* (Manchester, 1931).
[5] David Bogue and James Bennett, *History of Dissenters* (London, 1809), II, 19.

and was soon being "tormented in the bishop's court."[6] On October 14, 1697, he was cited to appear in the Ecclesiastical Court at Coventry "upon a suspicion of instructing youth," but managed to get "a stay of the proceedings and brought the matter up to King's Bench where it was depending three or four terms to his great trouble and charge."[7] Finally, the case was dropped with "a rebuke from good king William who intimated to the prelate that he was not pleased with such prosecutions."[8]

When, however, the tolerant Calvinist king was succeeded in 1701 by a thoroughly High-Church Anglican queen, Dissenting schoolmasters had cause to shake in their shoes. During the first year of Anne's reign, in fact, the lower house of Canterbury Convocation complained loudly against "ignorant and disaffected persons who without licence and contrary to the law" had set up schools where "not only academical learning is pretended to be taught to the prejudice of the two universities," but "such principles are also instilled into youth as tend to perpetuate the schism we now labour under and to subvert the established constitution."[9] This was followed, three years later, by a full dress debate in Parliament on the question of whether or not the Church was in danger, during the course of which Archbishop John Sharp of York, supported by the Duke of Leeds and the Bishop of Bath and Wells, voiced alarm at the growth of Dissenting academies "quite contrary to the law." Although in the Commons Sir John Packington and Mr.

---

[6] *Vide* J. W. Ashley Smith, *The Birth of Modern Education* (London, 1954), p. 121.
[7] Edmund Calamy, *op. cit.*, I, 403.
[8] Bogue and Bennett, *op. cit.*, II, 42.
[9] Edward Cardwell, *Synodalia* (Oxford, 1842), pp. 712–13; also reproduced in Norman Sykes, *From Sheldon to Secker* (Cambridge, 1959), pp. 93–94.

Bromley also professed the Church to be in great peril from "the increase of presbyterian schools and seminaries," many members agreed with Lord John Somers' criticism of those men who would "raise groundless jealousies" and in a time when the nation was at war "seek to embroil us at home and thus to defeat all our glorious designs abroad," and both Houses voted by comfortable majorities that the Church was safe.[10]

Nevertheless, the crux of the problem remained in the statement of Convocation that Dissenting academies tended "to perpetuate the schism we now labour under," for this implied that the Toleration Act was only a temporary and makeshift measure, not a permanent enactment. The clerical demagogue Sacheverell lost no time in broadcasting this view throughout the kingdom, insisting at his impeachment trial that the Act of 1689 was designed only "for the ease of those whose minds through the unhappy prejudices of education were already estranged from the Church, not . . . to indulge men in the most effective methods to propagate and perpetuate their schism."[11]

Any implementation of this High-Church and Tory interpretation of the Toleration Act remained impossible so long as Whig support was needed for prosecution of the War of the Spanish Succession, but when the fiasco of the Sacheverell trial was followed by the dissolution of Parliament, a general election, and a Tory majority and administration, Dissenters had just cause for alarm. During the excitements of the Sacheverell episode indeed mobs had burned down Dissenting meeting

---

[10] The Lords voted 61 to 30 that the Church was not in danger, and at length the Commons concurred by a vote of 212 to 160. *Vide* William Cobbett, *Parliamentary History* (London, 1810), VI, 493–510.

[11] *The Answer of Henry Sacheverell* (London, 1710), p. 10.

houses and attacked their congregations in spite of the legal protection accorded by the Toleration Act. What if this act should be repealed or its provisions restricted?

The first item of Tory policy, however, was peace at any price, and not until the last ministry and year of Anne's reign was the Schism Act passed in 1714 to abolish academies with one blow. It came as a desperate measure of the extreme Tories led by Henry St. John to oust Robert Harley and the moderates. "An Act to Prevent the Growth of Schism and for the further security of the Churches of England and Ireland," the measure required on penalty of three months' imprisonment without bail that all teachers hold an episcopal certificate which testified to their having received the Anglican sacrament within a year before application. Furthermore: "any person who shall have obtained a lycence . . . and shall at any time . . . willingly resort to any conventicle . . . shall thenceforth be incapable of keeping any publick or private school or seminary or instructing any youth as tutor or schoolmaster."[12]

While this harsh measure was being debated in Parliament,

---

[12] 12 Anne. c. 7. *Vide* W. C. Costin and J. S. Watson, *Documents, 1660–1914* (London, 1952), I, 122. Such a bill at once produced a fairly extensive pamphlet literature, e.g. *A Letter to a Member of Parliament . . .* (London, 1714) in which Richard Steele stressed the disastrous effects it would have on Dissenting education, stating that "as Englishmen they are possessed of a law in their favor which indulges them in the exercise of their religion; and where there is a right to a benefit, there are supposed to go along with it the necessary means of attaining that right; these means are interrupted when education towards enjoying the right is prohibited," p. 10. Thomas Reynolds, *A Discourse Occasioned by the . . . Act to Prevent the Growth of Schism* (London, 1714) furnished similar arguments. . . . The bill passed the Commons by 237 votes to 126, but squeezed through the Lords only by the narrow majority of 77 to 72. There it was amended to exclude persons instructing youth in reading, writing, and arithmetic, and the infliction of penalties was taken out of the hands of justices of the peace where the Commons had proposed to place it and committed to the cognizance of the superior courts.

London Dissenters did what they could to lobby against it. Despite the fact that by 1714 each of the three major denominations in the metropolis had established a reasonably efficient organization for itself through local associations, general assemblies, and fund boards, they had as yet co-operated with one another for ceremonial purposes only. The first record of any concerted action had occurred in 1689 when Presbyterian and Independent ministers joined in presenting a congratulatory address to William and Mary.[13] When Anne ascended the throne, Baptist ministers joined the other two denominations in presenting her with a declaration of loyalty, and further addresses were issued by the "Three Denominations" at the time of Blenheim, the Act of Union, and Ramillies,[14] but such activities hardly provided significant experience toward organizing themselves as a "pressure group" with given political ends in view.

Nevertheless, with the abolition of their whole educational system at hand, members of the Three Denominations hastily improvised some informal meetings, "one in the city, another about the Temple, and a third at Westminster," in which they "consulted with their friends so that nothing in their reach any way likely to ward off so threatening a stroke might be omitted."[15] In fact, at the first of these gatherings one rich Dissenter "declared he would willingly advance £1,000 than that such a law should pass," and at the other two petitions were addressed to Lord Treasurer Harley. Then, after the act had passed, "some wealthy citizens" at a fourth meeting prepared to petition Queen Anne for the use of her veto on their behalf. At this juncture Edmund Calamy and a

---

[13] Bogue and Bennett, *op. cit.*, II, 144–47, where the address is reproduced *in toto*.
[14] *Ibid.*, p. 149 *et seq.*
[15] Edmund Calamy, *op. cit.*, II, 284–85.

few other politically astute Dissenters consulted with Lord Charles Sunderland, who insisted that such a plan was "exceedingly weak and foolish, and if pursued would ruin both the Dissenting and the Whig cause."[16] After Charles Townshend, the Dissenters' other "friend at court," had joined in expressing these same sentiments, the "wealthy citizens" gave up their project, and on June 25, 1714, the Schism Act received royal assent by commission. Its operation was to commence on August 1, but the whole scheme exploded with the Queen's death on that very day and the act remained a dead letter until its repeal.

The other element in the Tory program was an attack upon the practice of occasional conformity by which Dissenters whose principles allowed them to communicate occasionally with the Church of England could fulfill the requirements of the Test and Corporation acts and thus qualify for any office of civil government. Since the Toleration Act of 1689 had made no change in the civil disabilities of Dissenters, some occasional conformists continued to creep into high positions, and the Tories resolved to close this gap. In November of 1702 a bill forbidding occasional conformity with a heavy fine attached as punishment was introduced into the House of Commons by representatives of the Universities of Oxford and Cambridge and passed by a large majority only to be rejected by a single vote in the Lords. Consequently it was reintroduced the next year, this time with a reduction of the fine from £100 to £50, but was again rejected in the Lords, now by a majority of twelve. A final flicker of Tory and High-Church resentment was seen the following year when an attempt to attach the bill to a vote of supplies was defeated in the

---

[16] *Ibid.*, pp. 286–87.

Commons on November 28, 1704, by 251 votes to 134. For
the next seven years the exigencies of war and the increasing
dependence of the Queen's administration on Whig support
for its prosecution in accordance with the military strategy of
Marlborough relegated occasional conformity to the background.

With the Tory triumph in the general election following
Sacheverell's trial, however, the Occasional Conformity Bill
assumed an immediate prominence; and in 1711, because of
an alliance between the Whigs and Nottingham, it passed both
houses easily.[17] The new measure was entitled "an act for preserving the Protestant Religion by better securing the Church
of England . . . and for confirming the Toleration granted to
Protestant Dissenters." Its champions claimed that they were
not violating or even restricting the Toleration Act, but simply
defining its original purposes and excluding illegitimate extensions. It provided that:

> . . . if any person or persons, either peers or commoners,
> who have or shall have any office or offices civil or military
> or receive any pay, salary, fee or wages by reason of any
> patent or grant from under Her Majesty, Her Heirs or
> Successors . . . or if any other person bearing any office of
> magistracy . . . shall at any time after their admission into
> their respective offices . . . knowingly or willingly resort to
> or be present at any conventicle . . . they shall forfeit fifty
> pounds to be recovered by him or them who shall sue for

---

[17] The Whigs wanted to overthrow the Tory administration because of
its proposed peace terms with France. For this purpose they desired the
support of the Nottingham faction who had been kept out of office because
of their uncompromising "High Tory" principles, even though such support could only be achieved by abandoning their Dissenting friends and
allies. Nevertheless, their political strategy was defeated when the Queen
followed the advice of her Treasurer, Robert Harley, Earl of Oxford, and
created twelve new Tory peers to carry the peace terms in the Lords.

the same in any of Her Majesteyes Courts . . . and shall be rendered incapable to bear any office or employment whatsoever.[18]

Thus the Tories had won their victory and had established their contention that the Toleration Act must be strictly confined to the legal protection of Protestant Dissenters in the exercise of their public worship only.

During the course of these several debates over occasional conformity the Tories had continually raised the frightening spectre of Sir Humphrey Edwin who while lord mayor of London in 1697 had "contrary to all law and custom"[19] carried the city regalia with him to worship at a conventicle. The open flaunting of such "presbyterian principles," it was declared, tended to subvert the constitution, and the Whigs replied by furnishing the example of a more tactful Dissenting lord mayor, Sir Thomas Abney, to prove that Dissenting principles and subversion did not necessarily go hand in hand. This Presbyterian chief magistrate had in fact helped to preserve the constitution, they argued, for when Louis XIV proclaimed the Pretender lawful sovereign of Great Britain in 1701, he responded at once by carrying a resolution through the Common Council in support of King William and the Protestant Succession.[20]

Now that the practice of occasional conformity was illegal,

---

[18] Costin and Watson, *The Law and Working of the Constitution: Documents, 1660–1914* (London, 1952), I, 118–119. The law also stipulated that not more than ten persons in addition to any one family could gather for private Dissenting worship without constituting a conventicle.

[19] Calamy, *op. cit.*, I, 400.

[20] Calamy reports that Abney's swift action "helped to animate the king's cause and gave new life to the Whig interest at home and abroad," *Ibid.*, I, 436; and, later, his conduct on that occasion gave vent to the assertion that "the House of Hanover owes the throne of Britain to a Dissenter." *Vide* Bogue and Gennett, *op. cit.*, IV, 4–5.

THE FIRST ATTEMPTS AT REPEAL 67

what was to be the proper course of action for Dissenting mayors, aldermen, or justices of the peace who still held office? Could they renounce public worship and retain their positions without appearing to deny their religious principles? Sir Thomas Abney and his brother alderman Sir John Fryer afforded the example of two magistrates who neglected public worship entirely for seven years. Far from being apostates, they reasoned that they were "offering a sacrifice to the interest of King George," which "the Resident of the Elector of Brunswick would not fail to report to his royal master."[21] By confining themselves to that private family worship which the law allowed they could retain their positions and be strategically placed, so they thought, to press for immediate relief from these and other hardships as soon as the Hanoverian succession should take place.

The Dissenters and their Whig allies watched with increasing anxiety events of the last year of Anne's reign. When on August 1, 1714, the schemes of Atterbury and Bolingbroke for a restoration of the Pretender were crushed and by a major miracle of history the Protestant Succession was peacefully settled in the house of Hanover, most Dissenters joined Abney and Fryer in the expectation that their steadfast loyalty to "Whig principles" would at last result in the repeal of all legislation which reduced them to the rôle of second class citizens. Dudley Ryder and other young nonconformist law students who met near the Temple for political discussions during the year 1715 placed great confidence in a report that Secretary Stanhope had requested Shute Barrington, Dissenting M.P. for Berwick, "to write down the reasons why it

---

[21] Jeremiah Smith, *The Magistrate and the Christian. . . . being Memoirs of the Life and Character of Sir Thomas Abney* (London, 1722), p. 57.

should be proper to have the Acts of Occasional Conformity and Schism taken off at this time and send them to him as heads for the Lords and Commons to argue upon."[22] Accordingly, it was expected "that parliament will take off these acts this year."

When such hopes failed to materialize, Ryder's friends attempted to press the matter as best they could. On April 25, 1716 Edward Leeds, Thomas Abney, and Michael Foster, all of whom were to pursue distinguished legal careers,[23] proposed to set up a club near the Temple "in order to encourage the cause," and several meetings followed. On May 10, 1716 it was proposed that "the Dissenters should have a general correspondence together through all the counties of England"[24] to promote their political interests, since "the court seems to regard only its own interest and to take care of the Dissenters only so far as it is necessary for this." The Whigs "cajoled Dissenters continually by promises of futurity, but neglected to make them good." In the face of this continued government inaction, Dudley Ryder reported high tempers at the November 8 meeting of "our Dissenters' Club at the Mitre." Messrs. Foster, Samson, and Abney declared themselves "very discontented Whigs so set against the present administration that they would gladly be revenged upon them . . . for their ingratitude to the Dissenters." Expressing the thought that they could not be "worse used by the Tories themselves," with righteous idignation, members of the club declared that "if

---

[22] William Matthews (ed.), *The Diary of Dudley Ryder* (London, 1939), p. 154.

[23] Leeds was admitted to the Inner Temple in 1710 and became King's Sergeant in 1748. Abney and Foster were also of the Inner Temple, the one becoming justice of common pleas in 1743 and the other a judge of the King's Bench in 1745. All three were "Protestant Dissenting Deputies" in later life.

[24] William Matthews, *op. cit.*, p. 233.

they don't repeal Occasional Conformity and Schism this session," the government would give all Dissenters "a full view and insight into the nature of the ministry and the Whigs, and . . . [we] will do our utmost to prevent the Dissenters voting for them again, [since] without their assistance they can never be chosen."[25]

The older generation of Dissenters also showed considerable impatience with the government; and, in 1717, when an address of congratulation on the end of the rebellion was under consideration by the Dissenting ministers of the Three Denominations "some were for having us speak plainly of the hardships the Dissenters lay under and of the little regard that was had to them notwithstanding their loyalty to His Majesty."[26] Although "moderate forces" at this meeting succeeded in passing a mildly worded resolution, it was evident that great dissatisfaction existed amongst Dissenters of conservative as well as those of more liberal persuasion.

That the impatience of nonconformists for repeal of discriminatory legislation could carry little weight with the government is hardly surprising. The primary interest of the Whigs was, quite naturally, to establish the new dynasty on as firm a base as possible. In pursuit of this policy, the first administration of George I had included the Earl of Nottingham, the principle author of the Occasional Conformity Act; and the first two years of Hanoverian rule were too disturbed to justify the risk of alienating Tory and High Church opinion by favors to the Dissenters. Indeed, feelings ran so high during the civil disturbances caused by the Jacobite Rebellion of 1715 that Dissenting meetinghouses were again burned and plundered. Not until the advent of the Stanhope-Sunderland Ad-

---

[25] *Ibid.*, p. 361.
[26] Benjamin Stinton MS (Dr. Williams' Library), p. 71.

ministration did things begin to look a bit brighter, and when the Ministry's position was greatly strengthened by Stanhope's diplomatic success in the spring of 1718 by the formation of the Quadruple Alliance and the naval victory over the Spanish fleet off Cape Passaro, it seemed that the Whigs could no longer find excuse for withholding their promise of relief to Dissenters.

Finally, on December 13, 1718, a bill was introduced into the House of Lords "for strengthening the Protestant Interest in these kingdoms," a measure which "was so bold as to take away the breath of all save perhaps Stanhope himself."[27] Not only did this measure propose to repeal the Occasional Conformity and Schism Acts, but it provided that any person who desired to receive the Anglican sacrament for the purpose of qualifying for office should give written notice of his intention to present himself at the altar on a given day; and, if the clergyman should refuse or not expressly agree to administer the sacrament at the time stipulated in the notice, "in every such case shall the notice refused be accepted and taken in place of receiving the sacrament of the Lord's Supper."[28] This bill, then, in addition to repealing the obnoxious acts of Anne's reign, presented a way of escape from the requirements of the Test and Corporation Acts without a direct frontal assault on them. Such a comprehensive measure could hardly fail to alarm the Tory bishops, and it was William Wake, Archbishop of Canterbury, who, despite his former reputation as a Whig in politics, acted as their chief spokesman. Employing as his major argument the assertion that the measure under consideration would upset a state of affairs most favorable to the Established Church, Wake declared:

---

[27] *Vide* Norman Sykes, *William Wake* (Cambridge, 1957), II, 122.
[28] *Ibid.*, p. 123.

The First Attempts at Repeal

... for five years past things have continued quiet and well under this law. Why should we now hazard the making them otherwise by repealing it? It is for the interest of the state to bring men as far to an union in the church established as might be. This the present act has in good measure done.[29]

It soon became evident that the whole bill would not survive the committee stage, and the Lords proceeded to delete what Bishop Nicolson of Carlisle called "several excresences in the bill, plastered upon it on purpose to be pared off, in order to its passing more glibly into law."[30] Accordingly, the measure emerged as a simple repeal of the Occasional Conformity and Schism Acts. It was opposed in the House of Commons by the Whig malcontents led by Robert Walpole, but passed by a majority of forty-four votes, restoring the ecclesiastical compromise of the Revolution Settlement and making religious toleration secure within these limits. Thus, one must look neither to May of 1689 nor to August of 1714 for the firm establishment of a toleration upon the statute book, but to December of 1718.

With the two obnoxious acts of Anne's reign safely repealed, the Dissenters' attention was now turned to securing relief from the two laws of Charles II which kept most of them from holding office, the Corporation and Test Acts. The older of these measures provided that all candidates must have taken the Anglican sacrament "within the year preceding their election to a corporate office." This requirement applied to "mayors, recorders, bailiffs, town clerks, common councilmen, and other persons . . . bearing any office or offices of magistracy or places or trusts, or other employment relating to or

---

[29] *Ibid.*, p. 126.
[30] *Ibid.*

concerning the government of . . . cities, corporations, and boroughs, and cinque ports. . . ."[31] The Test Act, designed to protect offices under the crown from religious subversives, stated that:

> . . . all and every person or persons . . . taken into any office or offices civil or military or shall receive any pay, salary, fee, or wages, by reason of any patent or grant of His Majesty, or shall have command or place of trust from or under His Majesty, his heir or successors . . . shall receive the sacrament of the Lord's Supper according to the usage of the Church of England within three months after his or their admittance in or receiving their said authority and employment in some public church. . . .[32]

On the face of it, therefore, this second statute was more liberal than the first, because a Dissenter need not overcome his scruples about taking the qualifying test until well after the reward of office was certain. Such fine points of law actually made little difference, however, for occasional conformity was not acceptable to all or even to many Dissenters. Although some "moderate men . . . in whom the Presbyterians chiefly confide" like John Shute (Viscount Barrington) and the Reverend Dr. Daniel Williams did not hesitate to write and preach in favor of it,[33] most Independents and Baptists found the

---

[31] 13 Car. II, St. II. C. 1. Costin and Watson, *op. cit.*, pp. 15–16.
[32] 25 Car. II. C. 2. *Ibid.*, pp. 40–41. This act did not extend to the peerage (clause XI), to non-commissioned army or navy officers who should make the declaration against transubstantiation (clause XV), or to any of the "nuisance offices" such as "high constable, petty constable, tithingman, overseer of the poor. . . . surveyor of the highways or any like inferior office . . . " (clause XVII).
[33] *Vide* Jonathan Swift's "Letter to Archbishop King" of Dublin in his *Works* (Edinburgh, 1824), XV, 318 for a good character analysis of Barrington and those "moderate men" who would "frequent the Church and the meeting indifferently." Barrington argued that it was perfectly proper to have communion "in any part of worship that is pure and un-

THE FIRST ATTEMPTS AT REPEAL 73

practice thoroughly distasteful. Moreover, many nonconformists from the Three Denominations, even when they had no objection to taking the Anglican sacrament, nevertheless opposed the imposition of any religious test—particularly the "profanation" of a sacrament—for admission to a state office.

Some historians have held that with the accession of George I these objections made little difference, for annual indemnity acts in fact released Dissenters from disabilities imposed by the Test and Corporation Acts.[34] It is quite true that an indemnity act was passed in 1714, but the second such measure did not appear until 1727; and, after that date, as both N. C. Hunt and David Thomson have pointed out, there were several

---

corrupted without countenancing the corruptions introduced in others . . ." After all, St. Paul himself had occasional communion with the Jews and "thus promoted his own edification and that of others by occasional conformity with the established church. But his conformity was always managed with a due regard and caution lest he should countenance and abet the mode of worship he only bore with." John Shute, *The Interest of England Considered* (London, 1703), pp. 55–56. Similarly, Daniel Williams, in *An Enquiry into the Present Duty of Protestant Dissenters* (London, 1712), p. 18, asserted: "We do not think the faults which we desire to be rectified to be such as to exclude those from being Churches of Christ who retain them; yea, we approve that our own members should testify their charity by occasional communion with them." Against this liberal Presbyterian viewpoint, Daniel Defoe spoke for many Baptists and Independents when he raised the question: "What have the Dissenters to do, as Dissenters, in the broils about who is or is not employed in the state? Is it not the interest of persons and the interest of parties that is the quarrel? . . . And moreover seeing which side soever prevails, the Dissenters are sure to have no share in the management: Why should they have a share in the hazard?" *A Letter to the Dissenters* (London, 1713), p. 27.

[34] F. W. Maitland, *The Constitutional History of England* (Cambridge, 1908), pp. 516–17; D. L. Keir, *The Constitutional History of Modern Britain,* 3rd ed. (London, 1946), pp. 321, 430; and W. A. Holdsworth, *A History of English Law* (London, 1938), X, 71. R. W. Cowherd in his recent work *The Politics of English Dissent* (New York, 1956) also asserts that such acts were "passed annually after 1727," p. 23.

more interruptions.[35] The Statutes at Large indicate that no indemnity acts were passed to cover any part of the years 1730, 1732, 1744, 1749, 1750, 1753, and 1757. Even after 1758, when indemnity acts actually did become an annual affair, their scope continued to provide very inadequate protection.[36]

To be sure, during the same parliamentary session in which Dissenters were relieved of the Occasional Conformity and Schism Acts there was passed an additional law which gave some slight measure of relief. An "Act for quieting and establishing corporations" provided that all office-holders who had not complied with the sacramental test, but whose tenure of office was not challenged within six months, were confirmed in

---

[35] N. C. Hunt, *Some Religious and Economic Organizations and the Government 1730–42* (Cambridge, Unpublished Ph.D. Dissertation, 1951), p. 131; and David Thomson in *The Listener* (London, 15 Nov., 1951), p. 843. Thomson's contention that "there were nine gaps between 1727 and 1760, and one more before 1789" does not appear to be strictly accurate. I find only seven such gaps in Danby Pickering's edition of *The Statutes at Large* (Cambridge, 1760–1807) between those years, nor is there evidence that an act failed to be passed at any time from 1760 to 1789.

[36] All of these acts, taking I Geo. I; St. II. c. 13, clause 23 as their model, simply indemnified those Dissenters who ought to have taken the sacrament, but had failed to do so by the time that the measure was passed; yet they were protected only if they actually did take the qualifying test by the date specified in each act. This might have been satisfactory if each law had provided for twelve full months of coverage, but such was not always the case. For example, the 1728 Act gave Dissenters until November 28 of that year, with a gap of two months before the 1729 measure was passed. The date for qualification was moved forward to September 29 in the Acts of 1733 and 1734, leaving three months exposed before parliament took action after the Christmas recess, while the 1736 Act laid down August 1 as the deadline, with over five months unprotected. Even after 1738 when the deadline for qualification was gradually moved toward the end of the year in which the Act was passed, gaps of from one to three months were common; e.g., there was a gap of one month in 1742, three months in 1760, and one month in 1766, 1771, and 1795.

their positions.[37] Since this was the one statute during the entire eighteenth century that gave sacramentally unqualified nonconformists any real security of tenure, and that only after an initial six months of vulnerability, it seems certain that when Dissenters held office or were members of corporations, they were nearly always occasional conformists. Even in areas where Dissent was strong, as Sidney and Beatrice Webb have shown, "the mere existence of the statutory prohibition, combined with the religious and political partisanship of the time, almost always served to exclude the definitely attached member of a nonconformist body."[38]

Although Presbyterians, Independents, and Baptists suffered the injustice of second class citizenship under the test laws, their lot was a happy one in comparison to that of two other Dissenting groups—Quakers and "Papists." It was not until after 1722, when their "right of affirmation" was made permanent in all legal requirements that the Quakers had secure power of protecting their property from constant petty persecutions; and their continued conscientious objection to the collection of tythes in the face of no government action to provide relief, even in the form of a compulsory system of inexpensive prosecution for their payment, was a source of grievance throughout the century.[39]

---

[37] 5 Geo. I. C. 6. *Vide* Pickering, *op. cit.*, XVI, 16–17.

[38] Sidney and Beatrice Webb, *The Manor and the Borough* (London, 1908), p. 391.

[39] R. M. Jones in *The Later Period of Quakerism* (London, 1921), I, 152, estimates that during the century between 1730 and 1830, well over £750,000 were exacted from Quakers in tithes and costs of collection. John Gough, their contemporary, in his *History of the People Called Quakers* (Dublin, 1790), IV, 289–300, lists about two dozen persons who incurred "grievous prosecutions for trivial demands," e.g., the case of Israel Fell in Lancashire, who, prosecuted for a tithe of only one shilling in value, at the suit of William Tufton, parson of Standish, was imprisoned for four years. Nevertheless, after 1722 Quakers ceased to be

The position of Roman Catholics was even more dismal. Despite Daniel Defoe's observation of "numerous popish chapels" among the religious buildings in the metropolis[40] and the fact that even Edmond Gibson, the staunchly Anglican bishop of London whose *Preservative against Popery* appeared in 1738, held that Roman Catholics should be tolerated so long as they lived quietly and obscurely,[41] the whole weight of the penal code continued to threaten them. As late as the seventeen-sixties Roman priests continued to be harassed by the accusations of informers;[42] and, if upon reaching the age of eighteen, any Roman Catholic refused to sign not only the oaths of supremacy and allegiance, but also the same declaration against transubstantiation required in the Test and Corporation Acts, he became legally incapable of inheriting land and his estate passed to the nearest Protestant relative, if he chose to claim it.[43]

Life under the Test and Corporation Acts, then, aside from constituting a brand of social inferiority, caused no such hardship in the ordinary business of daily existence for "orthodox" nonconformists. As a matter of fact, these acts can hardly be said to have inflicted great disabilities upon the rank and file of those affiliated with the Three Denominations, for many among the Baptists and Independents would never look for

---

outlaws of the state; and, although the petty annoyance remained their lot until subjection to the tithingman was finally removed in 1873, they were "rapidly acquiring the savor of respectability which attaches to estimable characters now freed from the reputation of disturbing enthusiams."

[40] Daniel Defoe, *A Tour Through the Whole Island of Great Britain* (London, 1738), I, 156.

[41] Norman Sykes, *Edmund Gibson* (Oxford, 1926), p. 295.

[42] J. W. Amherst, *History of Catholic Emancipation* (London, 1886), I, 84–88.

[43] *Vide* W. E. H. Lecky, *History of England in the Eighteenth Century* (London, 1892 ed.), I, 335 *et seq.*

civil or military offices, and there is strong evidence that those leaders among the Presbyterians who aspired to such positions were quite prepared to be occasional conformists. This no doubt does much to account for the very peaceful relationships between Dissenters and the government during the decade following repeal of Occasional Conformity and Schism legislation,[44] but by the early seventeen-thirties members of the Three Denominations became so worked up against the Test and Corporation Acts, that they spent much energy to agitate for repeal.

This sudden outburst of activity was probably sparked more by agitation from across the Irish Sea than from anything which occurred on home soil. In the autumn of 1731 Irish Presbyterians had sent a delegation to petition the London

---

[44] The peaceful relations between Dissent and the government can also be explained by the fierce doctrinal controversies that had begun to occupy the Three Denominations as a result of the famous Salters' Hall Meeting early in 1719 — disputes over subscription to the doctrine of the Trinity which revealed various degrees of heterodoxy among the Dissenting ministers, particularly among the Presbyterians who were leaning more and more in the direction of either Arian or Unitarian views. For a defence of the non-subscribers' position, the leading exponent of which was John Shute Barrington, see the anonymous pamphlet, *An Authentic Account of Several Things done and agreed upon . . . at Salters' Hall* (London, 1719). Thomas Bradbury, staunch defender of subscription, replied in *An Answer to the Reproaches Cast on those Dissenting Ministers who subscribed their Belief of the Eternal Trinity* (London, 1719). Roger Thomas has written an excellent article on the background and substance of the whole dispute: "The Non-Subscription Controversy amongst Dissenters in 1719: the Salters' Hall Debate" in *The Journal of Ecclesiastical History* (London, 1953), IV, 162–186. . . . Also, it was in this period that the Royal House showed Dissenters a particular favor. In 1723 George I made the initial grant of £500 to the widows of Dissenting ministers. This grant, the *Regium Donum,* was soon increased to £1,000 a year and its distribution was placed in the hands of nine ministers. *Vide* Edmund Calamy, *op. cit.,* II, 445. Calamy had also received £50 from the king for a sermon which he preached on the Trinity (*Ibid.,* II, 186). These favors no doubt helped to keep the Dissenters quiet.

government for repeal of the sacramental test. Walpole responded to their petition by expressing the view that "the time for relief to Irish Protestants had come and that in England such relief was considered universally right."[45] He proposed to tack such a bill on to one of the Irish measures then under consideration by the British Parliament, but this scheme miscarried largely because of fierce opposition by Churchmen in the Dublin Parliament who feared that Presbyterians might gain a dominant hand.[46] The whole affair nevertheless stirred up a spirited pamphlet warfare in which English Dissenters took lively interest.[47]

John Abernethy, a leading Presbyterian minister in Dublin, was particularly forceful on the subject of test legislation and his views received wide circulation in England. A law excluding free born subjects from civil offices for which they were otherwise qualified and enforcing that exclusion by penalties merely because of their scruples against receiving the sacrament according to the usage of the Established Church, Abernethy asserted, punished them for conscience' sake and so deprived them of "a basic natural right." No man, certainly, had the natural right to possess a state office, but that was hardly what Dissenters claimed. They asked only for the right

---

[45] Vide J. C. Beckett, *Protestant Dissent in Ireland, 1687–1780* (London, 1948), p. 91.

[46] As Beckett points out, even in England where Protestant Dissenters were a very small part of the population, it proved impossible at this time to secure a repeal of the sacramental test. It was not surprising, then, that in Ireland where they equalled or almost equalled the Churchmen in numbers, if not in wealth, there should be a deep reluctance to admit them to any opportunity for wider political influence. *Ibid.*, pp. 95–96.

[47] The first pamphlet in the Irish repeal controversy seems to have been John Abernethy's *The Nature and Consequences of the Test Considered* (Dublin, 1731), which was answered by Swift in his *Advantages Proposed by Repealing the Sacramental Test. . . .* (Dublin, 1732). Both were reprinted in London within a few months of their initial publication.

to be eligible, for a capacity in law of serving their sovereign should he deem them worthy :
> Their legal capacity is their right, of which they have made no forfeiture, unless by a religious opinion and practice pursuant to it which, whether it be itself right or wrong, is usually of no importance . . . to the civil interest of the nation.

Showing the unmistakable influence of Locke throughout, he concluded his argument by insisting that "a diversity of opinions in matters of religion is . . . inseparable from the nature of mankind and equally unavoidable with a diversity of faces." For a government to maintain legislation contrary to this basic psychological truth was not only unjust but sheer folly.[48]

Reacting to such agitation, Shute Barrington, who held an Irish peerage and was the most influential layman among English Dissenters, attempted to stir up his brethren in the cause of repeal. A practical politician, he realized that if the test could be eliminated, by opening up the magistracy Dissenters would be in a good position to protect themselves against petty persecutions at the local level, and also their interest would be strengthened in the corporations which themselves sent members to Parliament. For such reasons as these Barrington urged immediate action, declaring that "plain reason shows the Dissenters have a much stronger security if they shall obtain this explanation [that is, amendment] at the end of an old parliament than at the beginning of a new one . . ." in order that the government might be assured of their support in the coming general election.[49]

---

[48] John Abernethy, *Reasons for Repeal*. . . (Dublin, 1732), pp. 4, 43.

[49] *Vide* Barrington's *Answer to Some Queries* (London, 1732), pp. 21–30. Thomas Bradbury, always Barrington's bitter antagonist since they had taken opposite sides in the Salters' Hall controversy, accused him of

By the early seventeen-thirties the Three Denominations were not lacking in organizational machinery which could implement Barrington's efforts. Although from the beginning of the century their ministers had met only at irregular intervals for the presentation of loyal addresses to the crown, in 1727 Dissenting clergymen in London undertook to form a permanent association, agreeing that all approved ministers living within ten miles of the metropolis should constitute "the General Body of Dissenting Ministers of the Three Denominations in and about the Cities of London and Westminster." They also provided for a standing committee of seven Presbyterians, six Independents, and six Baptist ministers to handle any business of mutual interest which might arise between annual meetings of the General Body.[50] Besides passing a resolution in support of Irish Dissenters, however, no important action was taken until toward the end of 1732 when the pamphlet debate over test legislation had burst into full flame.

It was then that the General Body expressed the opinion that "a considerable number of gentlemen might meet to consider what steps were fit to be taken with relation to repeal of the Test and Corporation Acts the ensuing session of parliament."[51] Such a suggestion fell upon the willing ears of lay Dissenters in London and they lost no time in assuming the leadership of a campaign for repeal. On November 9, 1732, the "First General Assembly of Protestant Dissenters for Repeal of the Test and Corporation Acts" gathered at the meet-

---

interest in politics to the detriment of religion and came out with a strong defense of the status quo, declaring it "imprudent to hazard so many valuable privileges [e.g., the *Regium Donum* and general favor of the Royal House] for the sake of pushing that which, if you obtain it, will be of little advantage to you as a religious body." *Reasons offered against Pushing for Repeal of the Corporation and Test Acts* (London, 1732).

[50] *Minute Books of the General Body* (Dr. Williams' Library MSS), I, 11 July 1727.

ing house in Silver Street. The major item of business was to appoint a committee of twenty-one persons, with Samuel Holden as chairman, "to consider and report to a subsequent meeting when and in what manner it would be proper to make application" for repeal.[52] Both B. L. Manning and N. C. Hunt deal in detail with the development of this organization soon to be called the Protestant Dissenting Deputies, showing how the caution and apparent lack of enthusiasm of the committee which it appointed between 1732 and 1736 drew much criticism from contemporaries who tended to regard it as a mere agent of the Chief Minister.[53]

On November 28, 1732, Holden and a sub-committee of five met Walpole and were thoroughly discouraged by his pessimistic attitude. He clearly realized, of course, that Holden's

---

[51] *Ibid.*
[52] *Ibid.* for 9 November 1732. *Vide* also B. L. Manning, *The Protestant Dissenting Deputies* (Cambridge, 1952), p. 23.
[53] Lord Hervey in the first volume of his *Memoirs,* R. Sedgwick ed. (London, 1931), pp. 130–31, states that the committee presided over by Holden was "chosen by his [i.e. Walpole's] contrivance," but N. C. Hunt absolves Holden of this charge of being the Chief Minister's creature, stressing the fact that Holden and his committee, while under the most bitter attacks between the end of 1732 and the beginning of 1735, always had a majority of Deputies behind him. Also Holden, who was an occasional conformist, could not have felt a sense of immediate urgency in pushing for repeal, even though he regarded test legislation as grossly unjust. Hunt, however, finds the major reason for the committee's lack of enthusiasm in the fact that they were "political realists," realizing that the Bolingbroke–Pulteny opposition were utterly unreliable and that there was no hope for their project without government support or at least neutrality. Admittedly Holden and his friends on the committee were men of influence — six of them, including himself, were bank directors and he was also a governor of the Russia Company — and their high positions were probably what led the Deputies to entrust them with the repeal campaign. Unfortunately, their close connection with the government was such that they were not anxious to embarrass it even on so important a matter as repeal of the hated acts. *Vide* Hunt, *Sir Robert Walpole, Samuel Holden, and the Dissenting Deputies* (London, Dr. Williams' Library, Eleventh Lecture, 1957), pp. 23–30.

committee could have led an extremely powerful campaign during the 1733 Parliamentary session, backed by Dissenters in the country.[54] Not only would this have caused particular embarrassment to Walpole in the "excise session," but with the 1734 election on the horizon, he could hardly afford either to antagonize the Church or to offend the Dissenters. Therefore, courteously but firmly, the Minister declined to guarantee them his support "at the present time." The Deputies at first refused to accept this discouraging report, but the General Assembly finally agreed that the whole matter should be resolved by appointing four new members to the committee. This remodeling, however, did not serve to change the committee's views, and they passed a resolution "that application to Parliament in the ensuing session for repeal . . . is not likely to be attended with success." The Deputies accepted this and Holden, still chairman of the committee, drafted a "letter to the country" stressing that even a single petition for repeal in the 1733 session was likely to prejudice the Dissenters' hopes for future relief.[55]

A spirited pamphlet warfare, begun in the summer of 1732, now burst into full force. Bishop Thomas Sherlock led off with a defence of the status quo, insisting that in a Christian country it was fit and reasonable that those who were em-

---

[54] By the end of 1732, in fact, at least a dozen different meetings of Dissenters had taken place in the provinces, all of which passed strongly worded resolutions in favor of repeal. *Vide ibid.*, pp. 6–7.

[55] *Vide* Lord Egmont's *Diary* (H.M.C., London, 1920), I, 301–305 and *Minutes of the Deputies* (28 Dec., 1732). This failure to press for repeal was greeted by marked opposition from the country and several hostile pamphlets were circulated, e.g.: *The Right of the Committee considered in a Letter to the Deputies of the Three Denominations* (London, 1733); *An Impartial Account of the Late Transactions of the Dissenters in reference to their Committee* (London, 1734); and *A Narrative of the Proceedings of the Protestant Dissenters of the Three Denominations* (London, 1734).

ployed in the public administration should continue to give some public testimony of their being Christians. Surely the Lord's Supper was "the most proper proof of this." Rules and laws were not bad in themselves because bad men abused them. Besides, "if those who at this time inveigh so loudly against the Sacramental Test were *solely* or *chiefly* govern'd by a concern for the honour of the Ordinance, they would long e're this have propos'd in its stead some *other* pledge and security by which the end and intent of the Sacramental Test might be equally attain'd." Bishop Sherlock concluded with the old argument against the subversive nature of Dissenting doctrines in view of the preceding century with all of its civil strife. In view of their subversive behavior in the past, "however harmless and innocent the intention of the present Dissenters may be with regard to the Church, they cannot answer for the intentions of the next generation."[56]

An anonymous pamphleteer immediately took up Sherlock's argument, insisting that "if they [i.e., the Dissenters] would but consider that theirs is not the established religion of the country, they ought to be well contented . . . for what liberty and privilege is allowed them by the legislature." Indeed, how did they derive from the argument of their loyalty to the Crown a "natural right to some share in all public distributions with those of the established religion?" Their being good subjects was only what His Majesty deserved and might claim from them. Furthermore, "it is not only their duty but it is their interest, as well as it is ours of the Church of England, to be in a peculiar manner devoted to His present Majesty, since in him only is it . . . that both we and they are secured from

---

[56] Thomas Sherlock, *The History of the Test Act* (London, 1732), pp. 22–23; 28.

from a power which, if once it should prevail, would undo both them and us . . ."⁵⁷

Lord Egmont took a less conventional approach in upholding the test laws. He began his pamphlet by observing that Dissenters were never found complaining that restrictions upon Roman Catholics amounted to persecution or an infringement of the natural rights of mankind. But if the treatment of Roman Catholics did not deserve the name of persecution—which implies unjust severity—it must follow that "nothing can be deemed a persecution which is done for the advantage of society and that a society may lay what penalties, inflict what punishments, and prescribe what restrictions they please, when such penalties, punishments, and restrictions are only imposed for the general good." Egmont reasoned that it was in no manner lawful to persecute for opinions in religious matters or because opinions of other men were different from our own, but only because they were opinions with relation to civil matters which had "a tendency to the ruin of society." If, indeed, persecution consisted in depriving men of an equality which it might be supposed they possessed in a state of nature, there was not a country in the world where persecution did not exist, "nay, society itself is a state of persecution." It followed that "the natural privilege of mankind" vanished before "the supreme law of all, the safety of the people." The natural privileges of Dissenters were not consequently infringed, "but only abridged for the safety of the state."⁵⁸

Bishop Edmund Gibson then entered the fray, declaring that the whole matter could be summed up in a single

---

[57] *Some Account of the Dissenters* (London, 1732), pp. 10–12.

[58] John Percival, Second Earl Egmont, *A Full and Fair Discussion of the Pretensions of the Dissenters to the Repeal of the Sacramental Test* (London, 1733), pp. 7–12.

question: "Is not society and government itself founded in an abridgment of Natural Rights in such instances and such degrees as in the judgment of the legislature the safety and welfare of the whole requires?"[59] It was he to whom most Dissenting pamphleteers replied directly.

Samuel Chandler insisted that society in its nature required no abridgment of any natural rights, though it might determine the application or use of certain parts of those rights. For example, the fruits of every man's labor were his own, but the nature of society and government required that a part of private property should be appropriated to public services or for the support of society itself. Such application was no invasion of natural rights because every man who became a member of society was bound to contribute to the maintenance of it. But how did this duty prove that the nature of government or society required that man should be deprived of any natural rights when it was not necessary to the support of society; indeed, when the full enjoyment of them was necessary to the honor and security of the commonwealth? "Every subject hath thus such a right to serve the government under which he lives, and every government hath a claim to their service whenever they need it." It was an injury to society and a weakening of any government to deprive itself of "the services and talents of any body of subjects who have been long known to be loyal and faithful."[60]

Caleb Fleming adopted a slightly different emphasis in his answer to Bishop Gibson. All men, he insisted, were by nature

---

[59] Edmund Gibson, *The Dispute Adjusted about the Proper Time of Applying for a Repeal of the Corporation and Test Acts by shewing that No Time is Proper* (London, 1732), p. 95.
[60] Samuel Chandler, *The Dispute Better Adjusted* (London, 1732), p. 23.

equal, and no man could have a right over others until the people gave him that right for their own sakes. In other words, the people were the true fountain of all just power. But the sole end of government was the preservation of the rights of mankind, and whenever any government neglected to secure these rights, or in any degree actually abridged them, "so far is that government from being supported upon a just foundation that the very basis thereof has become insecure and dangerous." Therefore, Gibson's contention only served to state that "society is founded upon unnatural foundations." Ought not the mercantile and trading interests to be as naturally represented as the landed? And are Protestant Dissenters "whose number at the lowest calculation is much above 300,000 and whose wealth in land, etc. amounts to nearly £15,000,000; are they to be discarded the favour and equal protection of the legislature as an inconsiderable part of the community?"[61]

These same arguments were echoed by William Harris, but his basic contention in response to Gibson's challenge was a legal one. Since Dissenters were entrusted with the right to sit in Parliament where no sacramental test was required, but only the security of civil oaths, the same test deemed sufficient for members of the highest legislative body in the land ought also to be sufficient for members of corporations.[62]

Despite the position of great landowners and bishops against

---

[62] William Harris, *Brief Remarks upon the "Dispute Adjusted"* (London, 1733), p. 8.

[61] Caleb Fleming, *An Answer to the "Dispute Adjusted"* (London, 1732), pp. 13–14. His estimate of the Dissenting population seems somewhat inflated. The Evans MS, edited by E. D. Bebb in *Nonconformity and Social and Economic Life* (London, 1935) shows that in 1715 the adult Dissenting population was somewhere in the neighborhood of 250,000, about 14,000 of whom had the parliamentary franchise. *Vide* also Hunt, *op. cit.*, p. 7.

any sort of repeal, several anonymous pamphlets continued to push for it during the winter of 1732–1733, all repeating the same basic arguments: If the inconveniences the Dissenters had suffered from the disqualifying laws which were at first designed only to exclude Papists, if their quiet and peaceful behavior under a long series of discouragements "tho' they have seen rebels pardon'd and traitors to their country obtain money," if the firmness and vigor with which they had acted and "the numberless dangers to which they have exposed themselves for the support and defence of the Protestant succession," if their "known zeal and affection for his present Majesty and every branch of the Royal Family;" if none of these considerations have had weight enough to procure the desired repeal for the space of almost sixty years, "it is greatly to be feared that it will never be allowed to be a proper time so long as great men among the clergy oppose it or there are any Dissenters left in the kingdom. . . ."[63] "For God's sake, Gentlemen," wrote a country Dissenter in a pamphlet addressed to the Holden Committee, "let no plausible artifices of your enemies or their abettors deter or intimidate you, but use thankfully all the helps which providence has put into your power for the regaining your natural rights and liberties!"[64]

Regardless of all this strong feeling, Holden delayed in calling a meeting of the Deputies, of whom he was also chairman, after the year 1734 had begun. As a result, to express disapproval of his moderate policy, a faction of about fifty Deputies under the leadership of Captain James Winter met, elected a committee of fifteen, and called a general meeting of

---

[63] *Vide Reasons for Applying to Parliament* (London, 1732), p. 3; *The Rights and Liberties of Subjects Defended* (London, 1732), pp. 11, 19, 22; *Liberty the Support of Truth* (London, 1732), pp. 43–45; *A Letter to Protestant Dissenters of All Denominations* (London, 1733), pp. 15–16.
[64] *Reflections upon the Corporation and Test Acts* (London, 1732), p.22.

Dissenters from the entire country to convene in London on April 3, 1734. This meant, of course, that the attention of the majority group, now called into session by Holden, was completely absorbed by opposition to Winter and his followers rather than by the repeal question. They passed resolutions that the activities of the minority tended "to divide and weaken the interest of Dissenters" and "that it be recommended to Dissenters in the country at the ensuing election for members of Parliament to promote the interest of such persons as are known to be well effected to His Majesty's person and government and to the civil and religious liberties of our country."[65] Holden lost no time in getting off letters to the country to stifle Winter's scheme for a general meeting, and no evidence has been found to suggest that such a meeting took place. Although pressure from the country induced Holden to promise early action, he managed to avoid any application to Parliament in 1735.

Early in 1735, however, the breach was healed. Although they retained Holden as chairman, the newly elected Deputies for that year added Captain Winter to their ranks. The basis of this reconciliation lay in the results of an interview between Holden and Walpole in which the Minister had held, as usual, that it was not a proper time to afford the Dissenters relief, on this occasion offering the excuse of the press of business at the beginning of a new Parliament and also the crisis in foreign affairs caused by the War of the Polish Succession: "But as the Dissenters had in deference to the administration and at their desire deferred the application to Parliament from year to year and had at the late election behaved so exceedingly well they would not desire the Dissenters to put off the applica-

---

[65] *Minutes of the Deputies,* I (6 March, 1734/5).

tion any longer, but leave it to them if they saw fitting to make the attempt at the next sessions."[66]

Now that Walpole had indicated he would let the campaign proceed, Holden was willing to organize pressure in Parliament. He dispatched a letter urging country Dissenters "to use your best endeavours to engage as many members as you can to be in our interest, to concur with us in endeavours to remove that which has been so long and justly complained of."[67] At the same time members of the committee approached members of Parliament. Favorable replies came in from the country,[68] but there was a most discouraging interview between Walpole and a sub-committee at the end of December. As a result, on January 14, 1736, when Holden and his committee met the newly-elected Deputies, they submitted a gloomy report. The government would oppose them and no support could be relied upon from the opposition. But the Dissenters refused to be daunted and instructed the committee to make "early and vigorous application."[69] Again Holden tried to discourage the Deputies at a meeting on February 25, and again they insisted upon a "vigorous application."

Preparations to bring the repeal question before the House continued. On March 2, two propaganda pamphlets were distributed, and a week later a sheet was prepared for delivery to members of the House of Commons.[70] These not only repeated the arguments used by Chandler, Fleming, and Harris, but more tactfully emphasized that "repeal of the acts must not be considered as a benefit to the Dissenters so much as

---

[66] *Ibid.*
[67] *Ibid* (15 May, 1735).
[68] *Ibid*. (22 Oct., 1735).
[69] *Ibid*. (14 Jan., 1736).

restoring a fit right and power to the throne . . . to enable the King to choose whom he would for the support of Protestant government . . . ," the proved loyalty of Dissenters to the Crown making this all the more necessary.[71] The liberal Churchman Arthur Ashley Sykes also took up this argument, raising the question: "Is truth so much on their side, so little on the Church side, that as soon as ever they are freed from the Test Act, all must fall down before them?"[72]

Gibson's *Dispute Adjusted* was republished as a fitting reply by the High Churchmen, and other like-minded pamphleteers dwelt tiresomely upon the old "Church in danger" rallying cry. The Reverend Richard Grey referred to "the horrors of Cromwellian upheavals." " 'Tis not men's professions or prejudices that we are to regard, but the tendency of their schemes and the influence they are like to have on the public peace and safety."[73] After "the woeful experience we have had" with Dissenters in the last century, argued an anonymous pamphleteer, "must they be not only permitted to oppose the judgment of the legislature, but be paid for it too [i.e., by admission to offices] by the very legislature they oppose?"[74]

Finally, on March 12, 1736, William Plumer, M.P. for Hertfordshire, addressed a three-point speech to the Commons

[70] *Ibid.* (9 March, 1735/6).

[71] *Vide A Petition for Repeal of the Sacramental Test* (London, 1736), p. 16.

[72] Arthur Ashley Sykes, *The Corporation and Test Acts shown to be of no Importance to the Church of England* (London, 1736), p. 51. Sykes also uses the argument employed by Owen and Locke that "since public peace and order may be preserved without conformity to the standard of the State Religion (and we see it so in fact since the toleration has been granted) why is church conformity here made expedient to peace and order?", pp. 23–24.

[73] Richard Grey, D.D., *The Miserable and Distracted State of Religion in England* (London, 1736).

[74] *The Argument with Dissenters about Subscriptions and the Repeal of the Corporation and Test Acts* (London, 1736), p. 17.

in which he moved for repeal of the Test and Corporation Acts. First of all, Plumer professed himself "an enemy of all manner of persecution," and attempted to show his hearers that test laws constituted a "very high degree of persecution" by asserting the fact that if one of his majesty's loyal Dissenting subjects should work his way up to the position of a commissioned officer in a regiment while fighting for king and country abroad, immediately upon his return home the law required either that he become an apostate or resign his position. Secondly, Plumer had great reverence for the Lord's Supper and pleaded with the House no longer to "turn a sacred mystery to such prophane use as that of qualifying a man as an inspector of wine kegs or the bailiff of a little borough." Thirdly, he would always uphold "everything tending toward establishing the unity, peace, and trade of my country," and he cited history to show that to promote such desirable elements "we must allow men to judge freely in matters of religion and to embrace that opinion they think right without any hopes of temporal rewards and without any fears of temporal punishment."[75] Sir Wilfred Lawson at once seconded these liberal sentiments.

Sir Robert Walpole then rose to speak "as a sincere member of the Church of England" who wished that all Dissenters could be won over to it, but who would never seek to accomplish that wish "by any methods that have the least tendency towards persecution." According to Plumer's definition of "persecution," however, Walpole declared that there could be no established church or religion in the world without the government which supported it being charged with oppression. To exclude a man from a profitable post of employment was

---

[75] William Cobbett, *op cit.,* IX, 1047–50.

certainly a hardship, but was this not absolutely necessary to protect "our established church," the guarantor of stable government, "that all men be excluded from executive positions who think it their duty to destroy it?" Such action, motivated solely for the preservation of "our most excellent constitution," could no more be called persecution than the exclusion of Nonjurors and Roman Catholics from government offices. So far as profaning the sacrament was concerned, Walpole answered that this was no fault of the law, but was the responsibility of the Anglican clergy who were charged with the duty of admitting only sincere believers to the Lord's table. As to Plumer's last point, the Minister was persuaded that "the repeal of this law . . . would raise most terrible disturbances and confusions, for with respect to all posts and employments that go by election we should have all the Dissenters combining closely together to bring in their friends which would of course breed many riots and tumults."[76]

Lord Polworth spoke next followed by Alderman Heathcote, both asserting their understanding of Walpole's argument to be that "if the hardships imposed upon Dissenters by the law under our constitution are greater than what are necessary for preserving its being in their power to destroy the established church, it must be granted that . . . the law is a persecuting one." To determine that the Test Act was such a measure, they declared, one need look no farther than Scotland where judges and magistrates went openly to Episcopal meeting houses, while the Presbyterian establishment was so far from "any danger of being overturned by what is there the Dissenting interest that the former is daily gaining ground upon the latter, which evidently shews the weight and effect of a legal

---

[76] *Ibid.*, pp. 1053–55.

establishment with respect to religion once the minds of men are not irritated by any unnecessary hardship put upon them."[77]

Samuel Holden entered the debate to point out that the hardships put upon Nonjurors and Roman Catholics were not for the sake of conscience in any matter of religious concern, but because they were enemies of the state and to "the present happy establishment," but no party amongst Protestant Dissenters had "yet ever been suspected of being enemies to our excellent constitution." Holden, Polworth, and Heathcote all joined in insisting that every subject had the right "to a capacity at least of sharing in the honours and preferments of his country and that capacity ought not to be taken from him but by way of punishment for some very high crime or misdemeanor, for it is a punishment so severe that we never find it inflicted by our laws upon any crime of ordinary nature."[78] All such arguments were to no avail against the Chief Minister's opposition, however; and when, after a debate of more than four hours, the house divided on Plumer's motion, the Dissenters were defeated by 251 votes to 123, a government majority of 128. This was, of course, just as Holden had predicted, and he resigned on October 13, 1736.

Under Holden's successor, Benjamin Avery, there appeared a notable change in the committee's enthusiasm. They spent the year 1737–38 seeking the most effective way to mobilize the Dissenting strength of the country behind their program. By February of 1737 they had prepared an extensive list of country Dissenters with whom to correspond, and by April a solicitor had been appointed "to observe and carefully attend

---

[77] *Ibid.*, p. 1057.
[78] *Ibid.*, pp. 1058–59.

all motions in Parliament that can in any way effect Dissenters."[19]

At the beginning of November, 1738, thoroughly exasperated by the city of London's exactions from them for the Mansion House Fund,[80] a general meeting of the Deputies resolved unanimously to approach Parliament during the next session. Avery's committee at once sent off letters to the country which could only be contrasted with the counsels of candor and caution that had characterized Holden's dispatches. On November 28 a subcommittee with Samuel Chandler as chairman was appointed to wait on twenty-nine prominent individuals including principal members of the government and the opposition. Lobbying was begun promptly and the committee issued a short effective list of grievances.[81]

Two pamphlets by Churchmen then appeared in support of the Dissenters' position—one by the Reverend Robert Seagrave, who was becoming conspicuous as a supporter of George Whitefield,[82] and the other by Bishop Hoadly. Adopting the arguments of John Owen, Seagrave declared that: "We must

---

[19] *Minutes of the Deputies* (27 April, 1737).

[80] In April of 1730 the London Common Council had passed a resolution that all fines owing to the city for the privilege of being excused from serving in the office of sheriff (amounting to £400 per person) should be reserved for the building of the lord mayor's residence. By 1735 this had clearly developed into an extortionate procedure whereby the corporation deliberately nominated wealthy Dissenters who were clearly unqualified to serve and would thus be forced to "swear off" by paying the fine. A. J. Henderson, *London and the National Government* (Durham, N.C., 1945), pp. 165–68 shows that this procedure had netted the city upwards of £20,000 by 1738. Reacting in anger to such bold-faced extortion, Sir Thomas Sewell issued a pamphlet, *The Case of the Dissenters* . . . (London, 1739) in which he argued that "to make a man in this case liable to a fine is to punish him twice on the same account, once by excluding him from office and again by fine," p. 24.

[81] *Vide Minutes of the Deputies* (13 March, 1758/9). The list of grievances is fully reproduced in Manning, *op. cit.*, pp. 30–31.

make a wide difference between civil authority and ecclesiastical. The civil authority of a kingdom comprehends universally all persons born in it, but this is not the case of the ecclesiastical. . . ." Religion "reaches and comprehends" only every person who agrees to it; accordingly, mankind should be permitted "to arrange themselves in whatever religious societies they think fit, without the least envy or disadvantage, provided always they give proper security to the civil magistrate of their allegiance." What the legislature was in fact saying by the test laws was ". . . Judge for yourselves; but if you do not think and judge as we do, you shall suffer for it and be turned out of the house."[82]

Bishop Hoadly quite agreed with this reasoning, pointing out that "repeal will only remove a blot, a mark set upon them [i.e., the Dissenters], an incapacity of serving; but will no more actually put them into office than curing them of a fit of gout will do it." Civil power, insisted Hoadly, had no right even to exclude Roman Catholics "for religion only." If they took oaths of allegiance to the king, and declared that no power on earth had authority to release them from such an obligation, then all restrictions against them should be removed, and certainly this was true of all Dissenting groups. Indeed, toleration since the Revolution had diminished the members of Dissenters "and abated the zeal of those against the Church." Removing the test laws would likewise redound to the Church's advantage.[84] But staunch Churchmen answered these two extremists by redistributing the 1736 edition of Gibson's *Dispute Adjusted* and by remouthing their old argu-

---

[82] *Vide* Robert Seagrave, *An Answer to the Reverend Dr. Trapp's Four Sermons against Mr. Whitefield* (London, 1739).

[83] Robert Seagrave, *Observations upon the Conduct of the Clergy* (London, 1738), pp. 41–49.

ments in a new pamphlet, *The Church of England Vindicated.*[85]

In spite of the fact that support from these two "erring brethren" among the established clergy could only serve to make the Dissenters more unpopular with steadfast Anglicans, and in the absence of any encouragement from Walpole, they pressed on with their campaign. Indeed, to the deputation which waited on him late in December, 1738, Walpole made his stock reply: "The time has not yet arrived." "You have so repeatedly given this answer," said Samuel Chandler, the head of the deputation, "that I trust you will give me leave to ask when the time will come." "If you require a specific answer," said Walpole, "I will give it to you in a word—never!"[86]

Even in the face of such a flat denial, Chandler and Avery refused to lose heart. With an utterly unrealistic hope for success—a confidence partly encouraged by the fact that many of the Tories had temporarily withdrawn from the Commons[87] —they continued to lobby vigorously until the end of March, when the desired motion was finally introduced into Parliament. It was defeated without debate by 188 votes to 89, a clear indication that the cause was hopeless whether the opposition were present or not.[88]

Still refusing to accept defeat, however, in 1740 the Deputies went a step further by calling together a national

---

[84] Benjamin Hoadly, *The Objections against the Repeal of the Corporation and Test Acts Considered* (London, 1739).

[85] *Vide The Church of England Vindicated* (London, 1739), p. 21 *ff*. where Henry Stebbing's argument about the nature of the sacramental test is restated, i.e., that it is not a penalty but simply a safeguard against "licentiousness."

[86] Manning, *op. cit.*, pp. 29–30.

[87] *Vide* William Coxe, *Memoirs of the Life and Administration of Sir Robert Walpole* (London, 1789), I, 607–608 and N. C. Hunt, *op. cit.*, p. 199.

[88] *Journal of the House of Commons* (London, 1741), XXIII, 310.

meeting of the Dissenters for that year designed to associate their country supporters still more closely behind the London Committee."⁸ Country Dissenters did in fact turn up at this London meeting in December of 1740 and it was decided to set up a subcommittee "to consider what part it will become us to play with reference to the ensuing General Election." But the subcommittee reported back in January, 1741, that "upon mature deliberation [they] were of the opinion that the sending of a general letter on that subject to our friends in the country was an affair of too tender a nature for us to engage in and that they thought it not advisable for us to give any instructions relating thereto unless application be first made to us or there should be any case that shall appear to us to be peculiarly circumstanced."⁹⁰ The Committee accepted this report, and the minutes contain no further reference to any attempt at organizing the Dissenting vote during the 1741 election.

At last the Protestant Dissenting Deputies were forced to surrender to the inevitable. It had become increasingly clear that they did not have sufficient strength, no matter how logical their arguments may have sounded, to move the government to widen the toleration and admit them to state offices. They no longer had the heart to beat their heads against so adamant an opposition from Church and State. They would, then, bide their time, emphasizing with their spokesman Micaijah Towgood the right to freedom of conscience without state penalties, and awaiting the day when "a calm and unprejudiced examination of their case" should result in victory.⁹¹

---

⁸⁹ *Minutes of the Deputies* (2 April, 1740), and Manning, *op. cit.*, p. 31.
⁹⁰ *Ibid.* (24 Dec., 1740).
⁹¹ Micaijah Towgood, *The Dissenters' Apology* (London, 1739), pp. 14 et seq.

CHAPTER III

The Quiet Years, 1740—1760

FOR A GENERATION following their final unsuccessful attempt at repeal both the Protestant Dissenting Deputies and their parent organization, the General Body of Protestant Dissenting Ministers, made no effort to approach the government on this issue. Realizing full well that neither Newcastle nor Archbishop Herring would lend his support to any move which might constitute a slightest threat to the status quo, leaders of the Three Denominations had no desire deliberately to alienate the Hanoverian monarch and his chief ministers in Church and State. Besides, they had enough to occupy their attention in legal disputes over the extent to which existing toleration protected them from the "unjust demands and persecutions" of magistrates and parish officers. Indeed, these years record few instances in which the Toleration Act was not read at the close of the Deputies' general meetings, and it soon became evident that they considered themselves the guardians of its provisions. More than this, they took any concrete legal steps which might "in point of prudence" lead to a redress of grievances, and with few exceptions the General Body of Protestant Dissenting Ministers supported their more vigorous lay brethren.[1]

As B. L. Manning has pointed out, controversies over the right of burial in parish graveyards occupied the attention of

---

[1] *Vide Minutes of the General Body* (Dr. Williams's MSS 38. 105), II, 63–120.

the Deputies "more frequently and over a longer period of time than any other,"[2] the first definitive court decision not being made in the Dissenters' favor until 1809 in the case of *Kemp v. Wickes*.[3] But the Deputies went to law in many other types of cases as well. In 1741 when a mob broke the windows of a meeting house at Stratton in Wiltshire and insulted and "barbarously used" the congregation, since the Justices of the Peace refused to grant warrants against the rioters, the Deputies took the case to King's Bench. Here, however, as often, they failed to get satisfaction because those concerned could not be adequately identified.[4] In 1745 it was claimed that certain Dissenters had been illegally impressed, and the Deputies took up the matter in September of that year, the Secretary at War promising to release one who was a freeholder on an affidavit of fact in April, 1746. In November they learned that the man was in fact freed.[5] In addition, there were all sorts of requests for advice, such as the one from a Welsh minister in 1754, who, showing the tremendous prejudice against Dissent in his area, asked the Deputies whether they thought it was safe for him to speak over the grave of a person buried in the parish churchyard, even if the vicar had consented, or would such an action provide material for a case in the church courts?[6]

The major conflict between Dissenters and the civil power during this period was a struggle with the Corporation of London which dragged on for twenty-five years. In 1742, Robert Grosvenor, a prosperous London Dissenter, was elected

---

[2] B. L. Manning, *The Protestant Dissenting Deputies* (Cambridge, 1952), p. 286.
[3] *Ibid.*, p. 296.
[4] *Minutes of the Deputies*, 20 June, 1741; Manning, *op. cit.*, p. 114.
[5] *Ibid.*, 15 Sept., 1745; 2 April and 26 Nov., 1746.
[6] *Ibid.*, 9 Oct., 1754.

sheriff and refused to serve on the grounds that he was sacramentally unfit and that the Toleration Act protected him in declining to qualify. The Corporation cited him before the King's Bench, but he was supported by the Deputies and, after the case had dragged on for three years, the Corporation finally failed to get it remanded to the city courts and abandoned prosecution.[7] Refusing to admit defeat, however, the city then passed a by-law imposing additional fines on anyone who should decline election after being nominated, or who, after election, should decline to take the test. These fines were also to be devoted to the building of the new Mansion House, and for the six years after 1748 they accumulated about £15,000 for the city.[8]

Not all Dissenters had the same fighting spirit as Robert Grosvenor, and it was several years before the Deputies found a suitable case on which to challenge this by-law. But meanwhile they had not been idle. They set to work raising a national guarantee fund which amounted to nearly £4,000. Then came the year 1754 when three rich Dissenters, Messrs. Sheafe, Streatfield, and Evans, who had been successively nominated as sheriff, all refused to pay the fine. Such was their resolution, in fact, that each man paid the £400 and twenty marks levied against him to the Deputies instead of to the city in return for their backing. The cases were first tried in the Sheriff's Court, then in the Court of Hustings—both city tribunals—the municipal officials using every tactic to make the suit as expensive and awkward as possible.[9] Streatfield was proved to be out of their jurisdiction, but judgment was given against the other two.

[7] *Vide* Manning, *op. cit.*, p. 121.
[8] *Ibid.*, p. 122.
[9] E.g., they refused to shorten the procedure by consent or to take one case and let it decide the others. Three separate actions had to be sus-

The Deputies sued for a special commission, consisting of five judges, who with one dissentient ruled against the lower courts.[10] The city next applied to the House of Lords against Evans—Sheafe having died meanwhile—and in 1767 the case was finally argued in the supreme tribunal. Six out of seven judges gave their decision in favor of Evans, with Lord Mansfield pronouncing the verdict in scathing terms against the city fathers.[11] After vindicating the principles of religious liberty as enforced by the Act of Toleration, he declared nonconformity no longer to be a crime before the law.[12]

The Dissenters had borne all this litigation with a determined patience. Indeed, during the whole period of petty legal restrictions and annoyances, their records are punctuated with statements of great moderation almost reminiscent of the day when Samuel Holden was chairman of their committee for redress of grievances. "Use all gentle means first" was the Deputies' characteristic advice to distressed brethren who wrote to them from the country.[13] "Prudence" always dictated that it might not be wise to insist upon full legal rights. Often the issue was not worth the expense; and sometimes a legal victory would have cost local Dissenters more in reputation than it would have gained for them in other ways.[14] The Deputies never tired of reiterating that "the orderly, peaceful

---

tained. Also the defendants were compelled to apply to the Court of Chancery before they could receive authority to inspect the books of the corporation, and they were forced to have more than fourteen-hundred transcripts made in each case. *Vide Minutes of the Deputies*, 22 Feb., 1758.

[10] *Vide* Manning, *op. cit.*, p. 124, for Sir Michael Foster's pronouncement.

[11] *Ibid.*, pp. 128–129.

[12] *Vide* John Holiday, *The Life of William Late Earl of Mansfield* (London, 1797), pp. 251–256.

[13] *Minutes of the Deputies*, 12 Sept., 1759.

[14] *Ibid.*, 10 March, 1756.

conduct of Protestant Dissenters is the most likely means to lessen prejudice and silence those who clamour against us."[15]

This general spirit of moderation and forbearance during the seventeen-forties and fifties is also reflected in the literature of the age on all sides. Probably its greatest exponent was the Reverend Doctor Isaac Watts who, as a popularizer of Locke's educational philosophy, found favor with Dissenters and Churchmen alike. From the appearance of his *Essay against Uncharitableness* in 1707 to his death in 1748, Watts never ceased to press home in words almost directly taken from the *First Letter concerning Toleration* that " 'tis a very uncharitable practice to think that a man can never journey safely to heaven unless his hat and shoes be of the same colour as ours, unless he tread the very track of our feet, and his footsteps too be of the same size." It was not only bad psychology but "perverse fancy" to pronounce a man heretical simply "because all the atoms of his brain are not just ranged in the same position with the magistrate's."[16]

Prompted by the Dissenters' failure to push a repeal of the Test and Corporation Acts through Parliament in March of 1739, Watts brought out *A New Essay on Civil Power in things Sacred* in which he attempted to give a dispassionate view of the Dissenting position on penal laws and tests in civil and religious affairs:

> The author is very much desirous to try how far his reason would establish a natural religion and adjust and limit the common rights of mankind, both sacred and civil, under this establishment in any country whatsoever wherein religion may be professed in various forms; and at the same

---

[15] *Ibid.*, 29 Oct., 1760.
[16] Isaac Watts, *An Essay against Uncharitableness* (London, 1707), p. 7. Cf. John Locke, *Works* (London, 1823), VI, 29–33 and Lord Peter King, *The Life of John Locke* (London, 1830), II, 84–87.

time to maintain a perfect consistence with all due liberty of conscience and support the just authority of supreme rulers. . . ."[17]

Watts argued that God "by the light of reason hath led mankind into civil government," but he hastened to add that "though civil government is an ordinance of God and appointed by him according to the light of reason . . . yet in its proper aims and designs it hath no direct reach or authority beyond the benefit of men in this world."[18] An established church, then, could only assert the minimum requirements of worshipping God publicly, praying for the welfare of the nation, and attending public lectures on morality. There should be no persecution of any kind no matter what sort of beliefs were held by the citizens of Watts' ideal state, but he felt that Roman Catholics because of their "persecuting principles" and because they were subjects of a foreign prince who could absolve them from oaths should be barred from holding office. Nevertheless, he urged absolute liberty and tolerance in things religious, and concluded his essay with a thought from Bayle that in the final analysis "heretics have as much right to persecute the orthodox as the orthodox have to persecute them."[19]

In his quiet, compromising way, Watts was a great softening influence amongst Dissenters and Churchmen alike. Refusing to take part in the Salters' Hall controversy, he also steered clear of any direct pamphlet warfare. In his *Humble Attempt* of 1731 he had hinted that Dissenters led better lives than Churchmen and had provoked an answer from the Reverend John White, Fellow of St. John's College, Camb-

---

[17] Isaac Watts, *Works* (London, 1753), VI, 134.
[18] *Ibid.*, p. 137.
[19] *Ibid.*, p. 168; also A. P. Davies, *Isaac Watts* (London, 1948).

ridge, denying this allegation and upholding the Church's position.[20] It was, needless to say, Micaijah Towgood and not Isaac Watts who took up the cudgels and replied.[21] Indeed, loved as he was by his fellow Dissenters, his inclination to compromise caused some bitter feeling, particularly when he sought a union of Baptists and Independents, proposing that the former should surrender their insistance upon immersion and the latter belief in infant baptism as a basis for comprehension. Nevertheless, with all his moderation, Watts, like Locke, never tired of insisting that reason should always verify the testimony of custom.

Men were not wanting to take up Watts' spirit more vigorously, and Matthew Robles lost no time in doing just that. Defining bigotry and superstition as "religion exalted or elevated out of the verge of reason," he went on to declare that these twin perversions "have their just rise from prejudice of education." They are nourished "by custom, interest, and a desire of things being actually as they conceive them, which together strike an impression on the brain, at a time when the understanding is too weak to oppose them" with the result that early education "prepossesses the mind to such a degree that when reason would come to exert its right it has in most cases no admittance."[22] In order to cure such evils no man should fix his faith on any one thing before he has subjected it to "a strict and impartial enquiry."[23] Robles admitted quite frankly that formation of certain prejudices in our early years

---

[20] *Vide* John White, *A Letter to a Gentleman Dissenting from the Church of England* (London, 1742).

[21] Macaijah Towgood, *The Dissenting Gentleman's Answer to the Reverend John White* (London, 1746).

[22] M. Robles, *Bigotry, Superstition, and Hypocrisy worse than Atheism* (London, 1742), p. 2.

[23] *Ibid.*, p. 12.

was inevitable, but in good Cartesian fashion he insisted that "when we arrive at years of maturity, it is my opinion that for us first to doubt of the whole is the means in time to be certain of the truth. . . ."[24]

Following similar reasoning, the Archdeacon of Lincoln, George Reynolds, drew the same conclusion that "it is most ridiculous and absurd to blame any person, upon any account, for any opinion he entertains, especially when it is entertained by speculation."[25] As befitted a clergyman, he set out by observing that "Christian precepts about mutual forbearance, meekness, temperance, patience, and long-suffering are excellent rules of policy,"[26] but he switched immediately to a psychological emphasis:

> From the difference of men's natural endowment, education, and course of life frequently results a diversity of judgment, and this diversity, when it turns upon modes of religion, furnishes them with many opportunities to comply with the dictates of reason and Christianity in indulging each other in the use of different forms of worship according to their respective sentiments.[27]

He hastened to point out that as the welfare of society was likewise greatly interested in the performance of these duties, the civil magistrate could never want authority to enforce them for the sake of peace; but "whenever these differences proceed from nothing more than a different way of thinking and neither interest nor passion are thrown into the scale," he must let them alone.[28] If, however, peace and unity should be

---

[24] *Ibid.*, p. 13.
[25] George Reynolds, *An Historical Essay upon the Government of the Church of England* (London, 1743), p. 17.
[26] *Ibid.*, p. 201.
[27] *Ibid.*
[28] *Ibid.*, p. 202.

threatened with a return to Cromwellian chaos, "the magistrate's end in allowing different usages in religion will be in a great measure defeated, and consequently his motives to moderation be lessened in proportion." But Archdeacon Reynolds did not foresee this happening if the Church would only "candidly examine" her "unsettled state," amending those parts of her constitution—especially the ecclesiastical courts—which had given rise to such loud criticism from Dissenting ranks. Reform was the way to "peace and security."[29]

A large number of clergymen in the Church of England echoed Reynolds' views on candor and moderation in religious enquiry, although they did not lift up their voices for reforms in her administration. The Reverend Robert Eden in an assize

---

[29] ". . . If Dissenters were contented with the lenity they enjoy: if they forbore to make advances upon the Establishment . . . neither endeavouring to asperse its administrators, impair its revenues, nor undermine its securities, the motives for synodical regulations would certainly be less urgent. But if the tolerated sects, however divided in judgment or interest, combine to take advantage of the unsettled state of the Church . . . if the concealed Socinian strengthens his exception against the use of spiritual censures in the Church by observations upon the misapplication of excommunication; the Quaker furnishes himself with pleas against the recovery of tythes in ecclesiastical courts by dilatory, expensive, and precarious rules of practice there; the Methodist palliates his voluntary and uncommanded severity by imputations of a want of regular discipline in the Church; the Presbyterian covers his sin of schism by the continuance of those grievances in a Protestant church which gave occasion to the separation from Rome; and the abettors of arbitrary principles conspire with the Republicans to repeal the Test Acts and ridicule the decline of power and authority in prelacy which hath always been exerted to preserve the balance of the Constitution, defend the legal rights of the crown, and the liberties of a free people; in these circumstances the way to peace and security is to attend to demands of redress of the offensive disorders; that is, of such as gave occasion to the separation from Rome, and were not intended to be retained in the succceeding settlement. . . . This was the scheme at the Revolution, and can there be any ground to doubt whether it is reasonable to render the established church irreproachable . . . by a compliance with just exceptions against some parts of its ecclesiastical administration?" *Ibid.*, pp. 233-35.

sermon preached at Winchester in July of 1743 was to be found stating that:

> Every honest man, every real and unfeigned patriot will be inflexibly determined in his conduct by the dictates of conscience, the suggestions of true honor, and the principles of religion : He will change the narrow spirit of party and faction into a generous, diffusive zeal for the public good, and will upon all occasions sacrifice any views or inclinations, any prejudices or even resentments of his own to the real interest of this country . . . [In short, he will] . . . exercise the social virtue of justice and moderation, courtesy, and candour.[30]

In April, 1746, Samuel Lobb was glorifying Christianity in his assize sermon at Taunton, because "it leaves men the natural rights they were possessed of before its publication; it leaves to private persons their natural right of judging for themselves in matters of conscience. . . ."[31] As an illustration of the fact that the British Government recognized this essential aspect of Christianity, Lobb called special attention to "the glorious Act of Toleration passed in behalf of our brethren the Protestant Dissenters," ushering in an era where "there are no penal laws complained of as in force against any peaceable, orderly subject on account of their religious principles, excepting against those whose religious principles hinder them from giving the government reasonable satisfaction."[32] Even these latter restrictions were enacted and continue in force "not from any ill will to them, but purely on account of such inconsistency of those principles with public safety."[33]

Similarly, James Tanstall, preaching before the House of

---

[30] Robert Eden, *The Connection of Publick and Private Happiness* (London, 1743), pp. 17, 72.
[31] Samuel Lobb, *A Sermon on Benevolence* (London, 1746), pp. 20–21.
[32] *Ibid.*, p. 27.
[33] *Ibid.*

Commons at St. Margaret's Westminster, in May of 1746, insisted that:

> The true Church of Christ pretends no divine commission to entrench upon the natural or civil rights of men, dispensing an authority of reason to persuade, not of dominion to over-rule private judgments, and thankful for the borrowed aid of such an establishment as can maintain the exercise of her sacred functions without forcing the inviolable dictates of conscience.[34]

Preaching before the Lord Mayor and Aldermen of London in November of 1750, William Cockayne criticized sharply an "extravagant zeal for and violent attachment to the external parts of religious worship." He suggested that "true piety" consisted in following the dictates of "Christian candour—our great and only security against superstition on the one hand and impiety on the other."[35] And, addressing the Society for the Propagation of the Gospel in Foreign Parts in February of 1750, John Thomas, Bishop of Peterborough, urged "forbearance and moderation," exhorting his hearers to "avoid all force and violence and cruelty, remembering always that Christianity softens as well as purifies the heart."[36] Roger Pickering preached that "Compulsion may enforce submission, but not belief,"[37] and William Parker urged "candour" in his martyrdom sermon before the House of Commons, insisting that "from the active principles of prevailing influence which stained that unhappy age [i.e., of Charles I] states may learn

---

[34] James Tanstall, *A Sermon Preach'd before the Honorable House of Commons* (London, 1746), p. 15.

[35] William Cokayne, *Sermon Preached before the Rt. Hon. the Lord Mayor* . . . (London, 1750), p. 7.

[36] John Thomas, *A Sermon Preached before the Incorporated Society for the Propagation of the Gospel in Foreign Parts* (London, 1750), p. 24.

[37] Roger Pickering, *Reflections on Sentimental Differences in Points of Faith* (London, 1752), p. 3.

to be on their guard against the extremes of either *no* religion or *too much.*"³⁸

On January 30, 1750, the Reverend Doctor Thomas Pickering preached what was in many ways a typical martyrdom sermon before the Lord Mayor and Corporation of London, but it drew forth a vigorous polemic from the Dissenting controversialist Caleb Fleming. Stressing the theme of moderation, Pickering had stated that:

> No good churchman desires to afflict or grieve his weak brethren while they keep within the bounds of modesty and decency and do not offend against civil peace, nor vilify the Established Church. We do not envy them—we rejoice in their toleration. But, then, on the other hand, it would be great imprudence and downright folly (especially after the experience we have had of their good nature and abilities for Church government) to trust them with power. . . .³⁹

The only "sure method" which Pickering knew for preventing the "disorders and confusions" of the last century was "for members of the Established Church to look upon the Test Act as an essential—most sacred—most inviolable law."⁴⁰

In response to these pious assertions Caleb Fleming snarled back: "Why must emphasis be laid upon the weakness of

---

³⁸ William Parker, *A Sermon Preached before the Honourable House of Commons* (London, 1757), 12. It was, of course, customary in all martyrdom sermons to stress with Warburtonian determination the necessary alliance between the two essential parts of the constitution: Church and State. The remarks of James Beauclerk, Bishop of Hereford, before the House of Lords were typical: "We know what miserable confusion ensued upon the late downfall of *both,* which after various ineffectual struggles and attempts could not otherwise be recovered than by a restauration of both." But, like Warburton, the good Bishop found no objection to "the divine doctrine of toleration." *Vide* James Beauclerk, *A Martyrdom Sermon Preached before the Rt. Hon. Lords Spiritual and Temporal* (London, 1752), pp. 22–23.

³⁹ Thomas Pickering, *A Sermon Preached before the Rt. Hon. the Lord Mayor* (London, 1750), p. 13.

Protestant Dissenters? . . . Is it because Dissenters have less natural ability than churchmen?"[41] Fleming insisted that "unless it can be shown that under the instructions of an established clergy men have inculcated upon them more just and honourable sentiments of government or a more uniform and regular scheme of moral virtue and that in consequence of this members of the establishment are more judicious, pious, and charitable than their weak brethren," then Pickering must take back his words.[42]

The Reverend Caleb Fleming's fighting spirit was hardly typical of mid-century Dissenting ministers and laymen. With John Richardson and George Benson, the vast majority were quite contented to urge moderation, and to mouth the old phrases from Locke's *First Letter:*

> . . . Let the press lie open and let all sentiments be communicated without the least danger of conviction . . . except for those who write professedly against religion and virtue, for if persons endeavour to set aside the eternal and immutable differences between good and evil, to confound vice with virtue, or to disapprove the being of God, they then may be said to unhinge all society, and to reduce us to a state of anarchy and confusion, in which case the civil magistrate has a right to interpose for preserving peace and good order in a state.[43]

---

[40] *Ibid.*, p. 12.

[41] Caleb Fleming, *The Devout Laugh, or Half an Hour's Amusement to a Citizen of London from Dr. Pickering's Sermon* (London, 1750), p. 22. This suggests what was later to become so important an element in the arguments of Priestley, Price, Toulmin, and others—the idea of a career open to talents regardless of religious views. An anonymous pamphleteer of 1749 also hinted at the same thing: "If the civil magistrate adds superior knowledge to power, then only is he worthy of obedience." *Vide The Claims of Church Authority considered and the Rights of Private Judgment Defended* (London, 1749), pp. 31–32.

[42] *Ibid.*, p. 23.

[43] John Richardson, *Christian Liberty and Love Represented and*

... As to other controversies among professing Christians, as we have no business to require the aid of the civil magistrate, so the present happy government under which we live has too much goodness to concern itself with the unhappy difference among ourselves, unless by recommending moderation from the throne—a golden age in comparison with former times."

An anonymous Dissenting layman writing in 1755 contended himself with exhorting his readers to "an honest impartial enquiry after truth" and the insistence that force in matters of religion could only create hypocrites. But, then, the government of George II, "a most enlightened monarch in a most enlightened age," fully recognized this.[45] The rather truculent Samuel Bourn was satisfied with muttering that those who altered Christ's institutions were "traytors to his cause," that magistrates had no right to punish people for heresy, and that "uniformity cannot be necessary in unnecessary things."[46] Occasional conformity, rather than being subject to the charge of hypocrisy, was for Bourn "an indication of a sound and generous mind raised above prejudice and irrational party attachments." So long as Dissenters were able to fill offices in this way, he seemed quite satisfied with things as they were.[47]

Earnestly Recommended (London, 1752), p. 15. He goes on to quote from Locke's *First Letter* (1690 ed.), p. 67.

[44] George Benson, *A Collection of Tracts* (London, 1753), pp. 251 ff.

[45] Vide *The Foundations of Religious Liberty Explained by a Dissenting Layman* (London, 1755), p. 12.

[46] Samuel Bourn, *A Vindication of the Principles and Practices of Protestant Dissenters* (London, 1747), pp. 121, 125, 135.

[47] *Ibid.*, 163–167. He also insisted in another pamphlet that "Dissenters, by taking the sacrament at Church, do not pretend to be stated members of the Church of England, but only practice what they judge simply lawful, in order to evade the force of an act unjustly applied [as a species of High Church persecution] to deprive them of their birthright." Samuel Bourn, *An Answer to the Remarks of an Unknown Clergyman* . . . (London, 1749), p. 67.

All seemed to agree with that "learned and respectable man of moderate sentiments," the Reverend John Hodge,[48] who exhorted his congregation "to suitably prize the blessings we have of Protestant Religion and legal government and resolve to stand fast in defence of them as they are."[49] Even Dr. John Taylor, liberal as he was in presenting his theological views as tutor at Warrington Academy, glorified the status quo:

> ... Under the just, mild, and auspicious government of his present Majesty and that of his illustrious Father we have seen days of peace and prosperity not equalled in any part of the English annals and have enjoyed national privileges and happiness in as high degree as the best constitutions admit, and, I suppose, as the present state of things in this world will allow. Industry hath had full scope to extend itself in procuring the accommodations of life, and what industry hath procured we have been absolutely secure of possessing without any danger of molestation from lawless power. Clear of all unnatural restraints or discouragements from public authority, understanding and conscience have been in full liberty, and every person hath been perfectly free to be wise, pious, good, and virtuous under the direction of the best light he could discover. ...[50]

Taylor went on to exhort his congregation always to remember that all these blessings depended upon the succession of the Crown in "the illustrious House of Hanover":

> ... This is the life of the nation and we shall adhere to it

---

[48] *Vide* Walter Wilson, *The History and Antiquities of Dissenting Meeting Houses in London, Westminster, and Southwark* (London, 1808), I, 354–55 for an account of the Reverend John Hodge.

[49] John Hodge, *A Sermon Preached at Little St. Helen's* (London, 1751), pp. 21–22.

[50] John Taylor, D.D., *The Glory of any House erected for Public Worship and the True Principles, Religious, Civil, and Social of Protestant Dissenters represented in a Sermon preached ... in Norwich ...* (London, 1756), pp. 18–19.

and all the interests that are connected with it as our very life at the hazard and expence of our all. . . . Do all you can to make the burden of government easy; avoid whatever may perplex and distress it; abhor a spirit of disaffection and obloquy; do not rashly or wantonly censure the conduct of those who are at the helm. They are the ministers of God unto us for good ... labouring continually for our peace, safety, and welfare, and therefore as much as in us lies, we should assist their endeavours and strengthen their hands. What the wisdom of Parliament appoints, we should cheerfully contribute to the support of the government and defence of the nation. . . . At all times let us be well pleased that we, as Dissenters, are such large sharers in national privileges; nor let us expect or desire further favours when they cannot be allow'd consistently with the quiet of our country. . . .[51]

What signs of discontent there were both outside and within the Church seemed to embrace a characteristically "moderate" form. Walter Wilson shows in fact that the atmosphere between Church and Dissent was so friendly that the idea of comprehension could be discussed freely without violent feelings.[52] After the Rebellion of 1745, when the country had become quiet and no one remained to trouble the House of Hanover, Dr. Gooch, the Bishop of Norwich, presented a charge to his clergy in which he stated "that the leaders of the rebellion were Presbyterians as appeared by the conduct of those lords in the Tower, who, during their internment there, sent for Presbyterian confessors."[53] The celebrated Presbyterian minister, Dr. Samuel Chandler, happened to be present in Norwich cathedral at that time; and, after returning to

---

[51] *Ibid.*, pp. 21–22.
[52] Walter Wilson, *op. cit.*, II, 363.
[53] *Ibid.*

London, he wrote a polite remonstrance to the Bishop for misuse of the facts.[54] His remonstrance was given a civil reply, with the result that a friendly meeting was arranged between Chandler and the Bishop, during the course of which comprehension was discussed.

Another friendly meeting followed with Sherlock, Bishop of Salisbury, also present. "Our Church, Mr. Chandler," said Sherlock, "consists of three parts, doctrine, discipline, and ceremonies"; about the last two he suggested there might be no difficulty, but as to the first, "what is your objection?"[55] Chandler wanted the Articles to be stated in scriptural language and the Athanasian Creed to be discarded, and the bishops maintained that they were not unalterably opposed to either of these changes. They asked, however, what should be done about reordination of nonconformist ministers? Chandler was certain that none of his brethren would renounce their Presbyterian ordination, "but if your Lordships mean only to impose your hands upon us and by that rite recommend us to public service in your society or constitution, that perhaps might be admitted to."[56]

The two bishops then advised Chandler to confer with Archbishop Herring, which he promptly did, experiencing a most courteous reception at Lambeth. The archbishop said comprehension would be "a very good thing."[57] He wished it with all his heart, especially because this was a time which called upon all good men to unite against infidelity and immorality which threatened universal ruin.[58] To Chandler's

---

[54] *Vide* John Stoughton, *Religion in England under Queen Anne and the Georges* (London, 1878), I, 254-44.
[55] Walter Wilson, *op. cit.*, II, 373.
[56] *Ibid.*
[57] *Ibid.*, p. 354.
[58] *Ibid.*, p. 355.

request for the Articles to be rewritten in the words of scripture, Herring said: "Why not? It is the impertinence of men thrusting their own words into articles instead of the words of God which have occasioned much of the divisions in the Christian Church from the beginning to this day." He added "that the bench of bishops seemed to be of his mind, that he should be glad to see Mr. Chandler again, but was then obliged to go to court."[59] But Archbishop Herring, who always termed himself "a very insignificant and pusillanimous man"[60] was hardly constituted to conduct such a major reform of the liturgy. He, like Newcastle, thoroughly deprecated either controversy or innovation, and further negotiations on the topic were forever suspended.[61]

Discouraged by this delay, Chandler wrote:

... I think myself obliged, as a Christian and a Protestant, peaceably to withdraw from an establishment which ... alters the nature of indifferent things and makes new rites and postures in religion which are allowed to be indifferent, necessary terms of receiving her sacraments or joining in the privileges of her worship, and which then subjects herself to the magistrate as to make his law in the appointment of rites and ceremonies obligatory upon the consciences of all his numbers.[62]

He appealed to "the known learning, candour, moderation, and piety of the clergy of the national church, and particularly of those reverend prelates who now so worthily fill her sees and who some of them have treated me with great humanity and

---

[59] *Vide* A. H. Hore, *The Church in England from William III to Victoria* (London, 1886), II, 22.
[60] *Vide* Charles Smyth, "Archbishop Herring and the '45" in *The Church Quarterly Review* (London, April–June, 1946), pp. 30–47.
[61] *Vide* Norman Sykes, "The Duke of Newcastle as Ecclesiastical Minister," *The English Historical Review* (January, 1942), p. 62.
[62] Samuel Chandler, *The Case of Subscription* (London, 1748), p 10.

respect. . . ."[63] But, when his appeals fell upon deaf ears, Chandler nevertheless looked forward in supreme optimism to the day when "moderation, benevolence, charity, tenderness to the consciences of men, desire of peace, and love of liberty" would bring Church and State alike "to soften or rather remove those subscriptions that create any difficulties to good men. . . ."[64]

Isolated Dissenting ministers like the Reverend William Graham appealed for the repeal of subscription to the Thirty-Nine Articles in the name of "Christian candour and moderation,"[65] but they were completely lacking in any idea of how to achieve it. Most of them agreed with Chandler and Taylor that to upset the government in any way could only accrue to their loss, and there is no record of any attempt to negotiate for such a repeal in the minutes of their Ministers or Deputies. With Chandler they seemed to think that within a short time such an enlightened age could not refrain from automatically granting their wish. Meanwhile, life was hardly intolerable under the "benevolent Hanoverians."

Interestingly enough, it was within the Church itself that the roots of a vigorous anti-subscriptionist movement first took their rise. In 1749, the Reverend John Jones, Vicar of Alconbury, published anonymously his *Free and Candid Disquisitions relating to the Church of England* in which the liturgy was held up to scrutiny. "Divine offices should be free from all matters of dissertation," said Jones, "for however right a proposition may be in itself, it can scarce be thought right by men of peace and piety to interweave it in a dog-

---

[63] *Ibid.*, p. 1
[64] *Ibid.*, p. 147.
[65] William Graham, *A Sermon Preached at Kingston upon Hull* (London, 1759), p. 26.

matical form with our addresses to the Supreme Being."[66] When, however, he later referred to the Athanasian formula of "three persons in one substance" contained in the proper preface of the communion service for Trinity Sunday, Jones showed his moderate approach by saying: "Were it not likely to be more invidious than useful, it would be easy to point out other expressions in one of the most solemn offices of our Church, which are thought to be extremely improper in applying to the Almighty."[67] For such timidity he was accused by an anonymous pamphleteer of "being more afraid of offending man than God."[68] The same pamphleteer taunted Jones with the fact that, although he did not think the Athanasian Creed contributed to a proper understanding of Christian theology, he "humbly hopes it may retain its place in our Common Prayer Book."[69]

Pamphleteers were, of course, not lacking to accuse Jones of going too far in provoking "the moderate clergyman . . . without renouncing his calling . . . to pare off a great many elements . . ." which the orthodox clergy considered essential.[70] On the other hand, in a sermon preached to his congregation at the Parish Church of Halifax, the Reverend John Watson lashed out at "the rigid churchman," proclaiming that "as nothing has done more damage to the Christian cause than persecution, so nothing is more likely to promote the interest of it than moderation."[71]

---

[66] John Jones, *Free and Candid Disquisitions relating to the Church of England* (London, 1749), p. 7.
[67] *Ibid.*, p. 322.
[68] *Cursory Animadversions upon the Free and Candid Disquisitions* (London, 1753), p. 8.
[69] *Ibid.*, pp. 11-12.
[70] John Witherspoon, *Ecclesiastical Characteristics* (Edinburgh, 1753), p. 45.
[71] John Watson, *Moderation, or a Candid Disposition toward those that differ from us Recommended and Enforc'd* (London, 1750), p. 7.

> The rigid churchman is for taxing all as rebels to the Church that cannot think her liturgy and every appendage of it entirely perfect. He looks upon himself to be the greatest friend to the Church because he is the loudest in opposing those that wish for a comprehension, being absolutely positive that there can be no alterations for the better and firmly believing everyone that has asserted the contrary to be his natural enemies and such as would overturn him had they the power. He believes that we ought to give up nothing, not the most indifferent ceremony tho' it were to unite every sect to us; that Dissenters are in duty bound to give up all . . . He has learned to hate the man because of his opinions . . . He has in fact a greater regard to outward profession than to inward sincerity, believing in and contending for Church authority to oblige men to a particular communion. . . .[12]

Watson went on vigorously to defend the *Free and Candid Disquisitions* by pointing out that the Common Prayer, since it was first properly compiled in 1549, had undergone sixteen alterations as defects became apparent "and offence was thereby given to the promoting of separations and divisions."[13] He concluded by exhorting his congregation always "to behave candidly toward them that differ from you."[14]

Similarly, Robert Seagrave defended reform of the liturgy and a softening of subscription by the observation that "in proportion as mankind improve in their ideas of liberty and reason, 'tis observable that they grow more cool and moderate

---

[12] *Ibid.*, p. 9.
[13] *Ibid.*, p. 13.
[14] *Ibid.*, p. 23: "What is it to you by what name your neighbour chooses to be distinguished whilst he is quiet with his opinion. Has not the government thought fit to tolerate him? Is there no difference between the man and his opinion? The latter, if you believe it differs from the truth, you may hate; but the first, let him be Christian, Mahometan, or Jew, let him be what he will, you are commanded to love him."

in relation to many articles which before they lay no small stress upon;"[15] and the pseudonymous pamphleteer Britannicus expressed his astonishment "that in so enlightened an age as the present so absurd and contradictory a practice as imposing subscription to explanatory articles of faith should be continued."[16] He forcefully charged the clergy that:

> ... Your solemnly subscribing to articles which it is notoriously you do not believe, and your declaring publically your unfeigned consent to forms in divine worship which it is well known you disapprove of is one principal cause of infidelity and skepticism. ...[17]

The anonymous author of the pamphlet called *Advice from a Bishop in a Series of Letters to a Young Clergyman* put forward a much less troublesome doctrine. He declared that although the writings of the clergy over the past hundred years could in no wise be made to tally with the "calvinistical" parts of the articles, they had nevertheless gone on expressing their opinions and subscribing without due consequence. Why should they not continue to do so? Indeed:

> The legislature may be assured that there never was, and I will venture to say there never will be, a subscription to all the articles according to the plain sense and meaning of the first compilers; and as it hath never been declared that such alone is the subscription which is required, by depriving those whose public writings contradict this original sense, it is evident that a subscription is allowed in any sense which is agreeable to the Word of God. For he who subscribes the articles in a sense equally consistent with the public good and the rights and properties of his fellow subjects, equally answers the intention of the legislature in the law which

---

[15] Robert Seagrave, *The Principles of Liberty* (London, 1755), p. 35.
[16] Britannicus (Pseud.), *Friendly Admonitions to the Inhabitants of Great Britain* (London, 1758), p. 37.
[17] *Ibid.*, p. 34.

requires any subscriptions; and abstracted from the source of the Law, ecclesiastical impositions in a Protestant Church are impertinent and vain.[78]

Many clergymen found comfort in such reasoning, but before this pamphlet was written, in an almost unnoticed sermon preached on Christmas Day, 1753, the Reverend Francis Blackburne had declared his objections to the Book of Common Prayer, to the observance of that day and the other festivals of the Church, stating that many other things—especially the credal elements—were grievous to him.[79] Within the next two decades he was to produce anti-subscriptionist literature which was to circulate throughout the kingdom and to draw up a clerical petition to Parliament for relief from subscription.

The general calm of these years was interrupted by only one major outburst of religious intolerance which could recall the days of Sacheverell. This rose from an attempt of the Pelhams in 1753 to make legal the naturalization of Jews. The bill drawn up provided simply that Jews resident in Great Britain or Ireland for three years might be naturalized on application to Parliament without taking the sacrament.[80] These proposals were mild and unprovocative in the extreme, for only rich Jews could afford the expense of applying, and like all naturalized persons they would still be unable to become members of either House of Parliament, to hold any office of profit under the Crown, or to obtain grants of Crown lands. Besides, in view of all earlier legislation, there was no obstacle to the naturalization of a Jew by the Sovereign and Parliament.[81]

---

[78] *Advice from a Bishop in a Series of Letters to a Young Clergyman* (London, 1759), pp. 25–26.

[79] *Vide* Francis Blackburne, *A Sermon Preached on Christmas Day, 1753* (London, 1754).

[80] *Vide* William Cobbett, *Parliamentary History*, XIV, 1480 ff.

[81] W. E. H. Lecky, *History of England in the Eighteenth Century* (Lon-

The Quiet Years, 1740–1760

The bill passed the Lords easily. At its second reading in the Commons, however, a decided opposition began to develop under the leadership of Sir John Barnard, a member for London and a personal rival of the powerful Jewish financier Samson Gideon. When the second reading carried, the commercial classes, under the leadership of Sir Crisp Gascoigne, Lord Mayor of London, held protest meetings, while the Common Council condemned it as "disastrous to the Christian religion."[82] Despite all this, the bill passed.

Agitation was then transferred from Westminster to the streets and anti-government slogans were published throughout the country. The summer numbers of the *Gentleman's Magazine* gave vent to every sort of anti-Jewish libel from fables of ritual murder to attempts at proving Oliver Cromwell's Jewish extraction, and that all Jews were as naturally subversive to the constitution as he had been.[83] The old story of the crucifixion of Christian children by Jews was revived, and the bishops who had voted for the bill were libelled and insulted in the streets. Pork banquets became patriotic fare, and "no mass-house, no conventicle, no synagogue : High Church forever!" was the toast with which such convivialities closed.

As the tide of popular indignation rose higher and higher, the ministers pressed for and carried a repeal in 1754. Had they not done so, it is possible that they might have lost the general election then imminent. Furthermore, they argued that in the excited state of popular feeling the Jews could not live safely in England if the act continued in force. Such was the feeling that the High Church party actually attempted to carry their victory further by repealing, in so far as it related

---

don, 1892 ed.), II, 328, and Cecil Roth, *A History of the Jews in England* (2nd ed., Oxford, 1949), pp. 212–213.

[82] *Ibid.*, p. 216.
[83] *The Gentleman's Magazine* (August, 1753), p. 375 *et seq.*

to Jews, the act which naturalized Dissenters from the Anglican Church who had resided for seven years in the plantations, but the government resisted and succeeded in defeating the attempt.[84] In supreme disgust, the *London Magazine* observed that "when religion is brought into any dispute, reason is for the moment laid aside, and it becomes on both sides a sort of enthusiasm, the effect of which has been fatal to this nation. . . ."[85] Certainly the whole hysterical episode seemed to do much toward justifying the Whigs for not attempting more in the cause of religious liberty during their long period in office.

No sooner had the Jewish agitation subsided than the great disaster of the Lisbon earthquake occurred. The years immediately preceeding this cataclysm had not been wanting in prophets of doom who, like the Reverend Samuel Eccles, referred to his times as "the most licentious of ages,"[86] and Benjamin Bourn who felt certain that "the present age has risen to a greater pitch of luxury, profaneness, indolence, and immorality than any of the foregoing ones."[87] Such men were not slow to seize upon the earthquake as a sign of divine vengeance, and even the moderate Edward Weston who had entered the stream of pamphlet literature over the "Jew Bill" in order to counsel "candour and temperance,"[88] could not refrain from voicing his alarm to the bishop of London that, although "candour" did not justify pronouncing the present age "*in toto* more corrupt than the preceding," it was "far more culpable than formerly" in "the habit and fashion of

---

[84] *Vide* Cobbett, *op. cit.*, XIV, 1366.
[85] *The London Magazine* (December, 1754), p. 540.
[86] Samuel Eccles, *National Sins, the Cause of National Judgments* (London, 1750), pp. 5–6.
[87] Benjamin Bourn, *A Sure Guide to Hell* (London, 1750), p. 54.
[88] Edward Weston, *Some Reflections upon the Question relating to the Naturalization of the Jews* (London, 1754), pp. 48–50.

irreligion."[89] Sermon pyramided upon sermon warning the faithless and luxury-ridden to mend their ways before England should be visited by such disasters.

Saner preachers did not attempt to map out a direct connection between man's evil and visitation by natural calamities, but they used the occasion to cry out against "the alarming state of the moral world."[90] Most intellectuals agreed with the Reverend Thomas Seward, who, preaching at Lichfield on Sunday, December 7, 1755, maintained that it was mere "superstition" to connect the earthquakes with God's particular wrath against the Portuguese:

> It is hoped therefore that the publication of this sermon may tend some little to confirm that rational system of religion which excludes every species of superstition, a system which the infidel and enthusiast join their efforts to dispossess us of, and to substitute in its stead a Christianity not founded on argument.[91]

Seward closed his sermon with an exhortation both to his con-

---

[89] Edward Weston, *A Letter to the Right Reverend the Lord Bishop of London* (London, 1756), p. 10.

[90] *Vide* John Fludger, *The Judgments of God Considered* (London, 1755), p. 23; Peter Petit, *National Occasions of Terror considered as Intentional Warnings of Providence* (London, 1756), pp. 3–4; Thomas Fothergill, *The Qualifications and Advantages of Religious Trust in Times of Danger* (Oxford, 1756), pp. 12–13; and the anonymous *Earnest Exhortation to Repentance on Occasion of the Late Dreadful Earthquakes* (London, 1756), pp. 20 ff. The Reverend Doctor John Brown fulminated against "the vain, luxurious, and selfish effeminacy" which characterized his age, using the earthquakes and the outbreak of the Seven Years' War as signs of divine displeasure. *Vide* his *Estimate of the Manners and Principles of the Times* (London, 1757), pp. 56–57; pp. 201–216. Indeed, so great was his dispair that he committed suicide in order to escape the wrath to come. *Vide D. N. B.* Sir Thomas Kendrick, in his recent work on *The Lisbon Earthquake* (London, 1956), makes use of some British pamphlet materials in his concluding chapter, but he devotes most of his study to the impact of the earthquake upon Continental thought.

[91] Thomas Seward, *The Late Dreadful Earthquakes No Proof of God's Particular Wrath against the Portuguese* (London, 1756), p. 2.

gregation and to the government "to seize this opportunity of shewing to all the world the charitable and benign temper of the Church of England forgetting all distinction between Protestants and Papists, and only considering the Portuguese as our neighbours and brethren labouring under the most afflictive distresses that have for many ages fallen on any people."[92] His sympathies were echoed in many parts of the country, and Parliament voted £100,000 for relief of the distressed Portuguese, an act which Lecky terms "probably the only considerable trace of warm and disinterested philanthropy in the sphere of politics during the entire eighteenth century."[93]

Thus, what guilt feelings the prophets of doom had attempted to promote rapidly subsided, and most intellectuals returned to the "cosmic toryism"[94] of Stephen Hales, who preached about "the vastness and harmony of the great frame of nature" and man as "the noblest of all visible creatures."[95] True, the Lisbon earthquake had prompted Soame Jenyns to conduct his *Free Enquiry into the Nature and Origin of Evil,* but he had settled back upon a comfortable, though complacent and shallow, "whatever-is-is-right" philosophy which satisfied most of the men of his age.[96] Indeed, his *Enquiry* produced a typically mid-eighteenth-century God who loved abundance and variety better than happiness or progress, and a universe whose "goodness" consisted in its containing the greatest possible range of phenomena, many of which seemed evil to all but the philosopher.

---

[92] *Ibid.,* p. 22.

[93] Lecky, *op. cit.,* II, 132.

[94] The phrase is Professor Basil Willey's. *Vide* pp. 43–56 in his excellent work *The Eighteenth Century Background* (London, 1953 ed.).

[95] Stephen Hales, *The Wisdom of God in the Formation of Man* (London, 1751), p. 2.

[96] "Man," said Jenyns, "is one link of that vast chain, descending by

Equally important with all these developments for an understanding of the mounting pressure in favor of a more complete toleration was the growth not only of new means for mass communication and the sharing of ideas, but also of many clubs, societies, and educational foundations which gave opportunity for those barred from any direct connection with the government nevertheless to debate the issues of the day.[97] This new political consciousness can perhaps most readily be seen in the development of newspapers. By 1757 London had four evening papers and a series of bi-weekly and tri-weekly publications.[98] It was not only the metropolis, however, that had developed a vigorous press, for by 1760 there were forty well-established newspapers in several major towns.[99] These were distributed by itinerant newsmen who, with their stock of

---

insensible degrees from infinite perfection to absolute nothing. As there are many thousands below him, so there must be many more above him. If we look downwards, we see innumerable species of inferior beings, whose happiness and lives are dependent on his will; we see him cloathed by their spoils, and fed by their miseries and destruction, enslaving some, tormenting others, and murdering millions for his luxury or diversion; is it not therefore analogous and highly probable that the happiness of man should be equally dependent on the wills of his superiors?" *Vide* Soame Jenyns, *A Free Enquiry into the Nature and Origin of Evil* (London, 1757), pp. 71–72. In keeping with such a status quo philosophy, Jenyns was to be found on February 6, 1772, as a member of the House of Commons for Cambridgeshire, "vigorously defending the two Universities and showing that they could not alter an injunction founded on royal statute," in opposition to the views of Lord George Germaine, who held that undergraduates ought not to be required to subscribe to the XXXIX Articles. *Vide* J. W. Middleton, *An Ecclesiastical Memoir of the Reign of George the Third* (London, 1822), p. 126.

[97] Cesar de Saussure, *A Foreign View of England in the Reigns of George I and George II*, trans. Madame van Muyden (London, 1902), II, 162; comments upon the passionate interest of workingmen in politics and the fact that literacy was widespread, at least in London.

[98] *Vide* Alexander Andrews, *The History of British Journalism* (London, 1859), I, Chap. V.

[99] *Vide* G. A. Cranfield, *The Development of the Provincial Newspaper, 1700–1760* (Unpublished Cambridge Ph.D., 1952), p. 56 *et seq*.

patent medicines as well, covered an area of forty or fifty miles a day. For example, the *Northampton Mercury* was to be found on sale in Cambridge and Oxford, and Liverpool papers circulated in the Lake District. Furthermore, the important thing about this press was that its policy was almost invariably anti-government. Indeed, when Walpole purchased the *London Journal* in the seventeen-twenties in order to put a stop to its hostile propaganda, its sales fell by fifty per cent.[100] The *Liverpool Chronicle* printed all of Wilkes' letters to the press and paid no attention whatever to government arguments.[101] Here, then, is certain evidence of a public capable of understanding grievances and expressing them.

The fundamental reason why the press was so widely bought and read lay in new social and economic developments which demanded a modern system of education.[102] As J. H. Plumb points out, during the first half of the century there grew up a very extensive elementary educational system run mainly by private enterprise. Between 1720 and 1760 over a hundred educational establishments appeared in the pages of the *Northampton Mercury,* and from 1749 to 1756 the *Norwich Mercury* carried advertisements of sixty-seven institutions in which, for cash, instruction was offered in everything from accounting to Russian.[103] Surveying, mathematics, and navigation were taught along with languages for commerce. The need for a more progressive education also infiltrated the more progressive grammar schools like those at Manchester and Newcastle,[104] but it was the Dissenting academies—particularly

---

[100] D. H. Stevens, *Party Politics and English Journalism, 1702–1742* (Chicago, 1916), pp. 113–114.

[101] James Grant, *The Newspaper Press* (London, 1871), III, 195 *et seq.*

[102] Nicholas Hans, *New Trends in Education in the Eighteenth Century* (London, 1951), Chap. I.

[103] J. H. Plumb, *Sir Robert Walpole* (London, 1956), p. 31 fn.

[104] *Vide* Hans, *op. cit.*, p. 63 *et seq.*

Warrington, Northampton, and Hackney—which led the way.[105] And it was especially in these Presbyterian academies that a liberal spirit was manifested not only in the curricula of engineering and commerce, but also in matters of philosophy and theology—in short, in the whole basic approach to academic studies.[106]

Dr. John Taylor, the celebrated theological tutor at Warrington until his death in 1761, whom we have met as a loyal supporter of the Hanoverian monarchy and a staunch conservative in politics, nevertheless took an ultra-liberal approach to scholarship and teaching. The charge which he gave to his students at the beginning of each academic year was typical of that heard in many a Presbyterian academy:

I. I do most solemnly charge you in the name of the God of Truth and of our Lord Jesus Christ, who is the Way, the Truth, and the Life, and before whose judgment seat you must in no long time appear, that in all your studies and inquiries of a religious nature, present or future, you do constantly, carefully, impartially, and conscientiously attend to the dictates of reason; cautiously guarding against

---

[105] J. W. Ashley Smith, *The Birth of Modern Education: The Contribution of the Dissenting Academies, 1660–1800* (London, 1954), pp. 2–8. Irene Parker in her *Dissenting Academies* (London, 1914) did, of course, exaggerate their importance by such extreme statements as: "Without the story of the Dissenting Academies the history of education in England for those 140 years (1660–1800) would indeed be a dull and barren record. As it is, these academies prevent those years from being a reproach to us; for while other institutions were at a standstill they progressed, and it is therefore to them that the honor of furthering the development of educational opinion in this country belongs." Nicholas Hans comes nearer to the facts by attributing a large share in the development of modern educational curriculum to the Dissenting academies, while at the same time pointing out that Anglican and secular institutions were by no means uninfluenced by the trend toward a more practical and scientific education. *Op. cit.*, pp. 54–62.

[106] *Vide* Ashley Smith, *op. cit.*, pp. 129 *et seq.* for the curricula of these academies.

the sallies of imagination and the fallacy of ill-grounded conjecture.

II. That you admit, embrace, or assent to no principle or sentiment by me taught or advanced, but only so far as it shall appear to you to be supported and justified by proper evidence from Revelation or the reason of things.

III. That if at any time hereafter any principle or sentiment by me taught or advanced, or by you admitted and embraced, shall, upon impartial and faithful examination appear to you to be dubious or false, you either suspect or totally reject such principle or sentiment.

IV. That you keep your mind always open to evidence; that you labour to banish from your breast all prejudice, prepossession, party zeal; that you study to live in peace and love with all your fellow Christians, and that you steadily assert for yourself, and freely allow to others the inalienable rights of judgment and conscience.[107]

Henry Grove, tutor at Taunton Academy, had led a major reaction among Presbyterian academies to Calvinist theology in favor of free will doctrines during the seventeen-twenties and thirties.[108] At Bridgewater, John Moore, tutor until 1747, was an Arian, and at Exeter Academy, under the Hallets, students speculated freely upon the Trinity. Soon other academies like Taunton, Kendal, and Findern became Arian in tone, and in many of the earlier foundations like Doddridge's

---

[107] Reproduced in W. D. Jeremy, *The Presbyterian Fund and Dr. Daniel Williams's Trust with Biographical Notes of the Trustees and Some Account of their Academies, Scholarships, and Schools* (London, 1885), pp. 57–58. It should be pointed out, however, that not all Dissenting academies permitted such liberal instruction. By way of contrast, the Independent Academy at Mile End, later removed to Homerton, required each student to assent in writing to ten articles of a theological system — the strictest Calvinism — and to repeat his subscription every six months. *Vide* J. T. Rutt, *Memoirs of Joseph Priestley* (London, 1829 ed.), I, 21.

[108] *Vide* Henry Grove, *The Wisdom of God, the First Spring of Action in Deity* (London, 1734).

there was a general swing in that direction. As was the case with Dr. John Taylor, the attitude of lecturers in all of these institutions was to approve wide discussion of varying topics. Like John Jennings of Kibworth, they "encouraged the greatest freedom of enquiry and always inculcated it as a law that the Scriptures are the only standard of faith," not following the doctrines or phases of any particular party, "being sometimes a Calvinist, sometimes an Arminian, sometimes a Baxterian, and sometimes a Socinian as truth and evidence directed" them.[109] Like Jennings, they furnished their students "with all kinds of authors upon every subject without advising them to skip over the heretical passages for fear of infection," it being their main care "to inspire them with the sentiments of Catholicism and to arm them against that zeal which is not according to knowledge."[110]

As Nicholas Hans points out, adult education was also fairly extensive by the middle of the eighteenth century through the medium of clubs and various discussion groups. The Debating Club at Liverpool was to be found disputing whether political purity could ever be achieved without a secret ballot, and the famous "Society of Free and Candid Enquiry," better known as the Robin Hood Society flourished in London during the middle decades of the century, constituting what was unquestionably one of the great forums of the eighteenth century. An account published in 1752 described it as follows:

> The number of them is about 300 composed chiefly of shoemakers, apothecaries, lamplighters, and parish schoolmasters, a Baker at their head for president, they assemble every Monday evening, when they debate publicly on the most important subjects of Religion, Politics, and the Moral

---

[109] J. D. Humphreys (ed.), *The Correspondence and Diary of Philip Doddridge* (London, 1829), I, 155-156.
[110] *Ibid.*, p. 198.

Fitness of things, and each of the members is allowed five minutes to handle the subject according to his art and then the Baker reads up the whole of their arguments, mixes them with the leaven of his understanding and proportions them out into cakes according to the merits of each speaker.[111]

Another contemporary account states that "gentlemen, living in the country as well as foreigners of all nations, if in the least curious, learned or ingenious, resorted to it to hear debates that have so much attracted attention;"[112] and the *Gentleman's Magazine* commented that "this society is chiefly composed of lawyers, clerks, petty tradesmen, and the lower mechanics. . . ."[113] All denominations were represented, and Hans states that even a Roman Catholic priest was among the members.[114] Quaker pamphleteers like George Bridges, Churchmen like William Reder, a well-known writer on theological subjects, schoolmasters like James Barklay, the Reverend John Henley, an ordained priest, but very heterodox in his opinions, and avowed deists like Thomas Chubb and Peter Annet all met in this society and discussed religious and political topics on equal terms. Hans estimates that about five thousand people attended its debates annually.[115]

Furthermore, the higher brow society was in many instances discussing the same things as its intellectual and social inferiors

---

[111] *Vide* Hans, *op. cit.*, p. 169.

[112] *A History of the Robin Hood Society* (London, 1755), p. 2.

[113] *The Gentleman's Magazine* (London, 1754), p. 154.

[114] Hans, *op. cit.*, p. 170.

[115] *Ibid.*, p. 171. The number of publications excited by the Society is sufficient evidence to show that it made a stir in London and attracted general attention as a propagator of unorthodox opinion. *Vide* condemnatory letters in the *Whitehall Evening Post* (Dec. 29, 1749, and Jan. 30, 1750), and *An Apology* for the *Robin Hood Society* (London, 1751) and *Genuine and Authentic Memoirs of the Stated Speakers of the Robin Hood Society* (London, 1756).

in the Robin Hood group. For example, the seventeen-sixties witnessed the growth of the well-known Lunar Society at Birmingham,[116] where men like Boulton, Watt, Wedgewood, Samuel Galton, and Erasmus Darwin were to be found debating religious and political issues in addition to their scientific discussions;[117] and Lord Shelburne was soon gathering about him on his estate at Bowood and in his townhouse at Berkeley Square a group including Joseph Priestley, Richard Price, and Benjamin Franklin, who freely discussed all problems of the day.[118]

So it was that by the seventeen-sixties a critical, literate, and radical public opinion had grown up which was to become more and more indignant under the strain of constant failures in George III's policies from the Treaty of Paris in 1763 to the Treaty of the same name which ended the American Revolution twenty years later. And, in this movement of agitation for reform, it is hardly surprising to find Dissenters providing much of the leadership. They had learned the techniques of political agitation, how to lobby, to write propaganda pamphlets and letters to the press; and they had established a central London agency in their Deputies and Ministers to watch developments on the political scene. All that was needed were vigorous leaders, and they soon emerged in the persons of Priestley, Price, Furneaux, Kippis, Toulmin, and Towers, as well as Lindsey, Jebb, and Wakefield who defected from the Church to join their ranks.

---

[116] So named because its members arranged to meet on the day of full moon each month for safety's sake because of the bad roads. Erasmus Darwin, Thomas Day, and Dr. Edgeworth, lived some distance from Birmingham. *Vide* Conrad Gill, *A History of Birmingham* (Oxford, 1952), I, 135–137 for an account of the Society.

[117] *Vide* also *The Lunar Society of Birmingham . . . Papers . . .* (Birmingham, 1955).

[118] Lord Fitzmaurice, *Life of William Earl of Shelburne,* II, p. 333 *et seq.*

CHAPTER IV

Anti-Subscription and the Revival of Dissenting Activity

THE DECADE of the seventeen-sixties witnessed a phenomenon which Simon Maccoby has called "the birth of English radicalism."[1] It was not only that in 1760 the "Leicester House Party" of politicians no longer had a Prince of Wales around whom to rally in opposition to the government; inducements to political agitation went far deeper than this. The forcing of Pitt's resignation in 1761 incited London mobs to shout for "the Great Commoner," and substitution of the hated Scotsman Bute in his place roused them to new levels of indignation, especially after peace negotiations with France had been made public.[2]

Finally, on March 22, 1763, peace was officially proclaimed; two weeks later Bute resigned in order to end opposition, many thought, without surrendering actual power as chief adviser to the king; and on April 19 George III delivered

---

[1] *Vide* Simon Maccoby, *English Radicalism, 1762–1785* (London, 1955), Preface.

[2] "We have conquered everything and retained nothing," snarled Pitt, and the merchants and bankers who sat on the London Common Council glorified their fallen idol by resolving that: "The City of London . . . cannot forget that you accepted the seals when this nation was in the most deplorable circumstances to which any country can be reduced . . . The City must also remember that when you resigned the seals our armies and navies were victorious, our trade secure . . . and people readier to lend than ministers to borrow. . . . *Vide* J. H. Plumb, *Chatham* (London, 1953), p. 60.

a speech in which he praised the results of the peace and prorogued Parliament. Then, on April 23, Number 45 of John Wilkes' newspaper, the *North Briton,* launched a scurrilous attack upon the "ministerial effrontery" displayed in the king's speech and on "the tools of corruption" through whose continued presence in government "the Favourite" was attempting to impose upon king and people alike Scottish nominees and Stuart ideas of prerogative.[3] The ensuing story of how Parliament became more and more sensitive about its privileges in the face of mounting public criticism, of the high line which it took over the suppression of the *North Briton,* the expulsion of Wilkes from the House of Commons, and the validity of general warrants has been told too well by historians from Lecky to Namier to be repeated here. It should simply be pointed out that all this political furor could hardly fail to register its mark on the thoughts, writings, and actions of both Churchmen and Dissenters. A growing consciousness that government legislation was antipathetic to the spirit of the age was widely felt; and, so far as religious matters were concerned, this current of criticism was first to take the form of a threat to the internal constitution of the Establishment itself — a threat the more challenging because its leaders were the

---

[3] *Vide* Maccoby, *op. cit.,* p. 13 for a reproduction of the statement printed at the head of the *North Briton* on April 23, 1763. Men like Sylas Neville and his friends were in thorough agreement with such ideas. By 1767 they were gathering for dinner each January 30 to eat a calf's head in symbol of "the deserved death of that tyrant Charles I." Toasts were offered to "The Majesty of the People of this nation" and in moments of enthusiasm George III was likened to the Stuart tyrants. Richard Barron, editor of *The Pillars of Priestcraft and Orthodoxy Shaken,* also took a leading part at these dinners. Both he and Neville refused at all times "to drink George and Charlotte's health;" rather, at calf's head feasts on January 30 they drank to the toast: "May the example of this day be followed on all like occasions!" *Vide The Diary of Sylas Neville, 1767–1788,* ed. Basil Cozens-Hardy (London, 1950), pp. 3, 29, 90–91, 149, 196–197.

Church's own most liberal members.

An anonymous pamphleteer of 1761 showed the manner in which this critical spirit was to be focused upon the Church. In keeping with the traditions of "that incomparable patron of liberty, the great Mr. Locke," he urged like many before him that religion be "brought back to first principles" and that "the popish luxury and pomp" of the Establishment be done away.[4] Indeed, so enmeshed had the Establishment remained in "the trappings of popery" that a more complete reformation must be achieved — especially so far as "the shackles of creedal restrictions upon the human conscience" were concerned. More than this, bishops in particular and all clergymen in general had "waxed so fat" on the "worldly advantages" provided by the government that they could be relied on, "contrary to all the teachings of Christianity," to support it in "any measure of oppression." The pamphleteer suggested that the connection between the clergy and the State should be severed to the extent that the government might guarantee only their bare subsistence, removing all the "vain luxury and pomp" which bound a corrupt Church and a corrupt Court so closely together. He closed by pointing out with bitter irony that if his proposal were followed, then "perhaps clergymen could be trusted with the power of doing good, rather than merely being expected to support the Ministry in all its folly," in return for their comfortable position.[5]

Other pamphleteers were soon hurling charges of "priestcraft and oppression" at the Church of England.[6] Prominent among them was the Dissenting controversialist Caleb Fleming, pastor of Pinners Hall Meetinghouse, London, from 1753

---
[4] *Considerations upon War and Religion* (London, 1761), p. 312.
[5] *Ibid.*, pp. 313–315.
[6] Vide *The Character of Ecclesiastics* (London, 1763), Preface, p. iv, and *The Conduct of the Clergy* (London, 1764), pp. 4–6.

to 1777. Amid all the political upheavals of the early sixties he lost no time in charging the Church with "continually making indifferent things necessary" and "invariably standing upon the side of oppression."[7] As we have seen, however, until late in this decade the attention of London Dissenters was completely absorbed with fighting the City Corporation in the Evans Case, and their brethren in the country either devoted their time toward helping to raise money for this righteous cause or to fighting their own legal battles. Caleb Fleming's voice was therefore the only notable one from their ranks which was raised against the Establishment itself at this time.[8]

Dissenters had of course long taken a leading part in attacking "popery" and those areas in which they thought that the Church of England most closely resembled it. Vigorous Dissenting ministers like Benjamin Grosvenor, Samuel Wright, and Moses Lowman had written articles for the *Occasional*

---

[7] Caleb Fleming, *The Claims of the Church of England Seriously Examined* (London, 1764), pp. 27–28. Sylas Neville who frequented Fleming's sermons at Pinners Hall reported in his *Diary* for June 3, 1768: "Mr. Fleming acknowledges that very few of the Dissenters are truly free — that these 30 years he has been in town they have not invited him to assist in any part of worship — that but 2 or 3 of them would admit him into their pulpits . . . ." Apparently, said Neville, his outspoken "denial and complete rejection of every sort of church power" so far as relationship with the government was concerned, plus his Unitarian theology, was too much for them. *Vide* Neville, *op. cit.*, p. 33.

[8] That is, perhaps with the exception of the Reverend Richard Barron, erratic pastor of a Presbyterian congregation at Sydenham in Kent (1760–1768). According to his friend and fellow republican, Sylas Neville, he was "too zealous" and in preaching "apt to transport himself too far." Lord Chatham who owed him some personal favor had made an effort in that direction, but concluded that: "He is such a hot-headed republican, I cannot have anything to do with him." Consequently, his extreme fulminations against "the Stuart tyrant," George III, and the corruption of the Establishment served only to frighten the Dissenters rather than win their support. Nevertheless his edition of anti-prelatical tracts — *The Pillars of Priestcraft and Orthodoxy Shaken* — in 1768, the year of his death, sold widely and played its part in the discontents of those years. *Vide* Sylas Neville, *Diary*, pp. 13, 19–21.

Paper (1716-1720) which began the attack,[9] and during the following two decades they pressed their views through "anti-popery lectures" at Salters and Pinners Halls.[10] Also Trenchard and Gordon began their own occasional paper called *The Independent Whig or The Consistent Protestant* in 1721, and Thomas Gordon was still writing tracts of the same antiprelatical and unorthodox temper until his death in 1750, insisting that "nothing endangers the liberty of England more than the increasing power and opulence of the clergy."[11] Many of these tracts were republished in 1763 under the title *A Cordial for Low Spirits;* and in 1768 a more comprehensive collection, edited by Richard Barron, appeared in four volumes as *The Pillars of Priestcraft and Orthodoxy Shaken*.[12]

Admirers of the *Occasional Paper* and the *Independent Whig* continued a similar campaign in the newspapers, and a three-volume collection of their contributions between 1764

---

[9] *Vide* Benjamin Grosvenor, "An Essay on Bigotry" in the *Occasional Paper*, Vol. I, No. I, 2d ed. (London, 1718), Samuel Wright, "The Character of a Protestant" in Vol. I, No. II, (1716); and Moses Lowman, "The Danger of the Church Consider'd" in Vol. I, No. VI (1716) of the same publication.

[10] *Vide* Benjamin Grosvenor, *Cruelty in Religion No Service of God, A Sermon Preach'd at Pinners Hall* (London, 1725) and Samuel Chandler, *The Claims of the Church considered in a sermon preached at Salters Hall* (London, 1735) for two typical anti-popery tracts which cast aspersions on the Church of England.

[11] Gordon was perhaps best remembered for his essay on *The Character of an Independent Whig* (London, 1719) in which he insisted that "all Protestants ought to be equally employed in a state to which they are equally well effected," (p. 7). But "the clergy have made such a terrible and inhuman use of power in all ages . . . their nails must always be par'd and their wings clipp'd in this particular. Reason and liberty are the two greatest gifts and blessings which God has given us, and yet wherever a priestly authority prevails they must either fly or suffer. They are enemies to the craft and must expect no toleration. Darkness and chains are the surest pillars of the sacerdotal empire, and it cannot stand without them." (p. 6).

[12] *Vide* Sylas Neville, *op. cit.*, p. 17.

and 1770 was issued in 1774, probably under the editorship of Archdeacon Francis Blackburne and certainly containing many of his tracts.[13] It is most significant, however, that while maintaining the old anti-papist spirit, these letters thoroughly reflected the stirring political events of the day and snarled bitterly at Warburton's doctrine of an alliance between Church and State, maintaining that both were equally corrupt and in need of reform. Grumbling at the arrival of "the Scottish Millenium," Francis Blackburne complained that:

> The Favourite, whose principles are no secret to the public, though no longer visible at the steerage, has put a sort of men into a capacity of executing his purposes, who by their company and connections are known to have no predilection for the events in 1688 and 1714. . . . Clerics as well as laymen being enlisted must do the allotted duty. The latter are to write up the Crown prerogative to the highest pitch, and the alliance requiring that the prerogative of the Church should rise in proportion, the scribes of the sacred order have it in their instructions to magnify their office, to exalt the Church above Gospel and to represent the apprehensions of danger to the Protestant Religion from the increase of Popery to be groundless and ridiculous.[14]

Always a fanatical anti-Papist, Blackburne proceeded to charge Thomas Secker, the Archbishop of Canterbury, with being "a professed patron of this ecclesiastical drama" because of his strenuous attempts to provide bishops for the American Plantations against their will, and also because he approved

---

[13] The two copies of this work in Dr. Williams's Library both contain contemporary manuscript attributions to Blackburne. It was entitled *A Collection of Letters and Essays in Favour of Public Liberty* (London, 1774).

[14] *Ibid.*, pp. iii–iv.

"the establishment of Popery" in Canada.[15] Indeed, the effects of "this grand alliance, the combined powers of Church and State" was evident. "The connivance and indulgence of popery" constituted the "indispensable ingredient in this compounded policy," for "the spirit of popery" was utterly necessary if the present Establishment was to support itself.

> Papistical *imposition* and papistical *power* to enforce it are necessary now for her very existence in her present unreformed state; and while she continues in that state, to expose the errors and impositions of popery is of disservice to her; and the parties of whom she borrows the *power*, if she is disposed to avail herself of it effectually, must not disparage the *deed of conveyance* by which it came into their hands by lending it sparingly.[16]

How, he asked, could the Americans be blamed for resisting the establishment of such an oppressive form of church government on their soil?

It was in 1766 that Archdeacon Blackburne published the work which is credited with initiating the movement toward a "clerical petition" to Parliament for relief from subscription

---

[15] Blackburne poured his utmost contempt upon Secker's plan for sending bishops to America calling it "a mere empty, chimerical vision." If episcopal ministrations were vital to the Church, he argued, why were they so frequently omitted in England? How, for example, could confirmation be really indispensable when "in several dioceses there have been no confirmations for several years?" Furthermore: "Bishop Secker and other bishops, in vilifying and reproaching American colonists, shelter themselves under their fictious idea of Christianity, monopolizing the religion of Christ within a fixed model of civil establishment, confing Christianity, to a sect or party." *Vide* Blackburne in the *St. James Chronicle,* August 20, 1768. On the matter of Canada, he wrote to the *London Chronicle* on August 16, 1766, that: "To take a popish bishop into public protection and to authorize or allow him to exercise his function among *any* of His Majesty's subjects is directly contrary to the fundamental laws of our Protestant Government."

[16] Francis Blackburne, *A Collection of Letters and Essays in Favour of Public Liberty* (London, 1774), I, x–xi.

to the Thirty-Nine Articles. In this bulky volume he contended that churches had no right to make creeds and that every creed contained rigid pronouncements with which any intelligent Christian who had carefully examined the scriptures might reasonably take issue.[17] To impose interpretations of the Bible was to interfere with the right of private judgment so vigorously asserted at the period of the Reformation, and to adopt a latitudinarian defence of the Articles was to plunge into "embarrassed and fluctuating casuistry." If subscribers believed the Articles to be true, they certainly believed them to be true in one precise uniform sense; "if so," Blackburne asked, "what is there in our constitution to warrant an expositor to allow men to subscribe in different senses?"[18] Certainly the requirement by the Church of England of assent by either its clerical or lay members to a body of propositions on religion expressed in human language could not be justified :

The sum of the whole matter is this : place your church authority in what hands you will and limit it with whatever restrictions you think proper, you cannot assert to it a right of deciding in controversies of faith and doctrine, or in other words a right to require assent to a certain sense of Scripture, exclusive of other senses, without an unwarrantable interference with those rights of private judgment which are manifestly secured to every individual by the scriptural terms of Christian liberty and thereby contradicting the original principles of the Protestant Reformation.[19]

Several prominent clergymen came to Blackburne's immediate support, particularly a group at Cambridge under the leadership of the Reverend Doctor Thomas Edwards, Fellow

---

[17] Francis Blackburne, *The Confessional* (3rd ed.; London, 1770), p. 175.
[18] *Ibid.*, p. 241.
[19] *Ibid.*, p. 50.

of Clare, and Doctor John Jebb of Peterhouse who found the requirement of the University subscription particularly irksome. Preaching before the University on Commencement Sunday, June 29, 1766, Edwards left no doubt that he stood squarely on Blackburne's side, insisting that "the simplicity and purity of the principles and doctrine of Christianity" had been adulterated by "the heterogeneous unnatural admixture" of "Scholastic Jargon, Popish Superstition, and Calvinistic Enthusiasm":

> To get at knowledge of the truth, then, we must search the sacred oracles; and with honest and candid, with open and liberal minds, endeavour to discover the true genuine meaning and import of what is there. . . . Only by free impartial disquisition shall we know the pure uncorrupted doctrines. . . . And when we thus know them it will be our indispensable duty earnestly to contend for them . . . *against all opposition*—against those who enslaved by superstition and bigotry, or actuated by self-interested and wordly views are for obtruding upon mankind the adulterate heterodox doctrines of human systems: Who are professed enemies to all reformation in religion and would have Christianity rigidly adhere to the opinions of their fore-fathers, whether true or false, right or wrong: Who are for maintaining at all events what is established in the particular country or religious society they belong to, and for having the wisdom of past ages serve for all succeeding ones: Who would gladly check the progress of every free, though serious and very interesting enquiry: Who would have all new discoveries, though founded upon the solid and immovable basis of truth and of the utmost consequence and importance, diligently suppressed, and a stop put to all farther improvements in religious and spiritual knowledge.[20]

---

[20] Thomas Edwards, D.D., *The Indispensable Duty of Contending for*

No man agreed more with his colleague Dr. Edwards that the Church of England must free herself of the mistaken swaddling clothes devised by sixteenth-century clerics for an infant institution which had quite outgrown them than did the Reverend Doctor John Jebb, Fellow of Peterhouse. In fact, through his vigorous pamphleteering, he rapidly came to rival Blackburne as one of the centers of both a University and a national movement against subscription. Subjecting the Thirty-Nine Articles to minute scrutiny in a series of widely-published letters to the press, he declared:

> The first article of our church professes to treat of faith in the Holy Trinity; an expression not to be found in scripture, or doctrine not connected with the performance of a single duty in social life. A man may believe the contrary, and yet be a good christian, a good father, a good master, a good husband, a good citizen, and a good friend. . . .
>
> If the first article is faulty, the second is like unto it, and the subscription . . . should by no means be insisted on. It defines with a logical, or rather chemical precision, what never was comprehended, or ever can be comprehended, by the help of those rational powers which we now enjoy. . . .
>
> The ninth article treats of original, or birth sin; but the state has to do with those sins only when they are committed after birth.
>
> I would gladly avoid the consideration of the eight following articles . . . I am satisfied that, upon perusal of them, no English senator will see the necessity of binding these metaphysical subtilties upon the consciences of those, who are sent forth, by the civil power, to instruct the people in the necessity of obedience to the laws of God and man.

---

the Faith which was once delivered unto the Saints (Cambridge, 1766), p. 10 *ff.*

While they continue unintelligible, they are useless. When understood, they are prejudicial, nay, even dangerous. . . ."[21]

Support soon came in from the country. From his pulpit at Richmond in Yorkshire the Reverend Anthony Temple was raising the question: "Is it not the duty of a Protestant Clergy to wipe off all unfavourable aspersions that may have been cast on their profession for the suppression of speculative opinion?" To require men to act solely by the ideas and formulae of other generations was not to treat them as moral agents but as blind animals. "What good man wishes not to live till he see all the canker of former prejudices absolutely purged away and hear every minister of the Gospel boasting that he has no principles but what are justified by . . . scripture alone!" Temple could see "no harm Christianity would receive if fewer subscriptions were required," nor understand "what security any human bond could give to it." He looked forward to the day when his church should become "progressive" enough to open its doors to the "talents" of all Christians:

> Science of all kinds is progressive; like the human mind of which it is the object, it shall never arrive at perfection upon earth; never can it be said this is all a man shall know. Christianity has this in common with other sciences; every age adds something to the discoveries of the preceding, and the counsels of God are deep and impenetrable enough to excite all the talents of mankind to the end of time. Since it is that tho' the avowed design of our public constitutions be to prevent diversity of opinions, yet a considerable part of them are admitted by very few in the sense of the original compilers; that almost every man has an interpretation of his own: Hence the necessity of allow-

---

[21] John Jebb, *Letters on the Subject of Subscription to the Liturgy and Church of England first printed in the Whitehall Evening Post* . . . (London, 1770), republished by John Disney in *The Works of John Jebb with Memoirs of the Life of the Author* (London, 1787), I, 171–175.

ing latitude, if we would not deprive the Church of its ablest and most liberal defenders. . . .²²
Samuel Roe, Vicar of Stotfold in Bedfordshire quite agreed, urging that "in this inquisitive, curious, and enlightened age it is high time for learned and pious men to bethink themselves how to banish the clouds of ignorance, dissension and error from the Church."²³ And from his rectory at South Warmborough, Hertfordshire, the Reverend John Duncan also argued for "a reduction of our public religion nearer to the primitive model of the Gospel."²⁴

Such pamphleteering and sermonizing roused, quite naturally, the hottest opposition from more conservative sections of the clergy. Some were contented with the Reverend Benjamin Pye's simple assertion that "the mild spirit of the National Church and the liberal and condescending demeanour of its rules" were quite sufficient to embrace the vast majority of clergy, and tender indeed must be the conscience of the cleric who could not subscribe to them. Besides, the laws of self-preservation dictated that every society must establish its own rules for membership and those who must dissent were free to go elsewhere.²⁵ The definitive answer, however, was stated in somewhat more closely-knit reasoning after the pattern of

---

[22] Anthony Temple, *A Sermon Preached at the Visitation held at Richmond in Yorkshire* (London, 1766), pp. 17–24.

[23] Samuel Roe, *Another Letter humbly offered to the Public in Favour of a Revival and Amendment of our Liturgy* (Cambridge, 1768), p. 22. He went on to say: "Nor must we expect to see an end of our confusions, or to enjoy Christian concord, till the Book of Common Prayer, the mother of our devotions, be rightly cleared of such gross imperfections of human weaknesses and be rendered agreeable with the sound doctrines of the Holy Scripture. . ." He closed with a compliment to "the author of the Confessional" on his proposals for return.

[24] John Duncan, D.D., *An Address to the National Advocates for the Church of England* (London, 1769), p. 2.

[25] Benjamin Pye, *Five Letters on Several Subjects Religious and Historical* (London, 1769), pp. i–iii.

Stebbing and Warburton by the Archdeacon of Winchester, Dr. Thomas Balguy.

Beginning with the old familiar argument about the "mischief and peril" which lay in keeping civil and ecclesiastical power separate, Balguy went on to stress the point that no evidence could be found to prove that the founders of Christianity intended it to be governed "by any rules or principle opposite to those which reason and nature prescribe." They appointed ministers and officers of religion simply because it was impossible for any religious or other form of society to subsist without them. They also established a form of government and some basic modes of procedure in order to avoid complete chaos. True, their instructions were for the most part rather general, but "in this one point they are clear and explicit, that authority once *established* must be *obeyed*."[26] He then turned directly to the supporters of the *Confessional*, declaring:

> If they cannot lawfully comply with the terms of communion let them make an *open* separation; let them not profess to continue members of a church which they conscientiously disobey. In vain do men unite in civil or religious communities, if each individual is to retain entire liberty of judging and acting for himself. It is a liberty which defeats every possible good effect that such union might produce by substituting the caprice and folly of every disordered imagination to the uniform observance of rules and laws, settled on deliberated advice and enforced by legal authority.[27]

He freely admitted that the Church was by no means a perfect institution, but "common sense will ever teach us to accept the

---

[26] Thomas Balguy, D.D., *A Sermon Preached at Lambeth Chapel* (London, 1769), pp. 18–19.
[27] *Ibid.*, p. 19.

benefits of society on practicable terms and to be content with much less than perfection." No human institution was free from fault and therefore completely secure from the attacks of a willing adversary. "But the very worst establishment that ever existed is better than what these men seem to want, a state of anarchy and confusion."[28]

The Reverend Richard Shepherd fully supported these views, stating that the Articles approached nearer the truth than any private judgment "and in matters where we cannot arrive at exact truth, the nearest approach to it will satisfy a rational inquirer."[29] Like the High-Church pamphleteers of the seventeen-thirties he dwelt upon the horrors of religious warfare:

> Let supporters of the *Confessional* look back on those intestine fueds and civil broils . . . the State almost torn to pieces and the land deluged with blood ere the wished for "Reformation" could be effectively established; let them then dispassionately determine whether any thing but the grossest errors, offensive to the great object of religion or injurious to the State can justify innovation in religious establishments productive of evils as severely felt as those.[30]

He concluded with almost the very words which Henry Stebbing had used in 1724 by owning that he could not subscribe to the opinion that no religion was better than an imperfect or false one and by insisting that an establishment was the only alternative to religious anarchy.[31]

---

[28] *Ibid.*, p. 21.
[29] Richard Shepherd, B.D., *The Requisition of Subscription to the Thirty-Nine Articles of the Church of England not Inconsistent with Christian Liberty* (London, 1771), p. 12.
[30] *Ibid.*, p. 8.
[31] *Ibid.*, p. 14. "For as the existence of the Diety, a future state, and retribution of awards and punishments are the fundamental principles of all religions: those doctrines will better promote the interests of society; they will have a stronger influence on men's conduct than no religion."

Such traditional arguments reached their height in the sermons of the Reverend Nathaniel Foster. Starting with the good Lockean psychological principle that "opinion ought not to be forced simply because it cannot be forced."[32] he was soon sounding Henry Stebbing's warning that "the passions of men are always engaged on the side of their opinions" and "the consequences of such opinions to civil society and the public happiness are clearly within the bounds of civil regulation and control."[33] With Warburton he argued that "some religious establishment is necessary to the preservation of these two basic rights—the right of private judgment on the one hand and the right of self-preservation on the other."[34] Indeed, every state had as much right as every individual to judge for itself in matters of religion, to select its own official forms, to defend its judgment, and to preserve its choice.[35] Furthermore, it was just as reasonable for the officials and members of each given establishment to be required to observe certain regulations as it was for every officer in the state to do the same. A soldier was sworn to observe the articles of war and every judge that he would declare the law of the land, and with equal justice it was required that every teacher and preacher

---

Cf. Henry Stebbing, *An Essay Concerning Civil Government* . . . (London, 1724), 144. To justify his argument in favor of establishments Shepherd used the example of "New England where the religious establishment stands on the loosest footing and the old leaven of 1648 still prevails; parties are formed; sedition, I had almost said treason, was a very few years ago trumpeted from the pulpit; and civil government did among that licentious people then totter from its very foundations."

[32] Nathaniel Foster, *The Establishment of the Church of England Defended upon the Principles of Religious Liberty* (London, 1770), p. 7.

[33] *Ibid.,* p. 8.

[34] *Ibid.,* p. 9. "Until the experiment of a state subsisting without any establishment in matters of religion be tried, it is impossible to controvert the argument from general practice in their favour or to say that the great ends of civil society can be obtained without them."

[35] *Ibid.,* p. 14.

of the established religion should give similar security "that he acknowledges its truth and will regulate his instructions by its several articles and doctrines." Foster found no invasion of private judgment in this requirement, "not the minutest infringement of natural or civil liberty," unless indeed, as Stebbing had insisted, "man were pressed into the service of the church and obliged on pain of civil penalties to take up arms under its banners."[36]

If, then, the state had a right to say that Christianity should be its established religion, it also had "a right to say what those particular articles and doctrines are which constitute the Christian system and to require an acknowledgment of such doctrines from those who teach it."[37] He went on to challenge Blackburne directly by stating that:

> ... the end of our establishment would not in any degree be answered by such a general subscription as is contended for [i.e., to the Scriptures alone] by the writer I have been considering. For what is an establishment to guard against? Not Jews or Mahometans, but the various incompatible, I had almost said absurd sects of Christians, every one of them scriptural according to his own account and every one of which would be of the established religion if no subscription were required but to the words of the scriptures.[38]

While latitudinarian divines like Benjamin Dawson, Rector of Burgh in Suffolk, and Christopher Wyvill, Rector of Black Notley in Essex, were claiming the arguments of "the great Mr. Locke" for their side and replying to Foster that "the state which has established Christianity as it is contained in the scriptures only cannot regulate by any other formulary what the Christian religion is without establishing an inquisitorial

---

[36] *Ibid.*, p. 18; cf. Stebbing, *op. cit.*, p. 211.
[37] *Ibid.*
[38] *Ibid.*, pp. 20–21.

authority over the human conscience,"[39] others were taking more practical steps to organize a great campaign for repeal of subscription. In an address to the clergy of the Archdeaconry of Cleveland in 1767, Francis Blackburne had hinted that those who shared his feelings of "political dissent" should join in a movement "to solicit relief from those who have the power to give it,"[40] and shortly thereafter the Reverend John Jebb began his vigorous campaign for repeal of the University test at Cambridge which soon merged with a national movement for repeal of subscription.[41]

Early in 1771 Blackburne published his *Proposals for an Application to Parliament for Relief in the Matter of Subscription to the Liturgy and Thirty-nine Articles of the Church of England, humbly submitted to the Consideration of the Learned and Conscientious Clergy.*[42] The plan proposed was

---

[39] *Vide* Benjamin Dawson, *A Free and Candid Disquisition on Religion Establishments in General and the Church of England in Particular* (London, 1770), pp. 22, 62; and Christopher Wyvill, *Thoughts on our Articles of Religion with Respect to their Utility to the State* (London, 1771) in which he asks heatedly: "Who can doubt but religion is better understood now than it was two-hundred years ago. But to what purpose have we studied the immortal writings of Locke and Clarke, if we be still unwilling to remove the scholastic rubbish of the sixteenth century? . . ." p. 7.

[40] Francis Blackburne, *On the Duty of a Christian Minister under the Obligation of Conformity to a National Religion Established by Civil Powers* (Newcastle-upon-Tyne, 1767), p. 47.

[41] For the early activities of Jebb in organizing the repeal campaign vide John Disney, *The Works of John Jebb* (London, 1787), I, *Memoirs of the Life of the Author*, 30–37.

[42] The ideas behind Blackburne's *Proposals* were simply an abridgment of those contained in his *Confessional* that "the only objection made on the part of our Church governors (at least the only one worth notice) is that if the clergy should be released from their obligation to subscribe to the XXXIX Articles, the Church would want sufficient security for the orthodoxy of her ministers. But orthodoxy we apprehend is a term which in the mouth of a Protestant should mean only an agreement in opinion with the Scriptures," pp. 4–5.

simply to prepare a petition, circulate it in the country for from six to ten months, and then present it to Parliament.[43]

On July 17, 1771, a meeting of "conscientious and learned clergy" took place in London at the Feathers Tavern, where an association called by the name of their meeting place was formed and a petition to Parliament, written by Blackburne, was accepted and circulated for signatures. It read, in its main part, as follows:

> Your petitioners apprehend themselves to have certain rights and privileges which they hold of God alone—of this kind is the exercise of their own reason and judgment. They conceive they are also warranted by those original principles of reformation from popery on which the Church of England is constituted, to judge in searching the Scriptures, each man for himself, what may or may not be proved thereby. They find themselves, however, in a great measure precluded the enjoyment of this invaluable privilege by the laws relating to subscription whereby your petitioners are required to acknowledge certain articles and confessions of faith and doctrine, drawn up by fallible men, to be all and every one of them agreeable to the said Scriptures. They pray that they may be restored to their undoubted rights as Protestants of interpreting Scripture for themselves without being bound by any human explanation thereof."

As soon as the Feathers Tavern Association had been formed, the Reverend Theophilus Lindsey, Vicar of Catterick in Yorkshire, began a vigorous campaign by personal canvass and by correspondence to solicit signatures for the petition, and he is said to have traveled more than two thousand

---

[43] *Vide* Sir William Anson (ed.), *Autobiography and Political Correspondence of Augustus Henry, third Duke of Grafton* (London, 1898), p. 268.

[44] *Ibid.*, p. 267.

miles on horseback in furtherance of this object. Certainly his letters reveal much vigor and confidence in the progress of the scheme :

> I have received an answer to a letter I had sent to Mr. Sykes, the Vicar of Bradford, an old college acquaintance and contemporary who writes like one fully persuaded of the righteousness of our cause . . . The Master of Jesus College, Cambridge, and every resident Fellow has signed the Petition. The Bishop of Carlisle highly approved.[45] Some members of both Houses have also declared their approbation of our design.[46]

The final result was, however, that he could obtain only about two hundred signatures from clerics and forty or fifty from physicians and lawyers.[47] Nevertheless, in the face of a hostile press and hardly promising times the petition was made ready for presentation to the Commons on February 6, 1772.[48]

---

[45] Dr. Edmund Law was Master of Peterhouse, Cambridge, before he became Bishop of Carlisle in 1768. (*Vide* Disney, *op. cit.*, p. 28). His views tended in a markedly Unitarian direction and he gave consistent encouragement to Blackburne and Jebb. The support of so unorthodox a prelate probably did more to hinder than to assist their cause, however. Sylas Neville reported a conversation between himself and the Reverend Caleb Fleming in which Fleming gave a description of Bishop Law and exemplified his political views by this declaration of faith: "I adore Locke!" "Mr. Fleming and I," said Neville, "are glad that such a man is on the Bench and think his brethren would curse him for his sentiments." *Op. cit.*, p. 32.

[46] *Vide* Lindsey to his friend W. Turner, Esq., September–November, 1771, in Theophilus Lindsey, *Letters,* ed. H. McLachlan (Manchester, 1920), pp. 43–44.

[47] Lindsey later complained of being deceived in this matter. He is said to have lived to see four clergymen who had encouraged him and afterwards turned back, raised to the episcopate. Dr. Beilby Porteus, afterwards Bishop of Chester and London was one of them. *Vide* Lindsey to Tayleur, 25 May, 1795, in *Letters, op. cit.*, pp. 48–49. The Duke of Grafton reported in his *Autobiography* that "the more cautious" divines who originally supported the movement, "thinking it to be more proper to address the bishops than to bring the matter directly before Parliament" broke away from the Feathers Tavern group and met under the chair-

After the petition had been introduced by Sir William Meredith and seconded by Thomas Pitt, Sir Roger Newdigate, fiery member for the University of Oxford, rose to express vehement disapproval. Voicing profound shock at the principles of ecclesiastics who could continue to hold preferments while broadcasting the uncertainty of their faith, he insisted that:

> When we attend to the conduct of these gentlemen, we must acknowledge it was not without reason that our ancestors framed creeds and confessions. If they will not bind the consciences of such a slipery protean race, they

---

manship of the Reverend Francis Wollaston in Tenison's Library. This meeting apparently occurred after the failure of the Feathers Tavern Petition, for Bishop Porteus himself gave account of it as follows: "At the close of the year 1772 and the beginning of the next, an attempt was made by myself and a few other clergymen, among whom were Mr. Francis Wollaston, Dr. Percy now Bishop of Dromore, and Dr. Yorke, now Bishop of Ely, to induce the bishops to promote a review of the Liturgy and Articles. . . . This plan was not in the smallest degree connected with the Petition at the Feathers Tavern but on the contrary, was meant to counteract that and all similar extravagant projects . . . and to diminish schism and separation by bringing over to the National Church all the moderate and well-disposed of other persuasions. On these grounds we applied in a private and respectful manner to Archbishop Cornwallis. . . . The answer given by the Archbishop, February 11, 1773, was in these words: 'I have consulted severally my brethren the bishops, and it is the opinion of the bench in general that nothing can in prudence be done in the matter that has been submitted to our consideration." Reproduced from R. Hodgson, *Life of Bishop Porteus* (London, 1811), pp. 38–40 by N. Sykes in *Church and State in England in the Eighteenth Century* (Cambridge, 1934), pp. 383–384.

[48] *Vide The Gentleman's Magazine* for 1772, pp. 1–61; p. 225. The Methodists were to a man opposed to the scheme for a clerical petition, and Selina, Countess of Huntingdon, showed an uncompromising hostility to it, canvassing Methodists from the highest to the lowest rank against the measure. She even corresponded with Lord North and Edmund Burke, and received sympathetic replies. George III himself pronounced against tampering with the articles on the ground that "all wise nations have stuck scrupulously to their ancient customs." *Vide* A. C. H. Seymour, *The Life and Times of Selina, Countess of Huntingdon* (London, 1844), II, 284, 286–287.

will at least work upon their fears. Prudence will confine them within certain bounds and prevent the nation from being overwhelmed with a deluge of impiety and blasphemy. If you remove this institution I cannot see how the state can a moment subsist. Civil and religious establishments are so linked and incorporated together that when the latter falls the former cannot stand. . . .[49]

Nevertheless, even if one supposed that no general criterion of faith was necessary for the commonwealth to subsist, the Commons could not give the slightest countenance to such a petition without violating the law. This was so, Sir Roger asserted, because the king had sworn in his coronation oath to preserve the existing settlement in Church and State and no mistaken notions of any of his subjects could annul this sacred pledge. Furthermore, the Act of Union stipulated that the religious establishment in either kingdom could not be altered until each was first restored to the condition in which it stood before the union took place. But, thundered Newdigate: "The Union, as well as Magna Charta, I hold an irreversible decree, binding at all times and in all circumstances like the law of the Medes and the Persians!"[50]

Mr. Hans Stanley came to Sir Roger's support by denying that "any of the Reformers whose names are transmitted to posterity with respect ever adopted so wild an idea as that of a Christian society without any established church holding certain defined tenets."[51] Professing no "deep skill in theology," however, he would argue on the basis of "practical politics," proposing "the peace of mankind as a fortieth article . . . which I hold to be more important than any of the thirty-nine" objected to by those who with very blameable indiscretion were

---

[49] Cobbett, *Parliamentary History* (London, 1810), XVII, 252.
[50] *Ibid.*, p. 256.
[51] *Ibid.*, p. 257.

willing to disturb the public peace. He warned the House that political mobs were harmless as doves in comparison to those incited by theological hatred:

> Methinks the commotions raised by Sacheverell might be a sufficient lesson to reasonable men. Should you be bold enough to set fire to the train, I certainly shall not be one of the adventurers. . . . My study shall be to preserve public peace as the most sacred and inviolable article of religion.[52]

Charles Jenkinson also urged his colleagues not to "bring back that confused aera" of the past century, but to "cherish that system of ecclesiastical government which we have found so congenial to our civil establishment." He closed with the solemn warning: "Stir not the plague from the pit in which it is buried! If you once kindle the flame of theological dispute, you know not where it may end."[53]

Lord George Germaine voiced indignation that such obscurantist arguments could be offered in so "enlightened an age." The Clerical Petitioners should not be condemned but complimented for holding ideas "in common with the greatest divines and philosophers that England has produced":

> What think you of Clarke and Hoadly, of Locke and Newton? Would they subscribe in the literal and grammatical sense as the nature of the things requires? Their writings demonstrate the reverse. Is it not time then to remove so great a stumbling block? For my part it appears a melancholy thought and indeed a crying grievance that my son at sixteen must subscribe upon entering the university what I cannot understand, much less explain to him, at sixty. . . .[54]

---

[52] *Ibid.*, p. 261.
[53] *Ibid.*, p. 270.
[54] *Ibid.*, p. 266.

Thomas Pitt quite agreed with these sentiments, and Messrs. Dunning and Sawbridge pronounced "subscription to the articles indefensible, they are so strikingly absurd and palpably ridiculous!"[35]

The Prime Minister then rose to reiterate in milder fashion the arguments of Newdigate. He found the coronation oath a basic obstacle to the petition and pronounced the Act of Union "too fundamental a constitution to be lightly and wantonly altered." More important than these considerations, he agreed with Stanley and Jackson that the House must not "wake that many-headed hydra, religious controversy," in an age when any man, so long as he was a loyal subject, was "allowed to propagate his own doctrine." After all, every person could go to heaven in his own way; "the only restraint laid upon us is that we create no public disturbance."[56] North declared that the consequences of the petition would be the destruction of the very right of private judgment for which it contended by opening the Church to sectaries of every denomination and creating such dissensions as could be terminated only "by the heavy hand of an infallible authority."

Edmund Burke entered the debate to attack the notion that the Act of Union constituted an irreversibile decree, for "every legislature must be supreme and omnipotent with respect to the law which is its own creature."[57] Also, the king swore in his coronation oath to preserve the religion established by law, which could only mean that religion which had the sanction of his parliament. Indeed, would not the system proposed by the petitioners be the religion established by law if it passed through the three branches of the legislature?

Now that he had brushed these specious arguments aside

---
[55] *Ibid.*, p. 294.
[56] *Ibid.*, p. 273.
[57] *Ibid.*, p. 276.

and got down to consider the practicality of the plan proposed by the petitioners, Burke found it based upon "abstract principles" quite unworthy of the statesman's trust.[58] Nothing could be clearer to him than that some forms of subscription were necessary for order and public peace, because only a general standard which obtained throughout the whole community and not the partial creed of this or that bishop by whom a priest happened to be ordained, could produce any semblance of stability. In short, forecasting with remarkable clarity the attitude which he was to adopt in 1790, Burke declared:

> I would have a system of religious laws that would remain fixed and permanent, like our civil constitution, and that would preserve the body ecclesiastical from tyranny and despotism, as much at least as our code of common and statute law does the people in general; for I am convinced that the liberty of conscience contended for by the petitioners would be the forerunner of religious slavery. Men for the sake of peace and quiet would be forced to throw themselves into the hands of some dictator as they did at the Restoration into those of Charles the second. For my part I am no friend to innovations in religion when the people are not in consequence of some religious abuse much aggrieved. . . .[59]

This was the case at the Reformation, and Burke would have heartily concurred in the alteration at that time had he been

---

[58] Burke's refusal to enter into the abstract justice of the case showed, as Professor Sykes has said, that his whole approach to the matter lay in expediency rather than in truth. Shortly after, in a "speech on the Act of Uniformity," he was found saying: "I will not enter into the question how much Truth is preferable to Peace. Perhaps Truth may be far better. But as we have scarcely ever the same certainty in the one that we have in the other, I would, unless Truth were evident indeed, hold fast to Peace, which has in her company Charity, the highest of virtues. . . ." Reproduced in Sykes, *Church and State,* p. 382.

[59] Cobbett, *op. cit., pp.* 288–289.

a member of the House. But he must vote against the clerical petition, since the Articles contained "nothing contrary to scripture or that could shock a rational Christian."

With Burke's final statement C. J. Fox did not hesitate to agree. Although expressing hope that the two universities would "not much longer force the articles down the throats of young persons" unable to understand them, he found that they "savoured of Christian charity" and ought to be retained for members of the Establishment.[60]

Despite further efforts by Thomas Pitt, Sir William Meredith, and Sir Harry Houghton on behalf of the petitioners, it was clear that the Commons were in no mood to gratify their request. The assurances of Alexander Wedderburn, the Solicitor General, that the Act of Union afforded no legal impediment fell on deaf ears,[61] and Meredith's motion passed in the negative by 217 votes to 71.

This handsome majority of 146 votes nevertheless gave Sir Roger Newdigate, Lord North, and other friends of the status quo only eleven days in which to congratulate themselves before they were challenged from an unexpected quarter. On February 17, Henry Seymour moved to bring in a private member's bill for protecting his majesty's subjects against the dormant land claims of the Church. Seymour argued that "a limitation of this nature is necessary with respect to the church as it has been deemed so in regard to the crown, for there is no reason why the people should be disturbed in their possessions under the plea of immemorial time of the one than under the *nullum tempus* of the other." His

---

[60] *Ibid.*, pp. 293–294.

[61] "I am surprised to hear a doubt of the right to alter the Act of Union," said Wedderburn, "since it has already been altered both as to the English and Scotch churches; the former, by the act against occasional conformity, the latter by the act which destroyed elective patronages." *Ibid.*, p. 294.

purpose in bringing this matter to the attention of the House was "to put every subject in this free country upon the same footing in point of common law," after revealing "how oppressively this church power hath been used" by the revival of dormant and obsolete claims. Indeed, a family in his constituency were losers to the amount of £120,000 by a bishop's reviving such a claim, although they had been in quiet possession for more than a hundred years.[62]

George Onslow, William Dowdswell, Edmund Burke, and C. J. Fox all spoke in favor of Seymour's motion; but it was opposed by all the force which the administration could muster, Lord North and John Skinner crying out that the *nullum tempus* in the hands of the crown had been abrogated by statute law because it was "an engine in the hands of the strong to oppress the weak; whereas the *nullum tempus* of the Church is a defence of the weak against the strong," thereby keeping in proper balance the essential alliance between Church and State, protecting the former against encroachments by the laity.[63] Consequently the motion was lost, but this time the government's majority had dwindled to twenty-four votes.

Observing the administration's strength even in preventing the reading of a bill so evidently brought in on a public ground and for the general good, Theophilus Lindsey, most vigorous of the Clerical Petitioners, could see little hope for a movement which aimed to relieve a specific segment of the populace from a grievance less readily understood. Despite the resolution of his fellow petitioners to renew their efforts as soon as possible, Lindsey had "little hope of much in the future being done by us," even to the extent of getting another hearing before the Commons, "since Lord North is made

---

[62] *Ibid.*, pp. 301–302.
[63] *Ibid.*, p. 303.

Chancellor of Oxford and the whole bench of bishops declare themselves resolved to oppose everything that we shall propose . . . ."[64]

Lindsey did not await the result of a second application to Parliament by the Feathers Tavern Association, but resigned his living and withdrew from the Church of England on November 12, 1773.[65] In fact, by the time a second debate on the petition did take place, he had opened his Essex Street Chapel (Unitarian) in London. Although he despaired of success, nothing could keep him from the gallery of the Commons on May 5, 1774, and he reported what he heard there to his friend Turner.[66]

Again Sir William Meredith "opened the cause well upon the increasing hardships of the petitioning clergy," mentioning in particular the case of Mr. Lindsey "who was obliged to give up the emoluments of the church because he did not think the articles were right," and Edward Evanson of Tewkesbury who was currently under prosecution for deviating from rules prescribed in the Book of Common Prayer. He closed by stressing the absurdity of forcing articles drawn up by "Calvinist Reformers" upon "the Arminian clergy of

---

[64] Lindsey to Turner, October 23, 1772, *op. cit.*, p. 48. He complained in the same letter about "a dissentient party" amongst the petitioners, under the leadership of Dr. Beilby Porteus and the Reverend Francis Wollaston, "who are for receding from the rigours of our Protestant demand of subscription to the scriptures only and for trying to get what reformation they can, which will certainly only disgrace us and be none at all."

[65] In his *Apology on Resigning the Vicarage of Catterick* (London, 1774), Lindsey said: "I foresaw that if no relief was obtained, it would certainly terminate, as to myself, in the resignation of my office in the Church."

[66] Lindsey to Turner, May 10, 1774, *op. cit.*, pp. 49–51. This report is in many respects more detailed than the small space which Cobbett gives to the debate.

our present church"; and Sir George Savile seconded these sentiments.

Then Sir Roger Newdigate got up with his usual zeal, followed by Lord North, both emphasizing once more the unalterable sanctions of the coronation oath and the Act of Union. After they had finished, Burke, "in a masterly speech of upwards of an hour," ridiculed these arguments again in much the same language he had employed in the preceding debate, concluding with the plea for "a strict establishment narrowly watched, but with the most unbounded toleration to dissenters." Again Fox supported Burke's sentiments, "insisting vehemently on the Dissenters being relieved, saying that they had a connivance but not a toleration." When the question was finally called for aloud from all sides of the House, the gallery was ordered cleared; but on the question being put "there did not appear to be above twenty ayes and the noes made so strong a sound that Sir William Meredith declined dividing the House."[67]

Such was the end of the attempt to reduce the terms of subscription within the Established Church which had its origin in the Feathers Tavern Association. Its only concrete success lay in a slight easing of university subscription at Cambridge whereby candidates could proceed to the bachelor of arts degree by subscribing to a simple declaration of membership in the Church of England rather than to the Thirty-Nine Articles.[68] After the second failure of their application for

---

[67] Cobbett, *op. cit.,* p. 1327.
[68] This was accomplished in June of 1772 as an outcome of John Jebb's campaign. *Vide Annual Register,* 1772, Chronicle, p. 165. On February 4, 1773, it was proposed that Oxford should follow the example of Cambridge in substituting declared church membership as sufficient requirement for the B.A. but the University Senate was so shocked at the mere possibility of dissenting undergraduates, that they refused even to debate the issue. Not until 1858 was it possible to matriculate and

relief, John Jebb and Edward Evanson followed Lindsey in resigning their preferments and the Reverend John Disney brought up the rear. Their ideas, even on university subscription, were not to become "practical politics" for almost a century.

While clerical petitioners were threatening to rend the Church from within, momentous developments were also taking place among Dissenting ranks. In 1767 Lord Chief Justice Mansfield had pronounced that "it is now no crime for a man who is within the description of the Toleration Act that he is a Dissenter"; indeed, "nonconformity henceforth is legally established."[69] In other words, Mansfield handed down a decision which at last officially recognized Bishop Warburton's principle that an established church must be accompanied by toleration of those religious sects who would pledge themselves not to destroy it. But the Lord Chief Justice's ruling did not seem to make any immediate impression, at least upon the other leading jurist of the day, Sir William Blackstone. In *Commentaries on the Laws of England,* published three years after the Evans decision, that great lawyer spoke of the penalties for Dissent as being "suspended" only by the Toleration Act. Furthermore, after quoting from Warburton's *Alliance* to show that an establishment was fundamental to the peace and stability of all governments, he went on to state his belief that reviling the ordinances of the National Church was "a crime of much grosser nature than mere nonconformity."[70]

---

take the B.A. without a religious test; and not until 1871 were candidates for the M.A. and persons elected to fellowships relieved of all the old subscriptions.

[69] " The Toleration Act renders that which was illegal before now legal; the Dissenters way of worship is permitted and allowed by this act; it is not only exempted from punishment but rendered innocent and lawful; it is established; it is under the protection and not merely under the connivance of the law. . . . Now there cannot be a plainer position than

REVIVAL OF DISSENTING ACTIVITY   161

Such insinuations drew forth a heated reply from Joseph Priestley in which the radical Dissenter lost no time accusing Blackstone of speaking "in the voice of party rage."[71] Moved to thorough indignation by the political events of 1768 and 1769,[72] as were many of his fellow Dissenters regardless of their theological views,[73] he voiced alarm that since Blackstone was supposed "to possess the confidence of the ministry, his sentiments must be considered as a notification to Dissenters what

---

that the law protects nothing in that very respect in which it is in the eye of the law at the same time a crime. Dissenters within the description of the Toleration Act are restored to a legal consideration and capacity; and a hundred consequences will from thence follow which are not mentioned in the act. . . . The Dissenters are freed not only from the pains and penalties of the laws therein particularly specified, but from all ecclesiastical censures, and from all penalty and punishment whatsoever on account of their nonconformity which is allowed and protected by this act and is therefore in the eye of the law no longer a crime. . . ." *Vide* John Holliday, *The Life of William Late Earl of Mansfield* (London, 1797), pp. 255–256.

[70] Sir William Blackstone, *Commentaries on the Laws of England* (London, 1769), IV, 53.

[71] Joseph Priestley, *Remarks on Some Passages in the Fourth Volume of Dr. Blackstone's Commentaries . . . relating to Dissenters* (London, 1769).

[72] Assessing the political position of Dissenters in October of 1769, Priestley believed them to be "about as much in opposition to the court as the rest of the nation. . . ." Until then, Dissenters in general had been contented with things as they were, "satisfied to purchase their religious liberty by exclusion from public affairs;" but "the late vote of the House of Commons in favour of Mr. Luttrel" was "so evidently aimed to defeat the purpose of election of members of Parliament, which is the very basis of all our liberty," that almost all nonconformists were having second thoughts, "especially those of us who are called *Rational Dissenters* and have no legal establishment." No longer could this group count on "the moderation, the good sense, and the spirit of the times to be a kind of security that was nearly as good as the law." *Vide* J. T. Rutt (ed.), *The Works of Joseph Priestley* (London, 1823), I, 349–357.

[73] The Reverend Joseph Towers, far less moderate than Priestley, lamented that "the friends of the House of Hanover can no longer be considered as the partisans of liberty." Lashing out at the ministry for their "unjustifiable use of military power," which had not only "set the whole continent of America in flame," but alarmed everyone at home

light they are regarded in by those who are in power."⁷⁴ He pointed out that "in the present state of public affairs it is particularly unreasonable to irritate and disunite the subjects of this realm"⁷⁵ and charged the noted jurist with being "a man who, finding a house already in flames either wantonly or wickedly throws another faggot into it."⁷⁶ Like Mansfield, Priestley insisted that mere nonconformity was no crime in the laws of England since the Toleration Act, and it was certain "there is no penalty annexed to it."⁷⁷

"by the murders lately committed in St. George's Fields," Towers concluded: "When I consider what repeated attempts have been made wantonly to exasperate the people, I wonder at their moderation and am surprised that they have not committed greater violence. . . ." *Observations on Public Liberty, Ministerial Despotism, and National Grievances* (London, 1769), pp. 5–20. Also, in his reply to Dr. Samuel Johnson's pamphlet, *The False Alarm* (London, 1770), which attempted to justify the government's policy toward Wilkes, John Scott of Amwell, the Quaker poet, grew almost hysterical about the current political situation. Pointing out that no nonconformists had "forgotten what they formerly suffered from High Church principles whose offensive High Church advocate defends the obnoxious measures of the Administration," Scott declared that "the political second sight of Dissenters may well discern a schism bill or a repeal of the toleration in embryo. However, we have the consolation that dissolute and enervate as the populace of this age confessedly are, and as little as you think they have left of religion, should that little be ever again subjected to the iron hand of persecution, an opposition will probably be formed ten-fold more formidable than that of Wilkes and his Middlesex Freeholders." *The Constitution Defended and Pensioners Exposed in Remarks on the False Alarm* (London, 1770), pp. 30–31.

⁷⁴ Priestley, *Remarks*, p. 2. In his *Present State of Liberty in Great Britain and Her Colonies,* published the same year as his correspondence with Blackstone, Priestley warned all Englishmen about the "alarming attacks upon the essential rights and privileges of the subject" without "any prospect of their being called to account for their illegal and arbitrary proceedings." He enumerated their "persecutions" as follows: (1) "They have evaded the operation of the great writ of *Habeas Corpus* . . . (2) They have, by a *general warrant* in which no person was said to have been accused upon oath or so much as named, arrested the person of an Englishman and a member of the House of Commons . . . (3) They restrict the liberty of the press . . . (4) They have in these cases of libels contrived to evade the great privilege of Englishmen, that of being tried by their peers in the method of jury . . . and in the place of

REVIVAL OF DISSENTING ACTIVITY 163

Blackstone responded to this challenge at once, claiming "no general reflection on modern *Dissenters* . . . being persuaded that by far the greater part of those who now have the misfortune to differ from us in their notions of ecclesiastical government and public worship have notwithstanding a proper and decent respect for the Church established by law."[78] Nevertheless:

> After having made this sacrifice to the spirit of truth and moderation, I must beg leave to inform Dr. Priestley . . . that Nonconformity is still a crime by the Laws of England and has heavy penalties annexed to it notwithstanding the Act of Toleration (nay, expressly reserved by that Act) in all such as do not comply with the conditions thereby enjoined. In case the legislature had intended to abolish both the crime and the penalty, it would at once have

---

it they have extended the methods of trial by *attachment, information* and *interrogatories* in which juries are not used . . . (5) The great Bill of Rights has been invaded by a repeated refusal to admit the first county in England to judge of the fitness of the person who shall represent them in Parliament . . . (6) Recourse has unnecessarily been had to that great engine of arbitrary power, a *military force* in a manner contrary to the genius and spirit of our Constitution. *Vide* Priestley, *Works,* I, 389–391.

[75] On the matter of "irritation of the subjects," the Reverend Joseph Towers had much to say in his *Letter to the Rev. Mr. John Wesley in Answer to his Late Pamphlet entitled 'Free Thoughts on the Present State of Public affairs'* (London, 1771). "Your pamphlet," said Towers to the noted evangelist, who, like Dr. Johnson was attempting to justify Government policy, "merits the censure of every friend to freedom and the British constitution, and it is only calculated to please a corrupt ministry and their venal partisans." How could British subjects be otherwise than alarmed, asked Towers, when the king "pays no regard to the complaints and remonstrances of the people," "murders are committed by soldiers acting in the king's name and by his authority under the specious pretext of keeping the peace . . . ," and "public money is squandered in bribing the representatives of the people?" (pp. 5; 29–31).

[76] Priestley, *Remarks,* p. 3.

[77] *Ibid.,* p. 49.

[78] Sir William Blackstone, *A Reply to Dr. Priestley's Remarks on the Fourth Volume of the Commentaries on the Laws of England* (London, 1769), p. 10.

repealed all the penal laws enacted against Nonconformists. But it keeps them expressly in force against all papists, oppugners of the Trinity, and persons of no religion at all, and only exempts from their rigour such serious, soberminded Dissenters as shall have taken the oaths and subscribed the declaration at the Sessions and shall regularly repair to some licensed place of religious worship. But, though these statutes oblige me to consider Nonconformity as a breach of the Law, yet (notwithstanding Dr. Priestley's strictures) I shall still continue to think that reviling the ordinances of the Church is a crime of much grosser nature than the other of mere nonconformity.[79]

Again Priestley replied, this time in a letter to the press. He reiterated to Blackstone:

You have not convinced me that *mere nonconformity* is a crime in the Laws of England. I apprehend it to have been no offence at common law and that, since all penalties inflicted by particular acts of Parliament are declared by the Act of Toleration not to extend to those who comply with the terms of that act, that such persons are in no sense criminal. The Church of England has no authority but what it derives from the sanction of Parliament, so that our privileges stand exactly on the same ground. *Some Nonconformists,* it is acknowledged, are guilty of a crime in the eye of the law, and so are some men; but is it therefore proper to say that mere humanity is criminal?[80]

Priestley's contest with Blackstone attracted considerable attention, but it was the publication of Philip Furneaux's *Letters* in 1770 that provided a conclusive answer to the problems which had been raised. In the preface to his analysis of Blackstone's views on Dissent, Dr. Furneaux, in a far milder

---

[79] *Ibid.,* pp. 11–12.
[80] Joseph Priestley, "A Letter to Dr. Blackstone" in the *St. James Chronicle,* October 10, 1769, No. 1344, p. 2.

and more systematic manner than Priestley, pointed out that:
> The legal state of religious liberty in these Kingdoms is very little understood. Men naturally presume that in this free and enlightened age the rights of conscience, especially as they see them possessed without restraint or molestation, have the same legal security with civil rights. It will perhaps surprise many of my readers, if they are unacquainted with the laws of their country or have not read the late excellent commentaries upon them to hear that Deists and Arians, if they declare their sentiments, are by law incapable of holding any offices or places of trust, bringing any action, being guardians, executors, legatees, or purchases of lands, and are to suffer three years' imprisonment without bail. . . .[81]

What alarm must any "friend of civil liberty" feel when he reflected on the fact that many men had no security for the possession of their rights and privileges in the law and constitution of their country, but held them only "through the moderation of their superiors or the spirit of the times!"[82] Certainly no laws which were indefensible and incomparable with the rights of conscience should be allowed to remain unrepealed; for, if it was proper that such rights should be possessed in the extent to which they were through the leniency of the times, it was also proper that there should be a legal security for them "that they may not be trampled upon through the possible caprices of men in power or some unaccountable turn in the sentiments of the publick."[83]

Then Furneaux directed his remarks to Blackstone's interpretation:
> Your argument I take to be this: Because the legislature

---

[81] Philip Furneaux, *Letters to the Honourable Mr. Justice Blackstone concerning his Exposition of the Art of Toleration* (London, 1770), p. iii.
[82] *Ibid.*, p. vi.
[83] *Ibid.*, p. viii.

hath not at once repealed all penal laws against nonconformists, that is, as you go on to observe "against all papists, oppugners of the Trinity, and persons of no religion at all," therefore (a strange *non sequitur* surely!) the legislature did not intend to abolish the crime as well as the penalty in those who are no papists or oppugners of the Trinity or persons of no religion at all, but mere nonconformists to the established rules and modes of worship. These serious sober-minded Dissenters are only exempted from the rigour of the penal laws. They are still criminals it seems, only the penalties due to their crime are suspended and their nonconformity is still a breach of the law. . . .[84]

But the idea of suspension of penalties was not to be found in the language of the Toleration Act; it simply said that the penal statutes were not "to extend" to such persons as qualified. Furthermore, the protecting clauses of the Act showed the absurdity of Blackstone's interpretation, for surely the law protected nothing which was at the same time a crime in its eye.

Whether the Toleration Act was extensive enough for those who should be its objects was, of course, quite a different question from what was its meaning and intent with respect to those who were its objects. Mere nonconformists so far as worship, discipline, and government of the Church were concerned, certainly were its objects; and, said Furneaux:

I think that it ought not to have been limited as it is in regard to the doctrinal articles of religion. But still, with respect to those persons whom it does comprehend, that is the mere nonconformists to the constitution and rites of the Church, it also puts them on a very liberal footing, not on that of connivance only, but of protection also. And the

---

[84] *Ibid.,* pp. 8–9.

more the idea of legal protection is examined, the more it will appear to justify the strong expression which Lord Mansfield used concerning the dissenting worship that it is established.[85]

Dwelling upon the matter of penal legislation, Furneaux insisted that no civil punishments were adapted to enlighten the understanding or conciliate the affections. Almost in Locke's own words, he said: "Truth is so far from suffering by free examination that it is the only method in which she can be effectively supported and propagated."[86] He sneered at Warburton and Blackstone for supporting a doctrine which stated that "the success of true religion in the world depends wholly on the power of the magistrate or the majority, either of which may be as likely at least to be on the side of error as of truth."[87] Then Furneaux proceeded to make his most forceful statement, one which was to be carried into the halls of Parliament by Charles James Fox:

> If it be objected that when the tendency of principles is unfavourable to the peace and good order of society, as it may be, it is the magistrate's duty then and for that reason to restrain them by penal laws: I reply that the tendency of principles, though it be unfavourable, is not prejudicial to society till it issues in some overt acts against the public peace and order; and when it does, then the magistrate's authority to punish commences; that is, he may punish the *overt acts* but not the tendency which is not actually hurtful; and therefore his penal laws should be directed against *overt acts* only which are detrimental to the peace and

---

[85] *Ibid.*, p. 22. "If the justices of the peace at the quarter sessions or the registrars of the bishops court should refuse a dissenting place of worship, a *mandamus* always is and must be granted in Westminster Hall to compel them to discharge their duty, and is it not absurd to suppose that a *mandamus* must issue in a case which the law regards as criminal?"
[86] *Ibid.*, p. 45. *cf.* John Locke, *Works* (London, 1823 ed.), VI, 40.
[87] *Ibid.*, p. 46.

good order of society, let them spring from what principle they will, and not against principles or tendency of principles. . . ."[88]

In other words, punishing a man for the tendency of his principles is punishing him before he is guilty for fear that he may be guilty.

The writings of Priestley and Furneaux, therefore, far more than Mansfield's decision, served both to strengthen nonconformists in general toward embracing a movement for much broader legal toleration and to awaken "unorthodox" or non-Trinitarian Dissenters to the dangers which they might suffer from unenforced laws. Also, the currents of "candour and impartiality" in that "most enlightened of ages" seemed indeed to be moving swiftly to the Dissenters' advantage. Far more than the Evans decision, the petition movement within the Church itself seemed to portend that they would soon be relieved from the legal burden of subscription. After all, Archdeacon Blackburne's argument, although perhaps not logically sound for those within the Establishment, was certainly irrefutable when applied to those who held none of its emoluments. The sympathy and friendship of ultra-liberal Churchmen like Lindsey, Jebb, Evanson, and Disney, before they resigned their livings, led London ministers into a false belief that these men represented the attitude of most Anglican clergy.

Even after the clerical petition failed, their hopes continued to mount. Had not Burke and Fox, although opposing repeal for the Anglicans, voiced their support of such a measure if applied to Dissenters? More important than that, Dean Josiah Tucker, one of the Church's most noted doctors, while maintaining that the laws of self-preservation demanded retention

---

[88] *Ibid.*, pp. 53–54.

of subscription for all officials who constituted the nationally established religious organization, had expressly asserted: "Let the ministers of Dissenting congregations, if they choose to apply, be heartily wished a good deliverance from our subscriptions."[89] This they took as a direct encouragement.

Also, the whole character of the opposition to their claims was most edifying, expressed as it was in legalistic or historical objections like those of Blackstone and Lord North, rather than in the language of bigotry. Arguments that the king would violate his coronation oath in giving consent to a repeal bill or that the Union with Scotland would be dissolved by any changes regarding subscription, even as they related to Dissenters, were hardly calculated to stir up the passions of Sacherverell's day. Each group claimed, of course, that it had the principles of "free and candid reason" on its side, but the clerical petitioners had on the whole been obsessed with a most irrational anti-Papist fanaticism from which the majority of liberal Dissenting leaders were free.[90] Then too, the Church

---

[89] Josiah Tucker, D.D., *An Apology for the Present Church of England as by Law Established, occasioned by a Petition laid before Parliament for Abolishing Subscriptions* (Gloucester, 1772), p. 64. Tucker also said: "As to the case of those young gentlemen who are to be matriculated in our two universities . . . and also of all persons commencing graduate, either in arts, law, physic, or music—there doth not appear any strict propriety in the reason of things for requiring their subscriptions, and therefore were they permitted to be on the same footing with the rest of our lay congregations, or with the members of universities in other countries, I do not see . . . any danger that would attend their non-subscribing."

[90] As early as 1766, William Sharp had delivered a vigorous attack upon Warburton's *Alliance* in the course of which he defended an open toleration of Roman Catholics with the right of land ownership, although it is not clear whether he would have allowed them state offices. *Vide* William Sharp, *The Protestant, or the Doctrine of Universal Liberty asserted* (London, 1766), pp. 38–40. Somewhat less liberally, the anonymous author of a group of Dissenting tracts in 1769, reasoned as follows: "Who could take upon him to say that transubstantiation and other speculative opinions of popery, being once introduced, the king-killing,

seemed to be clinging more and more simply to its monotonous legalistic arguments. Since "true candour" was manifestly on their side, it seemed to Dissenters that in such an enlightened age the legislature could not much longer deny them what their apologist, the Reverend Joseph Fownes, called "the primary right of conscience":

> The matter indeed is reduced to this short and plain issue: either the just principles of toleration must be sacrificed or the laws from which Dissenters desire to be sheltered must be allowed to be indefensible. The truth of the one and the justice of the other cannot stand together.[91]

"Candour" demanded that Parliament should grant them this union of justice with truth.

---

deposing, etc. doctrines would not follow? Woeful experience has to our cost often proved this apprehension to be too well grounded. . . . But as neither their practical nor theoretical beliefs would ever stand any chance of obtaining in this enlightened age and realm, by dint of argument, it is a great pity they should not be indulged in the free use of it and their form of worship to prevent their propagating in the dark. . . . *Vide The Real Seeker* (London, 1769), pp. 351–352. In his *Essay on the First Principles of Government* (London, 1768), Joseph Priestley took issue with "the great Mr. Locke" over his exclusion of Atheists and Roman Catholics from a toleration, asserting in the light of contemporary experience that both could be good subjects, and in his *Remarks on Blackstone's Commentaries* he quite agreed with the anonymous author of the *Real Seeker*. Expressing his view that the penal code against Roman Catholics was far too harsh, he went on to say: "I think that that Anti-Christian power seems to be in its old age: that her malice is now impotent; and, since nothing but self-defence will justify hostilities that, in this case, persecution would be an unnecessary evil. Besides, it is cowardly to kick an old and dying lion" (p. 46). Fownes, Towers, Kippis, Furneaux and other liberal Dissenters, while most cautious on the question of trusting "papists" in the government, defended the right to practice their "religious opinions" in an unmolested fashion, and certainly none of them reach the hysterical heights of Archdeacon Blackburne's "menace of popery" fulminations.

[91] Joseph Fownes, *An Enquiry into the Principles of Toleration* (London, 1772), p. 108.

CHAPTER V

The Appeal to Candour

MEETING AT Dr. Williams's Library in Red Cross Street, London, on April 16, 1771, the General Body of Protestant Dissenting Ministers of the Three Denominations had unanimously voted a resolution of thanks "to the Revd. Dr. Furneaux for the great service he has done to the cause of religious liberty in general and for his able defence of the rights and privileges of Protestant Dissenters in particular in his excellent *Letters to the Honourable Mr. Justice Blackstone*."[1] In his acknowledgment, Furneaux had expressed "no small satisfaction" that "so respectable a body" should support his work and pledged himself to "continued vigilance in behalf of religious liberty."[2] Events of the next year were to prove this pledge far from an empty gesture.

Both Philip Furneaux and his colleague the Reverend Edward Pickard had watched the activities of Blackburne, Jebb, and Lindsey with great interest, and on February 6, 1772, they were to be found in the gallery of the Commons listening attentively to debate on the clerical petition. They heard Burke and Fox contend for the broadest possible toleration of Dissenters outside the Church, and even Lord North himself could not deny that Blackburne's appeal for freedom from subscription was logically valid when applied to those outside the National Establishment. Surely, then, Furneaux

---
[1] *Minute Books of the General Body* (Dr. Williams's MSS 38. 105, I, 89).
[2] *Ibid.*, p. 96. Furneaux's letter is dated Clapham, April 25, 1771.

argued, no reasonable man could question the desirability of mitigating such outmoded laws; and an anonymous Dissenting pamphleteer put the case in even stronger language: "Good God! that in a philosophic age, in a Protestant country, a country famed all over the globe for having given birth to the greatest masters of reason"—a country where the writings of Locke, Hoadly, and Butler had circulated freely among the people—there should be a brutal series of penal regulations hanging over the heads of every man whose conscience would not permit him to subscribe to a set of medieval theological dogmas! But then, all would soon be made right when the question "came before the British Senate to be discussed by persons of liberal and ingenuous minds" who would "consider the subject upon the principles of common sense and common honesty, without any regard to metaphysical subtleties or theological refinements."[3]

Encouraged by such cogent appeals and above all by the debate they had just heard, Furneaux and Pickard rushed to Dr. Williams's Library. With a confidence which proved utterly unrealistic they laid plans for a prompt meeting of the General Body of Dissenting Ministers in order to draft a petition to Parliament. So "favourable were the circumstances" that they urged swift action, and their entreaties fell upon willing ears.

No time was lost in sending out a summons to the ninety-five ministers of the Three Denominations "in and about the cities of London and Westminster," and seventy of them responded, gathering together at the Library early in March.[4] After some

---

[3] *Vide A Letter to the Right Honourable Lord North* (London, 1772), pp. 10–12.

[4] The movement was thus a wholly urban one and it was decided that time was too short to consult the views of country Dissenters because every moment lost would lessen the effectiveness of the appeal. But behind this official excuse was no doubt a dread of revealing the doctrinal strife within Dissenting ranks themselves, an element of basic weakness which

debate, with but one dissenting voice,[5] they passed the following resolutions:

Whereas intimation hath been given that the Administration appeared disposed to take off the subscription required of Protestant Dissenting Ministers by the Toleration Act and to give relief in the case of tutors and schoolmasters: Resolved that these are very desirable and important objects. Resolved that a committee be appointed to concert and pursue such measures and to make such applications as may be necessary to carry these purposes into execution. Resolved that the committee consist of fifteen, *viz:* Mr. Pickard, Dr. Amory, Dr. Price, Dr. Harris, Dr. Kippis, Mr. Pope, Dr. Conder, Dr. Gibbons, Dr. Savage, Dr. Furneaux, Mr. Toller, Dr. Stennett, Dr. Jeffries, Mr. Wallin. Resolved

---

the events of 1773 fully revealed. *Vide* Israel Mauduit, *The Case of the Dissenting Ministers* (London, 1772), pp. 54–58.

[5] The dissenting voice was that of the General Body's secretary, Dr. Henry Mayo, who actually wrote his feelings into the Minute Book and eventually gained the support of the Reverend Mr. Oswald and sixteen others. *Vide Minutes,* p. 123. Precisely what he wrote there will never be known as the majority had it expunged. Dr. Mayo's handwriting ends abruptly on page 111 and the next entry, for May 12, 1772, in the hand of Dr. Harris states that: "Dr. Mayo having resigned his office of secretary to the General Body: Agreed unanimously that Dr. Harris be secretary for the remainder of the year," (p. 112) a post which he held for the next twelve years. The recalcitrant former secretary would not be silenced, however, and lost no time in expressing his views in print. He emphasized that the application to Parliament "had but a very feeble foundation," insisted that "the disposition of the House after the rejection of the Clerical Petition could hardly be a valid reason for thinking that they would receive an application from Dissenting ministers," and deplored the fact that the General Body had not "consulted with their brethren in the country." He concluded by insisting that there were "many neutrals in the voting" of the voice resolution in favor of petitioning Parliament, and the actual proportion of these original "neutrals" is perhaps indicated in the recorded division of June 10, 1772, on whether or not to accept the resolutions of the March meeting as desirable for the General Body's future policy. Forty-seven divided in favor of the original resolutions and seventeen against them, with Mr. Oswald leading the opposition. *Vide Minutes,* p. 122, and Henry Mayo,, *Remarks on 'The Case of the Dissenting Ministers'* (London, 1772), pp. 53–54.

that the Committee being regularly summoned, seven may proceed to business an hour after the appointed time of meeting. Ordered that the Committee do convene the General Body as occasion requires.[6]

This distinguished committee set to work at once under the chairmanship of Edward Pickard. Its first step was to achieve as much solidarity as possible by "waiting on the gentlemen who are Deputies from the congregations."[7] Once assured of support from the leading laymen among London Dissenters, the committee of ministers next sought "advice and assistance from gentlemen respected for their rank and character" in the House of Commons, namely Sir Henry Houghton, Sir George Saville, Mr. George Onslow, and Mr. Jeremiah Dyson.[8] These gentlemen advised them "to pursue the design with all possible diligence." They should first draw up and print a statement of their case, "but secrete it from publick inspection till it should be first presented to the members of the House of Commons." Then they should lose no time in preparing a bill so that a motion might be made to introduce it into both Houses before the end of the session, keeping in mind that without a declaration of their Christianity, the bill would in all probability be refused consideration by either branch of the legislature. Accordingly:

They, after as mature deliberation as the time would per-

---

[6] *Minutes of the General Body,* I, 109–110.

[7] The *Minutes of the Deputies* report for March 11, 1772, that "The Revd. Mr. Pickard, the Revd. Dr. Furneaux, and the Revd. Dr. Stennett attended and acquainted this Committee that they came deputed . . . to request the advice, concurrence, and assistance of this Committee in carrying their purposes into execution. Resolved unanimously that this Committee doth entirely approve and will most heartily concur with the said design, apprehending it to be of the utmost importance to the liberty of Protestant Dissenters and they will by all means in their power assist in promoting it." *Vide* Vol. II, 201.

[8] *Minutes of the General Body,* II, 149.

mit, prepared the declaration contained in the printed case,[9] which declaration they persuade themselves is acceptable to their brethren as it is virtually a renunciation of human authority in matters of faith and an asserting of our great common principle—the sufficiency of scripture and the right of private judgment.[10]

The bill was first drawn up under the direction of the committee by one of the solicitors attending the House of Commons and afterwards revised by Michael Dodson whom Pickard described as "a very learned and skilful lawyer and a firm friend of religious liberty."[11]

On April 3, 1772 Sir Henry Houghton requested the Commons' permission to bring in a bill for the further relief of Protestant Dissenters. This motion, following so closely upon the clerical petition and an attempt to abolish the Church's *nullum tempus* claim, at once provoked great alarm among "the high church gentlemen" who "began to imagine that some settled design was formed subversive of the established religion."[12] Consequently the two hour debate which followed was a spirited one, with Sir Roger Newdigate providing his customary measure of hot temper. He declared that "the proposed regulations would pave the way for an increase of presbyterianism—in all ages the resolute foe of monarchy";[13] and Sir William Dolben came to his support, warning that such a proposal, supported largely by Unitarians and Atheists,

---

[9] *Vide* Israel Mauduit, *The Case of the Dissenting Ministers* (London, 1772).

[10] *Ibid.*, p. 37: "I A.B. declare, as in the presence of Almighty God, that I believe that the Holy Scriptures of the Old and New Testaments contain a revelation of the Mind and Will of God, and that I receive them as the rule of my faith and practice." A similar declaration had been suggested by Blackburne, *cf.* his proposal in the *Confessional*, p. 361.

[11] *Minutes of the General Body,* III, 150.

[12] *The Annual Register,* 1772, History Section, p. 89.

[13] William Cobbett, *Parliamentary History* (London, 1810), XVII, 432.

would "root out the Christian religion entirely from this nation!"[14]

Frederick Montague replied that he was tired of hearing "charges brought against the presbyterians for their connection with the wars of the last century when they had just reasons for arming themselves against a tyrannical king." But even supposing that they had then been misled by prejudices, it was "unfair to tax the children with the sins of the fathers," and George Onslow seconded these sentiments at once.[15] Constantine Phipps insisted that despite the vigorous attempts of High Churchmen to assert otherwise, the matter of business under consideration was completely different from that proposed by the clerical petitioners, who, as members of the Establishment were bound by every tie of honor and duty to obey its rules and laws, but contemporary Dissenters had always proved loyal and faithful subjects and were "only praying to be disengaged from ties which were foreign to their principles and institutions."[16]

After a brief speech by Lord Robert Clare attacking Sir Roger Newdigate for defending "unenforced laws," Edmund Burke rose to sum up for supporters of the motion, insisting that if this measure had been considered dangerous to the State, the Prime Minister would never have absented himself from the debate; and it was certainly of no danger to the Church, because, as Phipps had said, Dissenters did not partake of her emoluments. Speaking directly to Newdigate's point, Burke argued that "this absurd mode of subscription contributes rather to the propagation of presbyterianism than to the establishment of the national religion," for Dissenters

---

[14] *Ibid.*, p. 437.
[15] *Ibid.*, p. 434.
[16] *Ibid.*, p. 435.

were obliged to sign only thirty-five articles which favored the principles of the Church of Geneva, omitting completely the distinctive doctrines of the Anglican Church contained in the remaining four articles." Sir Henry's motion was thus carried without a division, and the Dissenters' bill passed its first reading on April 7 despite loud opposition from Newdigate and Dolben.

When on April 14, Sir Henry Houghton moved for a second reading, Sir William Dolben rose once more to decry a measure which would promote the growth of those who "blasphemed against the divinity of Christ." Sir William Bagot and Sir Roger Newdigate both asserted themselves with great zeal in his support, Sir Roger laying hold of this opportunity both to proclaim Charles I as "the only canonized saint of the Church of England," and to weaken the authority of John Locke by hinting that the great philosopher had in all probability been a presbyterian.[18] Despite the passion with which they were uttered, such irrelevant comments were treated with the lack of seriousness which they merited, and the House divided 70 votes to 9 for the Dissenters' bill, ultimately handing it on up to the Lords.

Pickard hastened from the gallery of the Commons to summon the General Body and report such encouraging news. On April 17, he rose to address the chairman before the assembled ministers in Dr. Williams's library as follows:

Thus far, Sir, this great affair has succeeded equal to our most sanguine expectations, but much remains still to be done. As we have no doubt of passing thro' the House of Commons, we have already been preparing for the House of Lords. We have waited upon every noble peer in town

---

[17] *Ibid.*, pp. 435–37.
[18] *Ibid.*, p. 438.

and either presented our case or left it for them. They must be again waited upon...."[19]

He ended on a confident note with an appeal for adequate financial support to see the measure through to success.

London Dissenters could hardly have hoped for more than what they saw plainly as an almost unanimous support in the Commons for their cause; but, as had been the case with their lay Deputies' attempt to push through repeal of the Test in 1739, so now the ministers were completely lacking in political insight. They took no notice of the increasing opposition which was being organized among supporters of "the established order in Church and State," and never considered the possibility that politicians might be using the apparent unanimity of the House as a mere maneuver to impress their Dissenting constituents on the eve of a general election that almost all M.P.'s favored so "liberal a measure in keeping with the times." That this was actually the case seems fairly evident from a letter which George III wrote to Lord North on April 2, 1772, the day before debate on Sir Henry Houghton's motion in the Commons:

> As I understand the petition of the Dissenters is to be presented tomorrow, I take this method of acquainting you that I think you ought not to press those gentlemen who are brought on that interest into Parliament to oppose the measure, as thus you may be driving them out of those seats on a new Parliament; but I think you ought to oppose it personally through every stage which will gain you the applause of the Established Church and every real friend of the Constitution. If you should be beat, it will be in doing your duty, and the House of Lords will prevent any evil...."[20]

---

[19] *Minutes of the General Body*, III, 151.
[20] W. B. Donne, *The Correspondence of King George the third with*

The House of Lords duly performed the rôle expected of them by His Majesty. On May 19, despite warm support of the bill from Chatham, Lyttleton, Shelburne, and Richmond, the opposition had found time to organize itself. Taking a leaf from Dolben's book, Shute Barrington, Bishop of Llandaff, offered proof that the principles of many Dissenting ministers were utterly subversive of orthodox Christianity by quoting a variety of passages from the publications of Dr. Joseph Priestley, a performance which Chatham himself interrupted with exclamations of "Monstrous, horrible, shocking!" The Bishop of London then rose to insist that, after taking some pains to inform himself whether the bill was promoted and patronized by Dissenters in general, "he had the authority to declare from the most respectable persons and ministers of that sect, who had waited upon him, that it was disagreeable to them and that they did not wish it to pass."[21] Consequently the bill was defeated by 102 votes to 29, but loyal Churchmen were not contented to drop the matter there.

Thomas Newton, Bishop of Bristol, who had been unable to address the House on the day of its debate, printed an intended oration which expressed the feelings of his colleagues on the Bench:

... What need is there ... to desire to be relieved from a

Lord North from 1768 to 1783 (London, 1867), Letter 131, pp. 101–102. His Majesty concluded the letter by pointing out that: "It is the duty of Ministers as much as possible to prevent any alteration in so essential a part of the Constitution as everything that relates to religion; and there is no shadow for this petition, as the Crown regulates a *nole prosequi* if any over-nice Justice of Peace encourages prosecution."

[21] William Cobbett, *op. cit.*, XVII, 441. When they found their views opposed by the majority of the General Body, Henry Mayo, Oswald and a few others had written to the Bishop of London asserting "that a great and respectable part of the Body of Protestant Dissenting Ministers in and about London disapprove of the application to Parliament for taking off the subscription required ... and do not wish it success. ..." *Vide Minutes of the General Body*, p. 153.

subscription which few [Dissenters] . . . have ever made? Easy and moderate as the terms of toleration are, yet scarce any have complied with them . . . Why not rest content with the general connivance without troubling the legislature to justify their neglect and omissions and to authorize their breaches of the law by passing another. They first break a law, and then, not content with impunity, must have a dispensation for so doing . . . If they are such friends to free toleration and full liberty of conscience, why will they not allow it to others as well as require it for themselves? We know very well what an intolerant spirit possessed the Dissenters in the last century while they had the power in their hands. We know it at this day by their opposition to the establishing of a bishop in America . . . I profess myself, my Lords, a hearty friend to freedom of inquiry and liberty of conscience . . . But liberty of thinking and judging is one thing and liberty of public preaching is another. . . . There are some secretaries who hold principles inconsistent with all civil government . . . and how do your Lordships know but some of these men may be of that sort, and would your Lordships grant your licence to such preachers? . . . Then there would be nothing that can hinder the revival of all the fanaticism and enthusiasm, of all the heresies and blasphemies which were broached in the last century and terminated in the ruin of the Constitution both in Church and State. . . . There is then no plea, no pretence for this bill, for I do not find that it would be agreeable to the generality of dissenters . . . I have been informed . . . that it is a measure in which they are far from being all agreed, that it is carried on chiefly by some ministers in and about London without the consent of many in the country and indeed without the approbation of the graver part of dissenters. . . . It is therefore improperly entitled a bill for the relief of Protestant Dissenters. It is more justly and truly a bill for the public preaching of Arianism, Socinianism, any schism, any heresy that any fanatic or incendiary may advance! . . .[22]

The Bishop of Hereford, Dr. John Butler, hastened to emphasize the same points in an open letter addressed directly to the London ministers:

> . . . It is honest to profess what you think; but surely it was injudicious to expect that the Legislature would abruptly set up the opinions of a small body of Dissenters against the fundamental doctrines of the Christian Church and even against the doctrines of a far greater part of the Protestant Dissenters, and in neglect of the experience of former times, lay a sure foundation for general discord and confusion. . . .[23]

So spoke the bishops, and it can hardly be questioned that the vast majority of temporal peers agreed with them.

The General Body of London Dissenting ministers lost no time in responding to this challenge. Edward Pickard was the first to rise and address a meeting at the Library on June 10, 1772:

> This body will join with me in lamenting the miscarriage of a Bill founded in and carried on by no party principles either political or religious; but upon the great principles common to all Protestant Dissenters and upon which alone our cause can be defended. It is not, Sir, for or against particular doctrines or names that we have been contending. It is not for or against Athanasianism or Arianism, it is not as Calvinists or Arminians, or Baxterians that we have applied and prosecuted this great affair . . . Sir, the prin-

---

[22] Thomas Newton, D.D., *A Speech designed for the House of Lords on the Second Reading of the Dissenters' Bill, May 19, 1772*, in *Works* (London, 1782), I, 137–141.

[23] John Butler, *A Letter to the Protestant Dissenting Ministers who Lately solicited Parliament for Further Relief* (London, 1772), pp. 17–18.

ciples upon which we have acted are Liberty of Conscience, the Right of Private Judgment, the Sufficiency of Scripture, and the Authority of our Divine Master and Saviour. . . ."[24] He went on to condemn "the dishonourable conduct" of Dr. Henry Mayo and his supporters who, despite the fact that the General Body had censured them by expunging Mayo's entries in the *Minute Book,* had carried "their disruptive doctrines" to the other end of town and presented them to the Bishop of London as representative of "many very respectable members of this Body." Pickard proposed a resolution that "the assertion that a substantial number of this Body is very well satisfied with the Toleration Act as it now stands is without foundation, and that the method pursued to obstruct this great project is highly censurable."[25] Thirty voted for the resolution, six divided against it, and six others remained neutral. The General Body then voted thanks to those peers who had supported them, and, mindful of the aspersions cast upon their unrepresentative character, "that proper measures be pursued to obtain the sentiments of our brethren in the country."[26]

More vigorous members of the General Body like Joseph Towers and Ebenezer Radcliffe continually dwelt upon the vote of the House of Commons as sufficient incentive to a second application.[27] Why should not the spirit of "Candour" which had shown itself in the lower House yet insinuate itself into the upper? There was, though, an essential change in the situation which these gentlemen had failed to notice. In 1772 their application for relief had come as a surprise with no

---

[24] *Minutes of the General Body,* II, 154–155.
[25] *Ibid.,* p. 153.
[26] *Ibid.,* p. 154.
[27] *Vide* Joseph Towers, *A Dialogue between Two Gentlemen concerning the Late application to Parliament* (London, 1772), pp. 26–27, and Ebenezer Radcliffe, *A Sermon occasioned by the Denial of Relief* (London, 1772), pp. 18–20.

opportunity for a formidable opposition to crystallize among High Churchmen, let alone within Dissenting ranks. Now they were not only confronted by a solid wall of resistance from High Church bishops led by Shute Barrington, but a resolute bloc of Calvinist Dissenters had proclaimed their opposition by issuing pamphlets and counter-petitions. Indeed, an anonymous pamphlet "by an Orthodox Dissenter," printed in September of 1772, asserted that "if heads were to be numbered, the Orthodox would tell at least equal to the Rationals, if ministers and people may both be included"[28] and that "the Orthodox Dissenters . . . have cause to wish that matters remain as they are."[29] In spite of such threats to Dissenting unity, the General Body moved relentlessly toward another approach to Parliament.

At a meeting on December 15, 1772, the General Body "agreed that any of our Country Brethren who desire leave to attend these meetings shall be admitted on sending their names to the Chairman,"[30] and Pickard reported "that the committee had received letters from a great number of country ministers of each Denomination declaring their approbation of and thanks for the late application."[31] At the next meeting on December 23, five country ministers were actually in attendance to hear Pickard announce that still more letters had

---

[28] *Candid Thoughts on the Late Application of Some Dissenting Ministers to Parliament . . . by an Orthodox Dissenter* (London, 1772), pp. 11–12.

[29] *Ibid.*, p. 18.

[30] *Minutes of the General Body*, II, 119. The General Body was, however, quite unwilling to concede anything beyond this mere permission to attend, and when at their meeting on November 30, 1774, the Reverend John Palmer actually moved "that any country Brethren who shall be willing to attend the Meeting of the General Body, on the business of an application to Parliament, be permitted to attend, to speak, and to vote on the business," it was "resolved that Mr. Palmer's motion be not put." *Ibid.*, p. 164.

[31] *Ibid.*, p. 120

come in "recommending a further application to Parliament whenever it should be judged by the majority of the General Body to be prudent and proper."[32] This recommendation was quickly turned into a resolution with fifty-five voting for and thirteen against it. Mr. Oswald, who led the Calvinist opposition, was allowed "to enter his Dissent from and protest against the resolution,"[33] but this made no impression upon the majority.

On January 27, 1773, the General Body by 43 votes to 17 resolved that "the application be renewed,"[34] with little apparent realization of their insecure position. After all, in spite of their attempt to pacify their "country brethren" through seeking their opinions by correspondence and actually allowing some of them "to attend" meetings without the right to vote or speak, there had been no change of personnel in the committee charged with the management of proceedings. This continued neglect to assume a more representative character was justified by the superior experience of the old committee,[35] an excuse hardly convincing enough to silence the opposition. In fact, only two days after the resolution for a new application was made public, Calvinist counter-petitioners were circulating a printed sheet which stressed the unrepresentative nature of those Dissenting ministers "who call themselves the General Body,"[36] and making known their intention to see that it was distributed to every member of Parliament.

---

[32] *Ibid.*, p. 122.
[33] *Ibid.*
[34] *Ibid.*, p. 128.
[35] *Vide* Joshua Toulmin, *Two Letters on the Late Application to Parliament* (London, 1774), p. 64.
[36] A copy of this sheet is filed under No. 3.6.21 of Dr. Williams' MSS and reads in part as follows: *Society of Protestant Dissenting Ministers, meeting at the New York Coffee House, Sweeting's Alley, Cornhill, London, January the 29th, 1773:* Whereas an application hath been made to Parliament by a number of Protesting Dissenting Ministers who

Nevertheless, on February 17, 1773, Sir Henry Houghton rose in the Commons to propose another bill "for relief of Protestant Dissenting clergymen, schoolmasters, and others in the affair of subscription." At once a member sprang to his feet insisting that "the very persons intended to be benefited by this bill are the very persons who think they labour under no grievance," for he had been handed a printed paper at the door of the House which stated that "orthodox" Dissenters opposed the application.[37]

Ignoring this assertion, the House gave leave to bring in Sir Henry's bill on March 2, and he presented it for their consideration on that day. Sir Roger Newdigate surprised no one by uttering a solemn pledge "to oppose the bill in every future

---

call themselves the General Body praying for relief in the matter of subscription, we think it our indispensible duty to make this public declaration: That we are all well satisfied with the present mode of qualification, prescribed in the Act of Toleration . . . : I—Because were the request of the aforesaid General Body (as they call themselves) granted, it would be going back to Popery, as it would set aside those *essential Doctrines contained in the Articles of the Church of England, on the faith of which the Reformation was founded.* II—Because it would justify the Church of Rome in her opposition to the Doctrines of the Reformation . . . and would reflect dishonour on the characters of those faithful Protestants who suffered martyrdom for the truths contained in those doctrines. III—Because it would tend to encourage the propagation of the principles of those persons who deny the doctrine of the ever blessed Trinity and other important truths. . . . IV—Because the excluding of subscription to the Articles of the Church of England and introducing the intended mode of qualification . . . suggests that these Articles are not contained in the scriptures. V—Because the end proposed in the bill would not be answered, i.e. universal satisfaction, as a very great number of Protestant Dissenters, Ministers and others, would be dissatisfied if the intended alteration took place. VI—Because it reflects dishonour on his Majesty and the present *mild and happy Administration* under which every Protestant Dissenter is protected from all persecution on a religious account. VII—Because it would give great offence to *The Reverend Clergy of the Church of England,* whose petition of a similar nature has been rejected . . . Published by order of the Committee, on behalf of the whole society. Richard Hutchings, Chairman, John Langford, Secretary.

[37] William Cobbett, *op. cit.,* XVII, 759–760.

stage, as well as every other attempt of the same tendency,"[38] and it passed a first reading despite his fulminations. But when it was brought up for a second reading on the following Tuesday, a much hotter debate ensued. Sir William Bagot, after once more stating his general reasons against the measure, contended that the time fixed for this second reading was too short, particularly because "many persons who were comprised within the description of those intended to be relieved by the bill were resolved to be heard by counsel against it," and they should have at least another week to muster their case.[39] Jeremiah Dyson and Thomas Townshend immediately accused Sir William of indulging in petty obscurantist tactics to kill the measure, but the House saw fit to grant the delay which he had requested. When on March 10, however, Sir William rose again to plead that the counsel for "orthodox" Dissenters needed a few more days for the preparation of his brief, tempers flared, and Edmund Burke pronounced it "a ridiculous impropriety in hearing counsel because nothing can be urged in favour of those who petition against the bill!"[40] The House then proceeded to allow a second reading by eighty-seven votes to thirty-four, with the provision that counsel might be heard at the third reading.

On March 17, Bagot chose to deliver a long speech in which he took great labor to identify the present bill with "the petition from the club at the Feathers," both of which aimed to "throw down the best barrier of Christianity [i.e., the Articles] and open a door for the admission of infidels of every species into the pale of the Church!"[41] After Francis Page had come to his support by asserting that "the divisions amongst the Dissenters

---

[38] *Ibid.*, p. 761.
[39] *Ibid.*, p. 764.
[40] *Ibid.*, p. 765.
[41] *Ibid.*, pp. 767–769.

themselves shows that in numbers the advocates of the bill are as inconsiderable as they are far from being unanimous,"[42] Edmund Burke replied that the reasonableness of the request and not the numbers who preferred it was the thing which ought to govern the attitude of the House. He could not but cry out against the lack of Christian charity shown by those petitioning against the Dissenters who said, in effect: "We enjoy every species of indulgence we can wish for; and as we are content, we pray that others who are not content may meet with no relief."[43] He ridiculed Bagot for arguing that since the Dissenters enjoyed liberty by connivance, they had no grounds for complaint: "You are desirous of keeping the rod hanging over their heads at the very instant you assure them they shall never smart under its stripes."[44] Why not release them altogether from the dread of those penal statutes, the cruelty of which so shocked the generous nature of the Commons that they thought it necessary to declare the unfeasibility of ever putting the law into execution?

The third reading of the bill was scheduled for March 25; and, on that day, petitions were presented from ministers and congregations of "orthodox" Dissenters at Bolton in Lancashire, at Exeter, at Dursley, and at Wotton-under-Edge in Gloucestershire, requesting that a bill so "detrimental to the establishment of religion in this kingdom" should not pass. After these petitions were read, Robert Chambers, Vinerian Professor of Law at Oxford, was called in as counsel for the Calvinist Dissenters, and his arguments reproduced almost to the letter Sir William Dolben's warnings about the perils for Orthodox Christianity latent in "a test proposed instead of the

---
[42] *Ibid.*
[43] *Ibid.*, p. 781.
[44] *Ibid.*, p. 780.

Articles, drawn up in a vague manner, and construed in such general terms that a Mahometan might sign it!" He also fell back upon Lord North's old argument that in England every man was at liberty to entertain what opinions he pleased and each could go to heaven in his own way so long as he did not disrupt public order by tampering with existing institutions;[45] but such vain repetitions, despite many quotations from Moses, Cicero, Chillingworth, and Warburton to buttress them, failed to impress the House. However, the majority of Chambers' audience could hardly have failed to grasp the incongruity of a situation in which a professor at High-Church Oxford was acting as spokesman for one group of Protestant Dissenters in order to oppose another group of fellow nonconformists, and they agreed with Burke in declaring against those who were themselves tolerated but refused toleration to others.[46]

Although the Dissenters' bill passed its third reading in the lower chamber by a vote of 65 to 14, it was again to be killed in the Lords. Despite strenuous efforts from Richmond, Mans-

---

[45] *Ibid.*, pp. 786–788.

[46] The Reverend Samuel Wilton, a prominent member of the General Body, marvelled that "the principles of divinity" held by the counter-petitioners could be "so much at variance with the obligations of humanity" and rejoiced that the Commons had not fallen prey to their shabby tactics. "The petitioners acknowledge that they are tolerated now and they will be equally tolerated if this bill should pass into law. The most they can say against it is that it will do them no positive good. But if it will do good to others and do no harm to them, what is the language of this petition but saying the misery of others is our happiness and the happiness of others is misery?" Wilton could hardly believe "that a learned professor of a famous university, not hitherto reckoned the most favourable to Dissenters, has actually appeared at the bar of a British House of Commons at the request of some who have called themselves Dissenters to oppose the grand principle of Protestantism and Toleration!" He concluded with an appeal to his recalcitrant brethren to consider the enormity of their position. *Vide An Apology for the Renewal of an Application to Parliament by the Protestant Dissenting Ministers addressed to the Thirteen Ministers who Protested against it.* (London, 1773), pp. 27, 94, 105–106.

field, Camden, Shelburne, and Lyttelton, the measure was rejected by a vote of 86 to 28, with the Bishop of Lincoln alone breaking away from a solid bloc of ecclesiastical peers united in opposition to it.[47]

At a *post mortem* held by the General Body on April 13, 1773, Pickard emphasized that without unity it was hopeless to expect any substantial achievement, and submitted his resignation with those of his fellow committee members. Immediately there were speeches of confidence in the old committee, compliments on "their ardent zeal," and the claim for real hope in the future under their leadership, actuated "by the consideration that above eight hundred of their brethren in various parts of the Kingdom had signified to them by letter their hearty concurrence with the resolution of this Body. . . ."[48] Consequently members of "the late committee" were re-elected by a large majority to watch the political horizon, but most of their old fiery faith in "candour" had completely departed. At the next five annual meetings they reported "that it doth not appear at present to this committee to be proper to renew our application to Parliament . . . but that the Committee will continue to keep the matter in mind to be pressed at the first convenient opportunity."[49]

Meanwhile, much soul-searching was taking place among

---

[47] Samuel Wilton blamed this defeat not only upon the Calvinist counter-petitioners but also the opposition of the bishops, who, like an obedient shoal of fish, would swim in any direction which the Administration beckoned them "even though it be contrary to the laws of God and men alike." He paid high tribute to Dr. John Green, Bishop of Lincoln, who alone had the courage and political nonchalance to stand out among all his colleagues in favor of the Dissenters' bill. In the face of such disloyalty, George III is said to have muttered: "Green, Green, he shall never be translated!" and he never was. *Vide* Wilton, *op. cit.*, p. 106 and J. W. Middleton, *An Ecclesiastical Memoir of the Reign of George the Third* (London, 1822), pp. 127-129.

[48] *Minutes of the General Body,* II, 136-137.

[49] *Ibid.,* p. 146 *et seq.*

Dissenting apologists. First to conduct an agonizing reappraisal of the old arguments for toleration was the Reverend Joseph Fownes in a second edition of his *Enquiry,* published in 1773. By reaching back over Locke's political thought, he found no difficulty in proving that toleration was the right of all good subjects and that the state must either grant it or deny the very principle of its own existence.[50] But he was quite satisfied to justify no more than full toleration and a legal security for religious beliefs without insisting upon the right of all good subjects to eligibility for state offices. All he desired was "that Dissenting ministers and their congregations be exempted from the penalties to which their not having complied with the Articles of the Church of England leaves them subject."[51] He had no complaint against "the spirit of the times," but only against "the spirit of the laws." Must it not soon be appreciated by the legislature — even by the Bench of Bishops — that non-execution of penal laws against nonconformists was a very different thing from proper exemption from them?[52]

The Reverend Doctors Philip Furneaux, Andrew Kippis, Robert Robinson, and other Dissenting apologists who took up their pens immediately after the disappointment of 1773 adopted similar attitudes. Furneaux insisted that the second application for relief from the Thirty-Nine Articles should have been considered by the opposition not as obstinacy "but as a

---

[50] "The right of conscience," said Fownes, "stands upon a foundation peculiar to itself and is so distinguished from every other right that it cannot be given up." In fact, he went so far as to insist that to secure this right alone men had formed the idea of a commonwealth, and so it formed the very basis of all government. *An Enquiry into the Principles of Toleration* (2d ed.; Shrewsbury, 1773), pp. 17–21.
[51] *Ibid.,* p. 74.
[52] *Ibid.,* p. 69.

renewed appeal to candour."[53] Referring to "the reasoning of that great man Mr. Locke,"[54] he showed that "though we may be safe by the powers of others, we cannot be religious by the consciences of others."[55] The bishops, by their late disgraceful action in the Lords, however, were trying to press just such an absurd doctrine, which ran counter to all the laws of human psychology. Why should they so fear granting more than "a mere connivance" to Dissenters who asked only for "a fully legal toleration," a toleration which entailed only protection from the penal laws, not emoluments of any sort in either Church or State?[56]

Notwithstanding the Calvinistic structure of their Articles, the majority of the established clergy were Arminian: "Why, then," asked Furneaux's colleague Dr Kippis, "may not Arians and Socinians be equally valuable members of society and equally worthy of protection?"[57] But he clearly did not venture beyond the limited doctrine of mere legal toleration for all religious groups.[58] Speaking of the attempts at repeal of the Test Act during the seventeen-thirties, Kippis regretted that Dissenters of those days had not "directed their attention and zeal to a much more desirable and important object." He professed himself quite prepared to endure the Test "because it only excludes those who cannot comply with it from the

---

[53] Philip Furneaux, D.D., *An Essay on Toleration with a Particular View to the Late Applications* (London, 1773), p. x.

[54] *Ibid.*, p. 1.

[55] *Ibid.*, p. 14.

[56] *Ibid.*, pp. 72–73.

[57] Andrew Kippis, *A Vindication of the Protestant Dissenting Ministers with Regard to their late Application to Parliament* (London, 1773), p. 46.

[58] "Religion in every form of it which is consistent with the safety of the State," said Kippis, "has an unlimited title to indulgence. I do not, therefore, think that toleration ought to be confined to Christianity. I am of the opinion that the magistrate hath no right to interpose in religious matters so as to lay any restraint upon or prescribe any test to those who behave as peaceful subjects. . . ." *Ibid.*, p. 63.

enjoyment of certain civil honours and preferments, whereas the penal statutes deprive us of the common rights of human nature and of Christianity...."[59]

"Whoever looks attentively," wrote the Reverend Robert Robinson, "will find that the leading principles of the petitioners for relief from the Articles ... are the allowed or professed principles of all mankind," and he was therefore confident that universal toleration, when thoroughly understood, would meet with less opposition than at first seemed probable from its recent defeat in the Lords. After all, any reasonable person must admit that diversity was a basic principle of human nature, and the notion that either priest or magistrate could produce any one article, let alone thirty-nine, on which any two men could exactly agree, ran counter to all known principles of psychology.[60] All three apologists quoted Locke to prove that the composition of the human understanding would render the enforcement of a uniformity of religious belief quite impossible.[61]

Such was the nature of the initial reappraisal after defeat,

---

[59] *Ibid.*, p. 16.

[60] Robert Robinson, *Arcana: or the Principles of the late Petitioners to Parliament for Relief in the Matter of Subscription* (Cambridge, 1774), p. 110. His basic argument ran as follows: "Civil society consists in a *moral* not a *sentimental* union, the preservation of which union is the business of the magistrate. Where a moral union prevails society is safe; where it does not no other unanimity contributes anything. What would it contribute to the peace of society if an uniformity of sentiment could be established in music, statuary architecture, or painting, unless at the same time an uniformity in moral obligations prevailed also? On the contrary, how would it injure the peace of society if every one had a different creed on these articles, suppose at the same time a moral unanimity prevailed?" p. 47.

[61] Furneaux, *op. cit.*, p. 30; Kippis, *op. cit.*, p. 48; Robinson, *op. cit.*, p. 46; *cf.* Locke, *Works, op. cit.*, II, 279. *Vide* also Ebenezer Radcliffe, *Two Letters addressed to the Right Reverend Prelates who a Second Time rejected the Dissenters' Bill* (London, 1773), pp. 100–102, which present the same sort of argument.

largely a retracing of the arguments which had ranged themselves behind the old appeal to "candour." But as these apologists continued to mouth their traditional arguments apparently unheeded, more radical voices were lifted to assert that, logically sound as the old reasoning seemed, it was far too limited in appeal. New principles must be set forth which advocated what the Reverend David Williams called "true rational liberty for all mankind," not the merely negative program of removing provisions of a penal code that threatened the ministers and congregations of three particular Dissenting groups. "All honest men, be they Calvinists, Arminians, Socinians, Papists, Jews, Turks, or Infidels" should never be excluded by law from "the right to rational liberty which they all possess as human beings."[62] Indeed, Williams professed himself to "rejoice that the Dissenting petitioners' efforts have miscarried," for they were based upon narrow and faulty principles:

The magistrate can have nothing to do with the opinions of those who renounce the advantages of the Establishment. Consequently the whole business of the Dissenters should

---

[62] David Williams, *Essays on Public Worship, Patriotism, and Projects of Reformation* (London, 1773), p. 21. But, said Williams with deep sarcasm, perhaps things were not so bad, for "in England every avenue to knowledge is thrown open and men carry on their enquiries with pleasure. Their devotion is however not suited to their knowledge. They may become as enlightened as a Newton and as rational as a Locke, but they must worship on the principles of a Calvin and in the words of a Cranmer. . . . Some of the clergy have attempted to throw open the Church to rational and philosophical principles, but they have not yet succeeded. Their attempts however have been treated with a decency and candour which does some honour to the present age. The virtues of the times are moderation and candour. Our governors hear petitions with temper and refuse them with decency, and though they will not legally tolerate, yet they connive at almost all principles and practices which save the appearance of religion. The language of their conduct seems to be: 'We will not alter our present constitution; but while we think you are good subjects and honest men, you may worship God as you please'." *Ibid.*, p.4–5.

have been to ask the repeal of the penal laws themselves, the free exercise of their worship, and the choice of their ministers, tutors and schoolmasters, and offer any security of their civil obedience which the government would require . . . To offer a declaration of faith to the magistrate as a condition of liberty was giving up their first principle . . . They say the faith was their own . . . they could conscientiously subscribe to the Word of God. . . . Here they deceive or are deceived by a quibble. Words of God—Words of man—Words of the devil—it makes no matter of difference: when the magistrate has adopted them, they are his words, and you desert your principles and injure your integrity . . . in taking even that Gospel you believe at the hand of the magistrate and making him the judge of your faith and conscience. . . .[63]

Start your business *de novo,* urged Williams to the Dissenting ministers. Have nothing to do with Mansfield, Onslow, Dyson, or any members of the legislature, but "bring your petition into the House on the single principle which justified your dissent and offer a *carte blanche* as dutiful subjects."[64]

Encouraged by developments in America, Williams once more addressed the Dissenting ministers:

Your very existence depends on your changing the reason of your dissent, which used to be an opinion of superior orthodoxy and superior purity of faith and worship, for another which is the only rational and justifiable reason of dissent—the inalienable and universal right of private judgment, and the necessity of an unrestrained enquiry and freedom of debate and discussion on all subjects of knowledge, morality, and religion. This may be called *Intellectual Liberty*. This should be the general reason of dissent; this would be an honourable, effectual, and perma-

---

[63] *Ibid.,* pp. 49–53.
[64] *Ibid.,* p. 56.

nent bond of unison among all your sects; it would render you the best friends and patrons of genius and virtue, and give you a kind of weight and consequence with the publick which you have never had or deserved. . . .[65]

Williams concluded with an exhortation to Dissenters of the Three Denominations to renounce the *Regium Donum* and any claim to "special privilege" under the government, to declare their principles to be "the right of private judgment" for all men without exception, and to seek repeal not only of the penal code, but all other discriminatory legislation like the Test and Corporation Acts which the principles of rational liberty could never justify.

Joseph Priestley also urged "the abrogation of all laws which do not tolerate all sects of Dissenters and Christians."[66] In a letter of advice to the General Body of London ministers, he wrote:

You have hitherto proffered your prayer as Christians; stand forth now in the character of men and ask at once the repeal of all penal laws which respect matters of opinion. This is the thing we all wish for, and in which we are most likely to unite, and nothing short of this will finally content us. I know we are not so narrow-minded as from choice to be secured from a danger to which our adversaries, the *unbelievers* are exposed, or so distrustful of the cause of Christianity as to think that anything is necessary for its security and flourishing state besides its own proper, rational evidence. Let us then act upon this generous principle, and at the same time assert the honour of

---

[65] David Williams, *A Letter to the Body of Protestant Dissenters and to Protestant Dissenting Ministers of all Denominations* (London, 1777), pp. 23-24.

[66] Joseph Priestley, *A Letter of Advice to those Dissenters who conducted the Application to Parliament for Relief from certain Penal Laws* (London, 1773) in J. T. Rutt (ed.), *Works of Priestley* (London, 1823), XXIII, 446.

our country and the dignity of human nature, by petitioning for a bill by which *unbelievers* shall be as much at liberty to attack as ourselves to defend either Christianity in general or our particular opinions concerning it. . . .[67]

Priestley offered the opinion that such a request, although more comprehensive than any the ministers had yet made, would nevertheless be more easily granted because in most cases religious sects entertained a greater antipathy to one another the nearer they were to agreement, for this made the few points of difference between them the more striking. But if people's sentiments were so remote from one another that they had few common principles on which to dispute, and had little or no intercourse together, they seldom thought of one another and consequently harbored no grudges:

Had the Jews, Mahometans, or Gentoos applied for a legal toleration of their respective religion and the Dissenters been silent, I dare say that a bill in their favour would have passed both Houses of Parliament without opposition and that the man who would have hesitated to tolerate these foreign religions would have been thought exceedingly cruel and illiberal. I will even venture to say that had the present Bishop of Llandaff [Shute Barrington], who it is plain would not have tolerated even his own father as a Dissenter, been applied to in behalf of these strangers, he would, without hesitation have promised them his vote and interest; but apply to him on behalf of a species of Christians and he is immediately startled. He does not know what mischief may be concealed in the proposal; and the apprehension of danger alarms men and puts them the more upon their guard, in proportion to its being indistinct and confused. For we are never more afraid than when we know not what we have to fear. Cancel, therefore, the

---

[67] *Ibid.*, pp. 442–443,

obnoxious name of Christian and ask for the common rights of humanity. At least, if you must hold yourselves out to be Christians, include *all* Christians and ask for the repeal of all the other laws which subject any Christians to pains and penalties, as well as that which is usually called the Act of Toleration.[68]

Then Priestley moved in the direction of those ideas which events in America and France were to make most popular with liberal thinkers in England. As a Christian only, he acknowledged that he should be contented with the bare toleration of his religion and be thankful for it. In that character he had nothing to do with the honors and emoluments of any state and no occasion to ask for the toleration of any sentiments but his own:

But when the Christian is satisfied, I cannot forget that I am likewise a man; and the generosity of the man and of the Christian happily concur in wishing for the toleration of all the modes of thinking in the world . . . Nor do I promise that even when these wishes are obtained I shall overlook what is due to civil society and especially to such a constitution as that of this country whose safety, honour, and happiness, it certainly imports not to deprive itself of the services of any man of ability and integrity on account of his religious opinions any more than on account of the colour of his hair, and how demonstrable soever the necessity of a *test law* may be thought, by those whose interest it is to have it demonstrated, I make no doubt but that at no great distance of time it will be seen to have been as absurd and mischievous in the politics of Europe as it is found to be altogether unnecessary in America; and that the obligation which now lies under the members of Parliament, civil and military, physicians, and doctors of

---

[68] *Ibid.*, p. 443.

music to subscribe the thirty-nine Articles of the Church of England, will be considered as equally ridiculous.[69]

Priestley maintained that Dissenters of the seventeen-seventies had no occasion to confine themselves within the bounds of Locke's principle of toleration. His treatise was certainly admirable for its time, but Priestley's contemporaries had made very poor use of Locke's arguments if they acquiesced in them still. It was hardly advisable to rest solely upon the authority of any man as though his sentiments and mixims were a perfect and unalterable standard. Locke was staggered at the thought of tolerating atheism, and for the same reason he might have hesitated to tolerate other opinions about which a wise civil magistrate would give himself very little concern.[70]

It was hardly surprising that other liberal Dissenting ministers, although not nearly so rabidly unorthodox in their theology as Williams and Priestley, were moving rapidly in the direction from appeals for a mere toleration toward a demand for complete religious freedom. The Reverend Benjamin Thomas of Malmesbury warned Shute Barrington that his obscurantist tactics in the House of Lords could have no lasting

---

[69] *Ibid.*, p. 450.

[70] Priestley illustrates the danger in Locke's position by showing how the Reverend Doctor John Brown had used it in his *Thoughts on Civil Liberty* (London, 1766) to justify a policy which was not only aimed against the toleration of Atheists and Papists, but which also clothed the civil magistrate with full authority to act against any opinion which he thought "might tend" in those subversive directions. *Vide* Brown, *ibid.*, pp. 43–46 and Priestley, *Letter*, p. 478. In his *Essay on the First Principles of Government and on the Nature of Political and Religious Liberty* (London, 1768), Priestley had made similar statements about Locke's restrictions upon the right to toleration: "These exceptions of Mr. Locke have an obvious tendency to multiply hypocrites in a state while the magistrate, instead of devoting himself to his arduous duty of controlling actions by established law, must become a vexatious inquisitor of opinions, constantly occupied in the investigation of their tendency and in ascertaining the religion or the irreligion of the individuals which compose the community," p. 63.

result, "for the Genius of the Age is not in their favour," and that the next attempt at repeal might be even more comprehensive "in keeping with the times."[71] Enumerating several instances of the prosecution of Dissenting schoolmasters in ecclesiastical courts, particularly in Wales, the Reverend Benjamin Fawcett vigorously upheld the right of all men to teach their religious beliefs to their children, proving his point by examples from the New Testament which showed that rational persuasion alone, and never a battery of penal laws imposed by the State, could lead to a knowledge of "true religious principles."[72]

Joshua Toulmin fulminated against "a mere state of temporary relaxation of tyranny and persecution," and cried out: "Give us back our full natural rights!" If most Dissenters were not actually fined or imprisoned, they were all continually in danger of both. Was this a condition in which "a prudent, ingenuous, and liberal mind" could acquiesce? "A man who is not indifferent to the rights with which the Author of Nature hath invested him and who knows that conscience ought to be left in the enjoyment of perfect freedom and ease will always seek something more than a partial toleration or a liberty by connivance!"[73] Even Samuel Wilton, Independent minister at Weigh House, London, who claimed to "receive the doctrine of the Trinity as the true doctrine of scripture" as fully as any Churchman,[74] revolted against "the

---

[71] Benjamin Thomas, *A Letter to Shute, Lord Bishop of Llandaff with reference to his Speech on the Dissenters' Bill* (London, 1774), p. 13.

[72] Benjamin Fawcett, *The Encouraging Prospect that Religious Liberty will be Enlarged considered . . . in a Sermon Preached at Kidderminster, November 5, 1773* (Shrewsbury, 1774), pp. 7-8.

[73] Joshua Toulmin, *Two Letters on the Late Application to Parliament by the Protestant Dissenting Ministers* (London, 1774), pp. 8-10.

[74] Samuel Wilton, *A Review of Some of the Articles of the Church of England to which a Subscription is required of Protestant Dissenting Ministers* (London, 1774), p. 87.

ungracious bigotry of the Bench of Bishops," and was moving markedly in the direction of Toulmin's call for a restoration of natural rights.[75]

A very short step, then, remained between the political sympathies of these Dissenting ministers and the ultra-liberal views of Dr. Richard Price, who pressed their claims to a logical extreme. He reasoned that individuals in private life, while held under the power of masters, could hardly be considered free, no matter how equitably and kindly they might be treated. This was strictly true of communities as well as of individuals—and particularly true of the British Government. Indeed, said Price:

> Religious and Civil Liberty must be enjoyed as a right derived from the Author of Nature only or it cannot be the blessing which merits this name. If there is any human power which is considered as giving it, on which it depends, and which can invade or recall it at pleasure, it changes its nature and becomes a species of slavery.[76]

So far as liberal Churchmen went, one would expect a man like John Disney, who was soon to enter the ranks of Dissent, to be perfectly capable of heaping abuse upon the head of

---

[75] *Vide ibid.,* p. 88.
[76] Richard Price, D.D., F.R.S., *Additional Observations o nthe Nature and Value of Civil Liberty and the War in America* (London, 1777), p. 4. Price followed a naïve "rationalist psychology" which reflected the marked influence of Rousseau. "Moral liberty," he held, "cannot be better defined than by calling it 'a power in every one to do as he likes without any restraint'. . . . Every man's will if perfectly free from restraint would carry him immediately to rectitude and virtue and no one who acts wickedly acts as he likes, but is conscious of a tyranny within him overpowering his judgment and carrying him into a conduct for which he condemns and hates himself." Tyranny from without, i.e., any political attempt to interfere with "religious and civil liberty" through penal codes and test laws must be done away before men can experience freedom from tyranny from within. *Vide ibid.,* p. 11.

Archbishop Cornwallis for "a fixed resolution to do nothing" in the matter of church reform and a further toleration. Nevertheless, warned Disney, the bigoted votes of the bishops against both the clerical petitioners and the Dissenters had "caused a trial of spirits to be made throughout the land into the nature and extent of our religious rights . . . and the times cannot help but foster a spread among the people of the idea that all religious groups have a right to teach and preach their beliefs."[77] One could, of course, hardly expect three learned doctors of the Establishment like Dean Josiah Tucker, Archdeacon William Paley, and John Sturges, Prebendary of Winchester, to go quite so far as this; but they too showed "the liberality of the times" by coming out rather forcefully in favor of "a more complete toleration."

Dr. Sturges summed up the attitude of his two other colleagues when he wrote:

> I wish that the Legislature had seen fit to comply with the Dissenters' application . . . for they asked only what was reasonable and consistent with the general principles of toleration. . . . If such an application be made again, I cannot help expressing my hopes that it will meet with a more favourable reception . . . in order to make the state of toleration in the Kingdom the more complete. . . . Let Popery also be legally tolerated as it is in certain parts of Germany and Holland . . . without injury to the State.[78]

---

[77] John Disney, *A Letter to the Most Revered Lord Archbishop of Canterbury on the Present Opposition to any Further Reformation* (London, 1774), p. 15.

[78] John Sturges, *Considerations on the Present State of the Church Establishment* (London, 1779), pp. 45–51. Tucker professed it the right of all religious beliefs "to enjoy a fixt and legal toleration instead of a temporary and precarious connivance," vide *Letters to the Revd. Dr. Kippis* (London, 1774), p. 33; and Paley pleaded for a full toleration "upon the general principles of justice and expediency alike," Vide *A Defence of the 'Considerations on the Propriety of Requiring a Subscription to Articles of Faith'* (London, 1774) in *Works* (London, 1877), p. 161.

All three divines admitted quite freely that Dissenting religious groups, even with this "legal toleration," would still find themselves "lying under some disadvantage through the Test and Corporation Acts," but they could not understand how dissenters could claim to suffer any injury from such legislation. After all:

> To exempt men from penalties which they do not deserve is one thing; to delegate to them authority is another. The first is a matter of justice, the latter of favour and discretion which the State may surely refuse to give if such authority be likely to operate to her own prejudice.[79]

The Reverend John Wood, and other Churchmen who did not see fit to identify themselves, at once took issue with these learned doctors and raised the old "Church in danger" alarm,[80] but most thoughtful clergymen of the Establishment saw eye to eye with Tucker, Paley, and Sturges, as the legislation of 1778 and 1779 clearly revealed.

---

[79] Sturges, *op cit.*, p. 47, *Cf.* Tucker, *op. cit.*, p. 67 and Paley, *op. cit.*, p. 156.

[80] *Vide* John Wood, B.D., *Institutes of Ecclesiastical and Civil Polity* (London, 1773), where he speaks of Dissenting religious groups as "insolent and rebellious" and on the whole markedly subversive to "our most excellent constitution in Church and State." He proves this assertion by declaring that most of John Wilkes' support had come from Dissenting ranks, and any group that would "contaminate the English Senate with a devil, or a monster, having refused to honor it with a gentleman and a believer," was worthy of no concessions from the government it sought to undermine, pp. 72–76. *Vide* also two anonymous pamphlets called *Thoughts on Religion wherein the Interference of the Civil Power and the Matter of Subscription are Candidly Considered* (Devizes, 1774), pp. 190–191 and *Antinarkia, or an Inquiry into the true Idea of Religious Liberty* (London, 1774), p. 20, both of which maintain a position similar to Wood's. The second takes Priestley vigorously to task for his doctrine that the magistrate has no right to enquire into the tendency of things, for "if tendencies exist at all, they can neither be vague nor imaginary and the magistrate must be very weak, that cannot fix and ascertain them." Priestley's system is obviously "destructive of all ordered society," pp. 65–66.

During the year 1774 it had become a matter of government policy to conciliate Ireland in order to promote unity at home, draw off sympathy for the Americans, and make the Irish more inclined to enlist in the regiments which it seemed likely would have to be sent across the Atlantic in large numbers.[81] The Irish Act of 1774, which "for the first time permitted Irish Catholics to swear allegiance to the sovereign and become subjects of the crown"[82] was a direct result of this policy. Although English Catholics amounted only to about fifty or sixty thousand in contrast to their Irish co-religionists who were rapidly approaching the impressive number of two million, it seemed expedient to gain even their goodwill after February of 1778 when the French solemnly acknowledged the independence of the United States and concluded with them an alliance which could only be treated as a declaration of war against England.[83]

Lord Petre, Sir John Throckmorton, William Seldon, and a few other leading Roman Catholic laymen immediately seized so favorable an opportunity to draw up an address to the Crown which dwelt upon their loyalty to the British Constitution in times of public danger,[84] and, on May 14, 1778, Sir

---

[81] *Vide* J. W. Amherst, *A History of Catholic Emancipation* (London, 1886), I, 65, where he states that although the object of the Act as professed in its preamble was "to promote peace and industry amongst the Irish," the real object was that soldiers might be more easily enlisted in the British army.

[82] Thomas R. England, *The Life of the Reverend Arthur O'Leary* (London, 1822), p. 50 *et seq.*

[83] *Vide* Donne, *Correspondence of George III*, Letter, 522.

[84] ". . . We beg to assure your Majesty that our dissent from the legal establishment in matters of religion is purely conscientious; that we hold no opinions adverse to your Majesty's Government or repugnant to the duties of good citizens. And we trust that this has been shown more decisively by our irreproachable conduct for many years past, under circumstances of discountenance and displeasure, than it can be manifested by any declaration whatever. . . . In a time of public danger, when

George Savile moved for leave to bring into the Commons a bill "to repeal certain provisions made in the Act of William III for further preventing the growth of Popery."[85] Sir George made use of "their late loyal and excellent address to the Throne" to demonstrate the good consequences which were likely to attend "this liberal procedure of Parliament"; and Dunning, in seconding the motion, pointed out that brutal penal laws "in times of so great liberality as the present and when so little is to be apprehended from them [i.e., the Roman Catholics] cry aloud for repeal. . . ."[86]

In the Lords, Dr. John Hinchcliffe, Bishop of Peterborough, spoke for his colleagues in favor of the measure:

> As a friend to civil and religious liberty, I am free, my Lords, to own that I think there ought to be neither penalty nor restraint on the intercourse between God and man's own conscience. I cannot, therefore, but disapprove of all laws which are calculated to oppress men from their religious persuasion; and to tempt any one with views of interest to trespass on his duty and natural affection by depriving his father of his estate or supplanting his brethren is a policy, in my opinion, inconsistent with reason, justice, and humanity. . . .[87]

Both Rockingham and Shelburne wished that "with a liberal

---

your Majesty's subjects can have but one interest and ought to have but one wish and one sentiment, we humbly hope it will not be deemed improper to assure your Majesty of our unalterable attachment to the cause of this our common country, and our utter detestation of the designs and views of any foreign power against the dignity of your Majesty's crown, the safety and tranquility of your Majesty's subjects. . . ." This address was signed by the Duke of Norfolk, the Earls of Surrey and Shrewsbury, by Lord Linton for the Scotch, by Lords Stourton, Petre, Arundel, Dormer, Teynham, and Clifford, and by 163 commoners. *Vide* Cobbett, *op. cit.*, XIX, 1138–1139.

[85] *Ibid.*, p. 1137.
[86] *Ibid.*, pp. 1139–1140.
[87] *Ibid.*, pp. 1143–1144.

toleration of religion, there should be given to a people who had demeaned themselves so well, a security and free disposal of their property."[88] This bill, repealing those clauses of the penal code which related to the prosecution of "bishops, priests, and Jesuits," which subjected any Roman Catholic keeping school to perpetual imprisonment, and which disabled any member of that religion from possessing real property by inheritance or purchase, passing such property on to the nearest Protestant relative, was thus passed into law practically without opposition.

During the course of debate on the Act of 1778, it had been pointed out that similar legislation would have to be passed for Scotland, since the penal measures repealed had been passed into law before the Act of Union. At once Scottish newspapers and pulpits showed uncompromising resistance to any sort of concession to papists. A solemn fast was proclaimed in Glasgow on October 18, 1778, with severe riots following both there and in Edinburgh. The *Annual Register* reported that by January of 1779 "the towns of Glasgow, Perth, Dundee, Dunfermline, Kilmarnock, Stirling, Dunse, etc., and a great many others" had "entered into resolutions to oppose to the utmost any relaxation of the laws against Roman Catholicks."[89] Parliament, however, turned a deaf ear. When Burke presented a petition from Scottish Catholics which requested the same measure of relief granted to their co-religionists in England and Lord George Gordon delivered a fanatically anti-papist speech demanding that Burke's motion be "thrown over the table," no one could be found to second his proposal.[90] Consequently, the Speaker refused to put it, and Burke's measure was carried without a division. But so cold a reception to his

---

[89] *The Annual Register,* 1779, Chronicle for January 8.
[90] Cobbett, *op. cit.,* XX, 327, 623.

demands did not serve to silence Lord George. He soon gave notice at a public meeting that he would present a petition to the House of Commons not only against further concessions, but for a repeal of the 1778 Act.

The violent feelings manifested in Scotland soon found their way southward and were rapidly embraced by members of the old anti-papist movement which Blackburne had led ten years earlier. Stimulated by vitriolic sermons from Scotland,[91] both Anglicans and Dissenters produced enough material of a similar nature to suggest that, if Catholic relief had not been carried through rapidly, virtually without previous notice to the country, it might not have been carried through at all. Typical of these productions was the *Anglican Antidote to Popery, or the Protestant's Memory jogged* which was early printed at threepence a copy,[92] and on the Dissenting side a pamphlet entitled *The Remembrance of Former Days,* which the *Monthly Review* termed "a good, honest, zealous, Dissenting declamation against despotism and against popery, the friend of despotism." It did not "absolutely protest against the indulgence lately extended to the Roman Catholics of this country," but it strongly recommended that everyone "keep a watchful eye upon them. . . ."[93] These sentiments, however, proved too moderate for those alarmed Protestants who were pursued by visions of a country flooded with Catholic priests, Jesuit colleges, and nunnery schools.

---

[91] Typical of these were the Reverend James Erskine's *Considerations on the Spirit of Popery* (Edinburgh, 1779) and the Reverend William Porteous's *Doctrine of Toleration applied to the Present Times* (Edinburgh, 1779), the latter of which considered Popery first as a false religion, secondly as a subversive faction in the State, and thirdly as a system of immorality. Such reasoning was followed by one Scottish preacher after another to prove that, even on the most liberal principles, toleration could not be granted to an organized system of immorality.

[92] The Protestant memory was jogged by "narratives and facts" about the persecutions of Protestants in the reigns of Henry IV, V, VIII, and

As this anti-popery agitation began to make itself felt, the paradox of having granted a measure of relief to Roman Catholics only five years after they had twice rejected a plea for the further relief of Protestant Dissenting ministers and schoolmasters became apparent to the Government. Perhaps if they were to act now, belated though it was, the goodwill created would help to subdue many of the present discontents over the Act of 1778 and the American War. The bishops even met to discuss the feasibility of bringing in a bill themselves, but thought it best that such a measure should originate in the Lower House at the initiation of the "Dissenters' friends."[94] Consequently, under the leadership of Sir Henry Houghton, Sir George Savile, and Frederick Montague, a motion was made on March 10, 1779, for bringing a Dissenters' relief bill into the Commons and leave was granted for March 17 by a vote of 77 to 6.[95]

Finally, the somnolent committee of the General Body got wind of what the politicians were doing, and they took their first action since the failure of 1773 by calling a special meeting of London ministers at Dr. Williams' Library for March 18. The first order of business was to report that Pickard, Furneaux, and Wilton, the three most vigorous members of the old committee were dead, and that one other had resigned. These four vacancies were then filled[96] and Dr. Andrew Kippis was appointed chairman with instructions "to watch carefully over the affair now in progress."[97] Kippis performed his assign-

---

Queen Mary—the Irish Martyrology—Popish treasons and conspiracies in England—Persecutions in France—an account of errors taught in the Church of Rome—etc.

[93] *Vide Monthly Review* (January, 1779), p. 80.
[94] *Vide Minutes of the General Body,* II, 196.
[95] *Ibid.,* p. 197.
[96] Dr. Rees, Mr. James Webb, Mr. Nath'l Jennings, and Mr. Noah Hill were selected. *Ibid.,* p. 199
[97] *Ibid.*

ment well, calling a meeting of the General Body on April 26 to report that:

> The bill was read for the first time on Monday, 22 March, when, after a short debate, it was agreed without a division that it should be read a second time on Tuesday, the thirtieth of the same month. . . . But on that day a petition from the University of Oxford was presented by Lord North, their Chancellor, praying that the bill might not pass in its present unlimited form. . . . Then your Committee, understanding that a declaration was likely to be moved for, to be added to the bill, drew up reasons to show that the bill ought to pass as it was first framed. . . .[98]

Kippis concluded by reporting that Lord North had in fact presented such a declaration and that it had been adopted by a vote of 88 to 58.[99]

The General Body reacted to this information by resolving that "if the bill could not be passed without a declaration" the Kippis Committee should make every effort "to get the declaration remodelled in such a manner as to render it unexceptionable to all who can submit to a general declaration of faith in the scriptures,"[100] and this they managed to do. Finding that the passing of the bill was impossible without the declaration, the committee's "friends" were at least able to get the word "whole" deleted. Consequently, the revised version required subscription to the belief that the scriptures "do contain the revealed will of God," and this encountered no difficulty in the Lords.

---

[98] *Ibid.*, p. 206.
[99] *Ibid.*, p. 207. The declaration read: "I A. B. do solemnly declare, in the presence of Almighty God, that I am a Christian and a Protestant, and as such that I believe that the Scriptures of the Old and New Testaments, as commonly received among Protestant Churches, do contain the *whole* revealed will of God, and that I do receive same as the rule of my doctrine and practice."
[100] *Ibid.*, p. 211.

THE APPEAL TO CANDOUR

Political circumstances in 1779 had thus, without the necessity of any primary action on their part, given the London Dissenting ministers that for which they had strained every nerve in 1772 and 1773. But, as we have seen, most thoughtful Dissenters were rapidly approaching a frame of mind in which only a broader appeal for the legal toleration of all religious groups, if not complete religious liberty, could satisfy them. In the words of Andrew Kippis: "The bill now passed does not come up to those ideas of complete and perfect toleration which we all think reasonable and just."[101] At least, however, it was a slight move in the right direction towards a widening legal toleration. But there remained a basic feeling of insecurity as Kippis showed in a letter to his "brethren in the country." Despite his initial emphasis that "the Committee had the pleasure of receiving the most explicit assurances from persons of the first consequence and status in the kingdom, including Lord North himself, that there could be no design of disturbing those who would not be relieved by the new law," and his dwelling upon the generally "favourable temper" of the government, he cautioned country Dissenters that:

... Tho' many will probably choose to avail themselves of the legal security now provided for them, it will perhaps be advisable for this not to be done anywhere by bodies of men, but separately and individually as each person shall think proper. By this means no particular notice will be taken of such as decline to qualify or are restrained from doing it by principles of conscience.[102]

This advice must certainly have been taken in one way or the other, as there is no indication in any of the voluminous pamphlet literature for the remainder of the century either of large numbers taking the oath or of what no doubt actually

---

[101] *Ibid.*, p. 214.
[102] *Ibid.*

did happen—a wholesale neglect on the part of Dissenting ministers and teachers to bother with it. The Act of 1779 seems in fact to have been passed over with little attention. It was far too limited to satisfy the aspirations of liberal Dissenters and it certainly did not fulfil the Government's hope of diminishing the anti-popery issue.

The rancor which Parliament was anxious to allay had shown itself in the riots at Glasgow and Edinburgh; it next assumed a threatening form in England under the label of the "Protestant Association" organized, under the presidency of Lord George Gordon, with the express purpose of preventing further concessions to Roman Catholics and repealing the Act of 1778. The Roman Catholic leader Dr. John Milner attributed the origin of the Association not so much to the speeches of Lord George as to the Methodist Movement:

> ... The pulpits of the lower sort, particularly those of John Wesley and his associates resounded ... with groans and lamentations on the pretended increase of Popery and the fatal consequences to be apprehended from the late indulgence granted to its professors, a religion which, they asserted, had slain its thousands by its cruelty, and its tens of thousands by its ignorances. By these and other inflamatory harangues ... the Protestant Society was instituted on the plan of similar associations in the last century, and particularly on that of the 'Solemn League and Covenant,' ... under the pretext of preserving the civil constitution and the Protestant religion by petitioning for a repeal of the late Act. ...[103]

---

[103] John Milner, *Letter to a Prebendary,* Letter vii, reproduced in Amherst, *op. cit.,* I, 145–147. To give added weight to Milner's statements, it should be noted that early in 1780, John Wesley wrote *A Defence of the Protestant Association,* an inflamatory pamphlet in which he contended that "an open toleration of the popish religion is inconsistent with the safety of a free people and a Protestant Government, for every convert

Although the Methodist community undoubtedly contributed most to the alarmist camp, there were numerous Churchmen who disregarded the silence of their bishops, and groups of Dissenting laymen who, when "the abominations of Rome" were in question, proved themselves completely unrepresented by liberal ministers like Priestley, Price, Kippis, Towers, Toulmin and their colleagues who were most in the public eye.[104] On the basis of local Protestant societies, therefore, it was not difficult to whip up prejudice and an *Appeal from the Protestant Association to the People of Great Britain,* issued in the autumn of 1779, called for the repeal of the Catholic Relief Act of 1778 in tones which should have been recognized as politically dangerous.[105] But Government leaders were too busy defeating the threat from another quarter — "Public Oeconomy" petitions inspired by the Reverend Chris-

---

to Popery is by principle an enemy to the Constitution of this country." Quoting from alarmist letters to the press by Wesley and his followers in favor of the Protestant Association, Milner charged the Methodist leader with being "the chief author of the riots in 1780." *Vide* Amherst, *op. cit.,* p. 147.

[104] *The New Annual Register,* 1780, History, p. 170, says that those who subscribed to the Protestant Association "were chiefly Methodists and bigoted Calvinists of the lower ranks of life. Hardly any of the clergy of the established church or of the dissenting clergy gave the least countenance. . . ."

[105] The author of *An Appeal from the Protestant Association to the People of Great Britain* (London, 1780) urged a return to "the zeal of our ancestors for the Protestant cause and for our glorious Constitution," justifying the enforcement of the severest penal statues against Popery "because they are mild when compared with the bloody edicts now in full force against Protestants in Popish countries," p. 44. He warned that if the present spirit of laxity continued: "By an influence in Parliamentary elections a future parliament may be found endued with such a liberal spirit of toleration as to remove the Test Act; to qualify them [i.e., Papists] for offices of magistracy and give them an opportunity of sitting in both Houses of Parliament . . . or Papists (as they can have dispensations for oaths) may think it a duty they owe to the Church of Rome and by jesuitical sophistry be taught that it is no sin to obtain seats in Parliament that they may serve the interests of Popery." pp. 54–56.

topher Wyvill's county movement for Parliamentary reform — to pay much attention to the Protestant Association's activities. It took the bloody mob-violence of the Gordon Riots to make them realize how dangerous this agitation really was.[106]

Military action by the king's authority on the seventh and eighth of June succeeded in putting down the riotous mobs, who, led by a distinctly criminal element from the London slums, had reduced the metropolis to a state of anarchy during the preceding week. With order once more restored, the Administration had little cause for anxiety, thanks to the readiness of Burke and Fox to take a strong line in support of North's refusal to grant any repeal of the Catholic Reliefs passed in 1778.[107] The result of the General Election of 1780 had served to improve the Administration's control of Parliament, and consequently, Burke's "Oeconomy Bill," which had been allowed a second reading unopposed before the election, was defeated by the Government without difficulty in 1781. Also, the second "Grand Deputation" of "Associated Counties" under the leadership of Wyvill and Dr. John Jebb which met in London in March of 1781 to make representations on the subject of "Public Oeconomy" and

---

[106] *Vide The Gentleman's Magazine* (June, 1780), pp. 265–268 for a graphic account of the "Rise and Progress of the Late Tumults."

[107] Parts of the Opposition, however, showed greater susceptibility to the wishes of "the people." Even Sir George Savile, if he did not go so far as Sir Joseph Mawbey, the Oppositionist representative of Surrey in accepting the views of the Protestant Association as those of the nation, still thought it incumbent on him as proposer of the Catholic Reliefs of 1778, to go farther in meeting Protestant anxieties than a mere projected resolution for declaring all anti-Catholic legislation not expressly repealed in 1778 to be still fully in force. Accordingly, he introduced a bill for disabling Catholics from undertaking the education of Protestants' children, but it was rejected in the Lords. *Vide* Horace Walpole, *Journal,* ed. by Doran (London, 1859), under June 20, 1780, for a good account of the debate.

"Parliamentary Reform" posed no great threat.[108] When, on May 8, the Wyvill petition was finally brought before the House, is was refused consideration by a majority of 212 to 135, and the status quo was safely preserved. The Government would abide by "the toleration acts" of 1778 and 1779, but it saw no necessity to make further concessions.

Meanwhile, the battle of the theorists continued with Dean Josiah Tucker producing a 428 page pamphlet upholding the Church against "the levelling principles of Mr. Locke," and the Reverend Dr. Joseph Towers responding with a lengthy vindication of Locke's political principles as a justification for dissent from the Establishment. Tucker began his great tome by conceding that Locke in his early days was witness to grievous persecutions. Locke saw the rights of private judgment exposed to continual vexations and argued that the interests of the state were not at all concerned in maintaining that rigid universal conformity for which the bigots of his day so fiercely contended—"that the principles of humanity, justice, and truth, as the suggestions of sound policy plainly required a more extended plan of religious liberty."[109] Thus Locke very justly insisted that every man had a right not only to think but even to act for himself in all such religious matters as did not oppose or clash with the interests of civil society. Had he stopped there and gone no farther all would have been well; but, said Tucker, he extended those ideas which were true only in what concerned religion to matters of a more civil nature and even to the origin of civil government itself "as if there had been the same plea for liberty of conscience in disobeying the civil laws of one's country as for not conforming to a

---

[108] For the literature of the first movement for the reform of parliament, vide Christopher Wyvill, *Political Papers,* 4 vols. (York, 1794–1802).
[109] Josiah Tucker, D.D., *A Treatise Concerning Civil Government* (London, 1781), p. 30.

church establishment or an ecclesiastical institution and that the rights of private judgment (I mean the open and public exercise of those rights) were equally unalienable in both respects."[110] The whole matter hinged, of course, upon whether the two cases were truly parallel. If so, a nonconformist in the one ought equally to be tolerated with a nonconformist in the other.

As to the first case, Tucker was prepared to assert with utmost vigor that no man, "not even the supreme magistrate," had a right "to molest me for worshipping God according to the dictates of my own conscience, provided I do nothing in that respect which can *fairly* be construed to hurt the prospects of another man or disturb the peace of society." Indeed:

> ... I may be a Papist as well as a Protestant in my speculative opinions and yet do nothing which can when justly interpreted be accounted to be injurious to others. Nay, I will not scruple to declare that I may be a Jew or a Mahometan, a Gentoo or a Confucian, and yet be a loyal subject to my prince, an honest man and a useful member of the community. Therefore, if toleration were ever to be extended as far as in reason and justice and good policy it ought to go, it ought to be so large as to comprehend every religious sect whatever whose doctrines, or rather whose practice . . . proves them worthy to enjoy the protection of the state. And there is a very particular and most important reason to be given why this liberty of conscience in religious matters ought to be extended as far as ever the safety of the State will permit; It is because in the affairs of conscience no man can act or be supposed to act as proxy for another; no man can be a deputy, substitute, or representative in such a case; but every man must think and act personally for himself. This is the fact, and in this

---

[110] *Ibid.*, p. 31.

sense it is very true, that the rights of private judgment are absolutely unalienable. But why unalienable? It is because they are untransferable and therefore every man must of necessity, after having used the best lights and helps he can obtain, be his own legislator (under God), his own governor, and his own director of affairs in religion."[111]

If, however, the cases between religion and government were similar, as Tucker held to be the position of Locke, no one individual could appoint another to judge for him what laws should be passed, what taxes should be raised, or what was to be done at home or abroad in peace or war. Every person who had these inalienable, untransferable rights of voting, judging, and fighting would have to do all these things for himself. Had not Locke's most ardent disciple in England, Dr. Richard Price, pressed these points as logical conclusions to be drawn from his master's hypotheses?[112] Surely a set of opinions more disruptive of all organized society had never been broached by man, and it was small consolation to reflect that "probably the original author . . . never meant to draw conclusions so horrid in their nature and so full of wanton treason and rebellion as the congresses have actually drawn from them in America

---

[111] *Ibid.*, pp. 32–33.

[112] "As no people can lawfully surrender their religious liberty by giving up their right of judging for themselves in religion or by allowing any human being to prescribe to them what faith they shall embrace or what mode of worship they shall practice," wrote Price, "so neither can any civil societies lawfully surrender their civil liberty by giving up to any extraneous jurisdiction their power of legislating for themselves and disposing of their property. Such a cession being inconsistent with the unalienable rights of human nature would either bind not at all, or bind only the individual who made it. This is a blessing which no generation of men can give up for another, and which, when lost, a people have always a right to resume." But, when dealing with the matter of civil rights, he spoke almost invariably in a collective rather than in an individualistic sense. *Vide* Richard Price, *Observations on the Nature of Civil Liberty* (London, 1776), pp. 21–22.

and as the Republican Factions would daily endeavour to draw from them here in England had they power equal to their will."[113]

The Reverend Dr. Joseph Towers hastened to Locke's defence, asserting that "the great man" had never maintained that anyone in any country had a right to disobey its laws. Rather, he had insisted that "no man in civil society can be exempted from the laws of it."[114] Nor was it Locke's sentiment that civil and religious rights were equally inalienable and indefeasible. It could readily be admitted that there is some difference between civil society and religious rights and that a

---

[113] Tucker, *Treatise*, p. 112. In a later work, he warned against Locke as "the idol of the Freethinkers or *les philosophes de France* . . . and also of the Levellers of England. . . . In the second part of his *Treatise on Government* he supplies them with such materials as put it in their power (were his schemes to take effect) to call for thousands and thousands of alterations in the forms and modes, management and administration of every government upon earth and to unsettle everything. In short, his principles or positions (whatever were his intentions) give them a perpetual right to shift and change, to vary and alter without end; that is, without coming to any solid establishment, permanence, or duration. Add to all this that as the rising generation are not bound (according to Mr. Locke's system) to acknowledge the validity of the acts of their fathers, grandfathers, etc., they must of course have a *new set* of unalienable rights of their own; for they are perfectly their own masters, absolutely free and independent of that very government under which they were born. In consequence of this, they also have a right to demand as many new arrangements and alterations as they please, agreeably to their own taste and honour; and if they are not gratified therein, have a right to stir up *new* commotions and to bring about another and another revolution. How could the most enthusiastic republican wish for more?" Dealing with "the manifold bad consequence of disturbing the public peace and tranquility under a pretence of procuring a more equal representation of the people in Parliament," Tucker charged the Reverend Christopher Wyvill and his county petitioners for parliamentary reform with trying to subvert the Constitution by Lockean principles. *Vide* Josiah Tucker, D D., *Four Letters on Important National Subjects addressed to the Right Honourable the Earl of Shelburne* (London, 1783), pp. 44–45; 110–112.

[114] Joseph Towers, *A Vindication of the Political Principles of Mr. Locke in Answer to the Objections of the Revd. Dr. Tucker, Dean of Gloucester* (London, 1782), p. 57.

man might with less criminality sacrifice the former than the latter. Surely Locke had said nothing contrary to this. But, wrote Towers:

> Civil rights are certainly so far indefeasible that no man can be deprived of them but by his own act. If a man may barter away his own liberty (which, however, necessarily implies in it meanness and baseness of spirit) he can have no right to dispose of the liberties of others, or of those of his posterity. 'Though it may be supposed that a body of people,' says Dr. Priestley 'may be bound by a voluntary resignation of all their interests (which they have been so infatuated to make) to a single person, or to a few, it can never be supposed that the resignation is obligatory to their posterity; because it is manifestly contrary to the good of the whole that it should be so.'[115]

However, since Dean Tucker had not produced a single passage from Locke to prove that he identified civil with religious rights, the matter need not be pressed. What should be stressed was that from Locke's "great principles" had sprung the idea that nothing could justify any sort of injustice or oppression which "deprived men of their lawful property and the use of those talents which the great Author of Nature had afforded them."[116] Towers concluded with a summary of Lockean precepts:

> It is the doctrine of Mr. Locke that all legitimate government is derived from the consent of the people; that men are naturally equal and that no one has a right to injure another in his life, health, liberty, or possessions; that no man in civil society ought to be subject to the arbitrary will of others, but only to known and established laws made by the general consent for the common benefit; that

---

[115] *Ibid.*, pp. 58–59. The quotation is from Joseph Priestley's *Essay on the First Principles of Government* (London, 1768), p. 17.
[116] *Ibid.*, p. 86.

> no taxes are to be levied on the people without the consent of the majority given by themselves or by their deputies; that the ruling power ought to govern by declared and received laws and not by extemporary and undetermined resolutions; that kings, princes, magistrates, and rulers of every class have no just authority but what is delegated to them by the people and which, when not employed for their benefit, the people have always a right to resume, in whatever hands it may be placed.[117]

It was the desertion of these principles which had led to "the present national degradation" and to the loss of America. Towers warned that if they were not soon embraced, "our dignity and reputation as a people will be completely ruined."[118]

Towers' hint at a right to the unhampered use of natural endowments or "talents" in the service of one's country was taken up and pressed by his colleague the Reverend Joshua Toulmin in a direction that indicated the broad new path which Dissenters would tread in their next approach to Parliament on the issue of civil rights. In his *Considerations on the Present State of the Church of England,* Dr. John Sturges had denied the right of all Dissenting groups to offices or emoluments of the State; but, asked Toulmin:

> Is it not wise in a State to avail itself of the wisdom and probity of any of its members? Have not all who are possessed of equal understanding and probity an equal claim to the employment of the State when their probity gives them merit and their understanding fits them to serve it? Can different ideas on speculative points, or different rituals in religion, be pleaded in bar against *political* merit? If so, then the man for conscience towards God is a sufferer for the State, and negative penalties form a degree and

---

[117] *Ibid.,* pp. 123–124.
[118] *Ibid.,* p. 143.

kind of persecution. So far the toleration is not complete nor doth the magistrate look upon all his dutiful subjects with an equal and impartial eye.[119]

Even Dr. William Paley, in attempting to uphold the Church's position on the Test and Corporation Acts, could find no justification for their continuance save only in cases of "most clear and apparent danger to the State."[120] Indeed, he went so far as to assert: "I perceive no reason why men of different religious persuasions may not sit upon the same bench, deliberate in the same council, or fight in the same ranks as well as men of various opposite opinions upon any controverted topic of natural philosophy, history or ethics."[121] He seemed to agree fully with Joseph Towers that "improvements are desirable in the science of government, as well as in all other sciences, and that system which will promote the

---

[119] Joshua Toulmin, *Letters to the Revd. John Sturges* (London, 1782), pp. 45-46.

[120] "There are two cases in which test laws are wont to be applied and in which, if in any, they may be defended. One is where two or more religious are contending for establishment and where there appears no way of putting an end to the contest but by giving to one religion such a decided superiority in the legislature and government of the country as to secure it against danger from any other. I own that I should assent to this precaution with many scruples. If the dissenters from the establishment become a majority of the people, the establishment itself ought to be altered or qualified. . . . The second case . . . is that of a country in which some disaffection to the subsisting government happens to be connected with certain religious distinctions. . . . If the government have no other way of knowing its enemies than by the religion they profess, the professors of that religion may justly be excluded from offices of trust and authority. . . . But even here it should be observed that it is not against the religion that government shuts its doors, but against those political principles which . . . members of that communion are found in fact to hold . . . and that these restrictions ought not to continue one day longer than some visible danger renders them necessary to the preservation of public tranquility. . . ." *Vide* William Paley, *Principles of Moral and Political Philosophy* (London, 1785) in *Works* (London, 1877), Chap. x, 177-178.

[121] *Ibid.*, 176.

happiness and wise employment of the greatest number of individuals appears to have a just claim to be considered as the best society."[122] Events were rapidly conspiring to convince not only Protestant Dissenters of the Three Denominations, but all Dissenting groups, that the times were ripe to cry out for a complete restoration of their rights—not primarily as Christians—but as men and citizens.

---

[122] Joseph Towers, *Vindication* . . . , p. 121.

CHAPTER VI

The Appeal to Human Rights

MID-FEBRUARY OF 1785 found the Reverend Doctor Andrew Kippis, as chairman of a special joint committee of London Dissenting Ministers and Lay Deputies, waiting "upon Mr. Pitt, the First Lord of the Treasury, to lay before him the resolutions agreed to by the General Body on the 9th Feby.,"[1] and by the Deputies on the following day.[2] These resolutions had been prompted by "an Act for granting his Majesty a Stamp Duty [of three pence] on the Registry of Births, Marriages, Burials, and Christenings," which made specific mention of Anglicans and Quakers only.[3] The Deputies' standing committee had complained that under such a law none of their vital statistics could be admitted as "legal evidence in any court of law or equity,"[4] and the General Body had passed resolutions stating their "most affectionate disposition to share in the burden of this and every other tax" and "as most loyal friends of the government" both to enjoy its "protection" and "to be afforded opportunities of service in common with our

---

[1] *Minutes of the General Body,* II, 285.
[2] *Minutes of the Deputies,* II, 384.
[3] 23 Geo. III. c. 67, the Registry Act, with the sole exception of a clause embracing "the people called Quakers," was phrased in the language of the acts of 6 and 7 William and Mary which required "all persons in Holy Orders, deans, parsons, vicars, curates, and their substitutes within their respective episcopal parishes, precincts, and places to keep a register in writing . . . etc." Thus no records kept by any other religious societies, whether on stamped paper or not, could be admitted as legal evidence. *Vide* Pickering, *Statutes at Large,* XXXIV, 328-332.

fellow subjects."[5] Kippis then presented these resolutions to Pitt, who "expressed the greatest respect for the Protestant Dissenters and the utmost readiness to comply with their wishes." Certainly he had every cause to feel well disposed toward this group. Had they not rallied almost unanimously to his support in the General Election of 1784?[6] Wishing to retain their goodwill, he saw that no obstacle should stand in the way of fulfilling this small request.[7]

So it was that once again liberal Dissenters in London thought they had found a probable ally in the Chief Minister. His consistent advocacy of parliamentary reform, his extremely courteous reception of the Kippis Committee's petition, and above all the fact that he seemed "a product of the times" when liberty had been vindicated in America and was soon to lift up her voice in France, offered substantial encouragement. But, warned by Price, Priestley, and Toulmin, London Dissenters made certain that their new appeal should not be limited simply to freedom from penal legislation for three specific religious denominations. In keeping with the spirit of the times they must embrace at least all Protestant Dissenting

---

[4] *Minutes o fthe Deputies,* II, 384.

[5] *Minutes of the General Body,* II, 249–250.

[6] The great body of nonconformists had naturally rallied to the banners of "the virtuous young minister" along with Christopher Wyvill and most of the supporters of parliamentary reform. They remembered that he had refused to hold office in the same ministry with North, that he had tried in vain to force the question of parliamentary reform on the uncanny coalition ministry of Fox and North, and that he had spoken out as strongly as Fox himself on the necessity of suppressing corrupt royal influence in the House of Commons. Men like Sir Cecil Wray and Dr. John Jebb, who loudly condemned Fox's alliance with North, were thus attracted to Pitt.

[7] 25 Geo. III. c. 75, a measure "to extend the provisions of an act made in the 23rd of his present Majesty . . . to the registry of burials, births, marriages, and christenings of Protestant Dissenters from the Church of England," received the royal assent on August 2, 1785. Pickering, *Statutes,* XXXIV, 340.

groups. They would appeal not only for freedom from penal laws for conscience sake, but for freedom to serve the state with whatever talents they might be endowed; they would insist upon restoration of their rights not as a particular group of Christians, but as men and citizens. Indeed the currents of destiny appeared to move in their favor. Once they had got hold of so universal an appeal, who would check them? Who would divert them? Who would stop them? Surely not "the enlightened young minister."

In this spirit a group of more than two hundred Dissenting laymen and ministers met at the King's Head Tavern, London, in mid-December of 1786 to discuss the situation. As a result, a general meeting of the Deputies was called for January 5, 1787, with the express purpose of considering an application to Parliament for repeal of all test legislation.[8] After the question had been put and "fully debated," it was "resolved unanimously that an application be made . . . for a repeal of the Corporation and Test Acts, so far as they concern Protestant Dissenters," and that the matter be referred to a special committee of twenty-one members of the Deputies, including the dissenting M.P., Benjamin Hopkins, who were "to take the most effectual measures for carrying the above resolutions into execution."[9] Under the vigorous leadership of their chairman,

---

[8] Strangely enough, there is no reference to this general meeting in the official *Minute Books* of the Deputies, the earliest entries on support for a movement to secure repeal of the Test not occurring until those for December 18, 1789. The Jeffries Committee, however, within a few weeks of its inception, assumed an "aggregate" membership which placed it outside the immediate jurisdiction of the Deputies. Clearly they did not regard the Committee's business as a part of their own proceedings.

[9] The minutes of this 5th of January meeting were reproduced in the *Gentleman's Magazine* (March, 1787), p. 237, with the following list of those elected to the repeal committee: Benjamin Boddington, Thomas Boddington, John Bond, John Bradney, Richard Cooke, John Dowson, James Bogle French, William Fuller, Edward Grubb, Benjamin Bond Hopkins, M.P., Edward Jeffries, Chairman, James Johnson, Stephen

Edward Jeffries, who was also chairman of the Dissenting Deputies, the repeal committee set to work at once and within a week's time had printed a succinct list of grievances for distribution to both Houses of Parliament. It gave the following reasons for quick legislative action :

I—Every man hath an inalienable right . . . to judge for himself in matters of religion; and, as the Dissenters have always proved themselves well affected to the present government and have been ever ready to take the oaths required by law, it is unjust and oppressive to deprive them of civil rights on account of their scruples to receive the Sacrament. . . .

II—The Sacrament of the Lord's Supper having been solemnly appointed by our Blessed Saviour only for remembrance of his death ought not to be applied to Civil purposes.

III—The receiving of the Lord's Supper occasionally according to the usage of the Church of England is no proof of our approbation of the whole institution and frame of that church, since many Christians conform in this particular who do not approve of other parts of the establishment, and other Christians, as well as unbelievers, may copy for interested or ambitious purposes. . . .

IV—The repeal of the laws by which the Sacramental test is imposed would not injure the established church. That church was established long before the imposition of this test and would continue to be established though it should be removed. . . .

V—In no other country is the Sacramental test required as a qualification for civil employment; and it must be particularly marked that episcopalians in North Britain who are dissenters from the church established there are not

---

Lowdell, Joseph Paice, John Raymond, Thomas Rogers, James Smith, John Towers, Matthew Towgood, William Wilson, John Yerbury.

liable to any incapacities in consequence of not qualifying themselves by receiving the Sacrament according to the usage of that church . . . yet in England the natives of Scotland . . . cannot be members of the privy council or hold any commission in the army or navy of Great Britain, to the support of which they contribute their proportion, without receiving the Sacrament according to the rites of a church to which they do not belong. . . .

VI—In the year 1779 an act was passed in Ireland for the relief of his Majesty's faithful subjects, the Protestant Dissenters of that kingdom (by which all civil and military offices should lie open to "all and every person and persons being Protestant"). This measure was designed to give additional security to the Church of Ireland by conciliating the Protestant Dissenters of that country, and it is apprehended that it had the desired effect. The Protestant Dissenters in England, therefore, cannot but consider it as ungenerous and unjust to treat them as enemies to the establishment here when the friendship of their brethren has been acknowledged and their assistance courted by the establishment in the sister kingdom.

VII—The absurdity of the test laws as they now stand is most glaring; for, though a Dissenter may be a Legislator in either house of Parliament without taking the sacrament according to the rites of the Church of England, yet he cannot legally without it have any share in the direction of the Bank of England, the East India, Russia, or South Sea Companies, etc. . . .

VIII—The large and indefinite terms in which the act is expressed may give occasion to the grossest abuses and render it an instrument of the most grievous persecution and oppression. If the act should be rigorously enforced, many Protestant Dissenters might be compelled to violate their consciences or to abandon even the ordinary occupations by which they now support themselves and their families . . . The act extends not only to persons who bear offices civil and military, but to those who have command or place of trust under his Majesty *or by authority derived from him* . . . Indeed, "so low have these holy things been prostituted" that, Mr. Locke tells us, "men have been driven to take the sacrament *to obtain licences to sell ale.*"

IX—It is manifestly unjust that the rights of innocent persons should be destroyed or affected by the criminal conduct or neglect of others; yet no man can recover a debt in an inferior court over which an unqualified corporator presides; nor can the election of a corporate officer, before magistrates who have neglected to qualify be supported. It is unjust that punishment should be inflicted for crimes which the offender could not possibly know he is in a capacity to commit. . . .

X—The penalty inflicted by the Test Act is enormous and humanity cannot contemplate it without horror. The party is not only deprived of office, but he is incapacitated to sue in any court of law or equity, to be guardian of any child . . . to take any legacy or deed of gift, etc. . . .

XI—The situation of foreign countries with regard to Britain offers strong arguments for repeal of these oppressive laws . . . The United States of America . . . make no distinctions as to religious sects in relation to public offices . . . Moreover, in France, Germany, Prussia, Russia, Holland, Poland, and other countries, many persons dissenting from their respective establishments have been employed in the highest offices, who by the most signal services have manifested this important truth : THAT A DISSENTER FROM THE ESTABLISHED RELIGION OF A COUNTRY MAY BE A TRUE FRIEND TO ITS GENERAL INTERESTS AND PROSPERITY.[10]

---

[10] *The Case of the Protestant Dissenters* (London, 1787), single sheet.

Before the month was over this list had been so well received by at least a dozen M.P.'s that Jeffries conceived the idea of making his committee a genuinely non-partisan body by adding to it other Dissenters not immediately connected with the Deputies and even liberal members of the Establishment who sympathized with the cause. After some discussion, his colleagues agreed, and "additional gentlemen" were invited to join "an aggregate committee formed of the Deputies, of delegates from the country, and of distinguished individuals . . . dropping the partial style of 'The Three Denominations'. . . . "[11] Certainly, argued Jeffries, the ruinous charges of non-representation levelled against the anti-subscriptionist committee of 1772 and 1773 could never be voiced against his group. Of his twenty-seven "additional gentlemen," eleven were M.P.'s, nearly all of them recognizable as sympathizers rather than adherents.[12]

The *ad hoc* minutes which one assumes were kept by this enlarged committee appear to have been lost, but there is substantial evidence that they were not idle. If frequent meetings of the whole group were not held during the first three weeks in March, at least some of the forty-eight members were feverishly active in feeding the press with their propaganda.

---

[11] *Vide The Monthly Repository of Theology and General Literature,* New Series, I (January to December 1827), 133, which reviews the attempts at repeal from 1787 to 1790, "after a sleep of nearly fifty years."

[12] I can recognize only Sir Henry Houghton and William Smith as Dissenting M.P.'s among the following twenty-seven names added to Jeffries' original committee: James Adair, Nathaniel Barnardiston, Henry Beaufoy, M.P., Edmund Calamy, Michael Dodson, Sir James Esdaile, Aldermen, Samuel Heywood, Sir Henry Houghton, Bart., M.P., Timothy Hollis, Thomas Brand Hollis, John Lee, M.P., John Maitland, James Martin, M.P., William Mount, Thomas Rickards, Sir John Sinclair, Bart., M.P., Samuel Shore, jun., Samuel Smith, William Smith, M.P., Samuel Thornton, M.P., Robert Thornton, M.P., Henry Thornton, M.P., Benjamin Vaughan, James Watson, James West, Thomas Whitmore, M.P. *Vide Gentleman's Magazine* (March, 1787), p. 237.

Within two weeks of the new committee's formation there appeared, under its imprimatur, *An Appeal to the Candour, Magnanimity, and Justice of those in Power to Relieve from Severe . . . Penalties a Great Number of their Fellow Subjects, who will give . . . a security . . . of their Fidelity . . . to the Present Establishment which does not oblige them to Violate the Rights of Conscience.*[13] Beginning with a formidable "outline of penalties which may be inflicted on those who refuse to qualify," the authors offered as proof that Parliament considered such laws as "basically too hard and cruel to be put into execution" the fact that "an annual indemnifying act passes generally, though not always, at the end of every session."[14] It was well known, however, that these acts had "occasionally been suspended for two years," and although they were said to be intended to relieve the Dissenters, how could this be true? Surely no Dissenter as such could really be relieved by giving him a longer time to do that which his conscience told him was an unlawful "profanation of a religious rite."

A more practical question which the British Government must answer was this: Did the civil incapacities and penalties affecting the Protestant Dissenter as a man, a father, a relative, and a member of a community bear any proportion to the actual danger which he posed to society as a nonconformist in matters of religion? Test legislation was enacted in days when "the horrors of popery prevailed," but certainly there was no need for it now. "All the enlightened sentiments of refined

---

[13] *Vide* John Disney, *An Arranged Catalogue of the Several Publications which have Appeared Relating to the Enlargement of the Toleration of Protestant Dissenting Ministers and the Repeal of the Corporation and Test Acts* (London, 1790), p. 10.

[14] *An Appeal to Candour, Magnanimity, and Justice* . . . (London, 1787), p. 5.

liberality" were at last prevailing in France, where Protestants were being "restored to equal privileges and opportunities with their fellow citizens." The Emperor Joseph II was also reforming abuses in religious matters. With knowledge and truth spreading throughout the world in such a fashion as this, "if the English remain in their ancient errors and prejudice" much longer, they would surely "lose the claim of being the freest and most liberal of nations."[15] It was wholly contrary to the principles of an "intelligent, free government" that "a respectable body of men, bearing equally with their fellow citizens all the taxes and burdens of the state, and being equally good members of the community by a willingness to take all oaths of fidelity to the established government," should be excluded from all offices in the state, "and the benefit of their services be lost to their country."[16] It was even more unjust that they should be under "reproach and contempt and be liable to the severest penalties for mere matters of opinion in religious affairs which no one has a right to control, as it concerns only God and themselves." Every consideration of "humanity, justice, and policy" united to plead for the repeal of such obnoxious legislation.

Within two weeks after the appearance of this *Appeal* the committee issued its most ambitious literary attempt, a 228 page essay containing "an historical review of the situation of Protestant Dissenters under the laws imposing the Sacramental Test on persons admitted to offices, showing the imposition of that Test to be unjust with respect to the Protestant Dissenters of England, and the Natives of North Britain, as well as inexpedient, with an answer to the Objection urged from the Act of Union with Scotland and proofs that the present is the proper

---

[15] *Ibid.*, p. 8.
[16] *Ibid.*, p. 9.

time for applying to Parliament for the necessary redress."[17] The "Advertisement" to this bulky pamphlet, written in the name of the Jeffries Committee, apologized for the hasty manner in which it was compiled but stressed the necessity of getting an "impartial account" before the public in advance of the "imminent action" in Parliament. "The compilers of these sheets" then went on to point out that they were "not intending to express any opinion respecting Papists at present;" they were pleading for Protestant Dissenters only. But with supreme goodwill the editors emphasized that they "could not suppress their wish to see a more generous spread of prudent civil toleration; for though the *object* of toleration be religion, yet the *rule* by which toleration is to be fixed should be civil; and civil men, whether we judge from theory or experience, seem the only men proper to apply the rule."[18]

Furthermore, in the name of the Jeffries Committee, they insisted that the present condition of public affairs should inspire Dissenters with the most sanguine hopes of success. The Church was in no danger from Papists or sectaries of any kind; there was no longer a formidable pretender to the crown; and the nation was in profound tranquility both at home and abroad. The king had "with unexampled liberality" granted the inhabitants of Quebec an establishment of their religion and restored to the Protestant Dissenters of Ireland their rights as full citizens: "Could it be conceived that a prince who has graciously lent an ear to the complaints of catholic subjects on the other side of the Atlantic would be deaf to those of the Protestant Dissenters of England, or would withhold from them those rights which their brethren in Ireland are permitted to enjoy?"[19] This appeared most unlikely; but, even if through

---
[17] *The Right of Protestant Dissenters to a Compleat Toleration Asserted* (London, 1787), title page.
[18] *Ibid.*, p. iii.

some unforeseen twist of circumstance the king and his ministers should show themselves in opposition and succeed in defeating the Dissenters' first attempt to obtain a restoration of these rights, Edward Jeffries reasoned that "after a full and fair discussion of the question," public opinion in that "enlightened and liberal age" would soon carry them through to success, for "magna est veritas et *prevalebit*"[20]; and the committee agreed that "by perseverance they must be victorious":

> Should king, minister, and prelates be arrayed against them, let them not shrink from the contest; their claims fear not discussion; and they may cheerfully appeal to the impartial decision of public opinion which . . . is paramount to princes and potentates, and to which kings, ministers, and prelates must ultimately bow . . . Dissenters ought never to abandon their object, but repeat their application until the voice of reason can be heard.[21]

When, as a proper response to this increasing volume of Dissenting propaganda, the Established Church republished Bishop Sherlock's arguments against repeal of the Test in mid-March of 1787, the Jeffries Committee immediately printed a *Postscript* to *The Right of the Protestant Dissenters* in which they asserted their defiance of arguments "more than a generation old." Could the Establishment offer nothing better than the moth-eaten, legalistic platitudes of 1732? Dissenters would certainly have no trouble in producing something more in keeping with the times.

At last the great day dawned. It had been decided that the attempt to secure repeal should be by motion rather than by

---

[19] *Ibid.*, p. 202.
[20] Edward Jeffries MS 94. H.4a, Dr. Williams's Library. The italics are Jeffries' own.
[21] *The Right of Protestant Dissenters* . . . , pp. 207–208.

petition, and Henry Beaufoy, a liberal member of the Established Church and one of the new recruits to Jeffries' "aggregate committee," brought in the bill on March 28 with a speech in which at the outset he assured his listeners that there was no division among Dissenters in their desire for repeal. To prove this he quoted directly from minutes of "the Assembly of Delegates meeting at the King's Head Tavern in the Poultry on February 2, 1787, under the chairmanship of Mr. Jeffries" which had "unanimously resolved that the mode of proceeding in the House of Commons for repeal of the Corporation and Test Acts be by motion, and that Mr. Beaufoy be desired to make the motion for that purpose."[22]

Thus authorized, Beaufoy declared that the grievances of which Dissenters complained were of a civil and not of an ecclesiastical nature. Consequently they posed no threat to the Church of England. True, the establishment of a church required a legal provision for its ministers, but it did not require for its laity an exclusive right to civil and military trusts. Its financial security rested in its tithes, prebends, canonries, archdeaconries, deaneries, and bishoprics. They constituted its establishment before the Corporation and Test Acts existed and would equally guarantee it should these acts be repealed. The Church had a right to its establishment and the Dissenters had a right to complete toleration, a right which it was impossible to assert they enjoyed so long as they were subjected to civil incapacities on account of religious opinions.

"Every man," insisted Beaufoy, "has a right to the common privileges of the society in which he lives; and among those common privileges a *capacity in law* of serving his sovereign is undoubtedly one of the most valuable." No man, certainly,

---

[22] *The Substance of the Speech delivered by Henry Beaufoy, Esq., in the House of Commons upon the 28th of March, 1787* (London, 1787), p. 5.

had a natural right of appointment to state offices, but that was hardly what Dissenters claimed. They asked not for the right to be chosen but only for the right to be eligible. Since, then, "Dissenters have a right as *men* to think for themselves in matters of religion, and since they have a right as *citizens* to a common chance with their fellow subjects for offices of civil and military trust, if their sovereign should deem them worthy of his confidence,"[23] Beaufoy moved that the Commons should go into committee on the bill; and Sir Henry Houghton gave the motion a vigorous second, contending that "if the present age" were really "most eminently enlightened," as everyone was claiming, "it seems indispensably requisite to wipe away these anomalies for ever."[24]

Lord North then rose to express opposition to the measure, adopting the familiar rôle of guardian of the status quo in which he had been so markedly cast during the anti-subscription debates of 1772 and 1773. If the present motion went no farther than the free exercise of the rights of conscience, North professed himself the last man on earth to oppose it; indeed, his motive for rising was simply "to play the part of a good citizen," rather than to lay heavy hands on the consciences of any individual whatsoever. But this motion prayed for repeal of an act which was the great bulwark of the constitution and to which all Englishmen owed "those inestimable blessings of freedom which we now enjoy"; it recommended procedures "contrary to the happy experience of a century."

And what was the Dissenters' grievance? A "general toleration" had been granted them eight years ago in the Act of 1779:

[23] *Ibid.,* pp. 46–47.
[24] *Debate on the Repeal of the Test and Corporation Act in the House of Commons, March 28th, 1787* (London, 1787), p. 44.

If there remains any thing which can operate as a burden on any man's conscience, in the name of Heaven let it be done away; but let not the admitting of persons of particular persuasions into the offices of the State be confounded with the restriction of conscience. If this Government finds it prudent and necessary to confine the admission to public offices to men of particular principles, it has a right to adhere to such a restriction; it is a privilege belonging to all states. . . . If dissenters claim it as their undoubted, their natural right to be rendered capable of enjoying offices, and that plea be admitted, the argument may run to all men. The vote of a freeholder for a representative to Parliament is confined to those who possess a freehold of 40s or upwards; and those not possessing that qualification may call it an usurpation of their right by preventing them from voting also. . . .[25]

The Commons were called upon by Mr. Beaufoy to proceed as France had done, but he would rather proceed according to the experience of England which had enjoyed peace and harmony in the Church by these acts. The Dissenters had no complaint of ecclesiastical tyranny; they "could offer no instance of church persecution."[26] Let them not confound toleration of religious principles with civil and military appointments. North concluded with his usual note of

---

[25] *Ibid.*, pp. 45–46.

[26] In direct contradiction to North's assertion *vide* Henry Peckwell's *Account of an Appeal from a Summary Conviction on the Statute 22 Car. II. c. to the Honourable Court of Kings Bench* (London, 1787), pp. 12–69 and Durnford and East, *Reports,* I, 320–322 for a treatment of the same case: the *King* v. *Samuel Hall,* in which the defendant was successfully prosecuted by the Reverend Robert Benson, Vicar of Hockington in Lincolnshire, for holding a prayer meeting in violation of the Conventicle Act. Hall was heavily fined by Quarter Sessions, and when his case was appealed to King's Bench, in the Easter Term of 1787, Lord Mansfield saw no alternative but to uphold the original sentence, since Hall had confessed to violating the law.

warning: "Let us be upon our guard against any innovation in the church. The constitution is always in danger when the church is deprived of her rights!"[27]

Brief arguments by Lord Beauchamp, Mr. Smith of Clapham, and Sir James Johnstone followed in favor of repeal. Then all eyes focused upon the Prime Minister. This was not an application to relieve a class of men "from any reproach or distinguished odium," observed Pitt, nor to relieve them from penalties. The Dissenters were at present in possession of all indulgences; they had nothing to fear either from the spirit of religion which members of the state church professed or from the constitution, and the question now to be considered was very different. It was simply this: whether it was "expedient to deprive the Legislature of the exercise of a discretionary power now vested in them." This had to be considered as a political power, not the right of the individual, and "a distinction must be drawn between political and civil liberty." From a consideration of these two types of liberty Pitt then concluded that it was impossible "to separate the ecclesiastical and political liberties of this country." He observed that there had to be restriction of rights in all societies and that all modes of representation must include or render necessary some mode of qualification, but:

Is a man to be considered as marked with infamy because he does not vote for a city, a county, or a borough? The true question now to be considered is, is there any substantial interest that makes it necessary for one part of the community to be deprived of participation? Certainly this deprivation should not take place unless there is reason to see substantial inconvenience in the participation. . . .[28]

Lord Beauchamp had asserted that he never knew as large

---
[27] *Debate on the Repeal of the Test and Corporation Act* . . . , p. 50.
[28] *Ibid.*, p. 53.

a body of men so easily gratified as those who now applied; but, said Pitt:

> There is another class, equally respectable and numerous, whose fears upon this occasion will be alarmed. The members of the Church of England, a part of our constitution, will be seriously alarmed and injured; and their apprehensions are not to be treated lightly. If I were arguing upon principles of *right*, I should not talk of alarm; but I am acting upon principles of *expediency*. The Church and State are united upon principles of expediency, and it concerns those to whom the well-being of the State is intrusted to take care that the Church should not be rashly demolished. There is a natural desire in sectaries to extend their religion. The dissenters have never been backward in this, and it is necessary for the establishment to have an eye to them. It must be conceded that an established church is necessary; that provision for the ministers is of the essence of church government. To exclude the violent, the bulwark must be kept up against all; and I am endeavouring to take every prudent and proper precaution.[29]

It was the right of every legislature and every state to make those tests which they thought most conducive to the public good, and Pitt professed himself unable to vote for repeal without "alarming a great body of the legislature." He concluded by saying:

> I must also enter my objection to those arguments which state that a seclusion from office unless certain restrictions founded on the policy of State are compiled with is a punishment in itself. It has been deemed a necessary and proper measure by those who have held and those who now hold a great stake in this country; and I do not see any reason to consider the seclusion of the dissenters more

---

[29] *Ibid.*, pp. 53–54.

as a mark of infamy than any other distinction that upholds political government.[30]

Fox then rose in support of Beaufoy's motion. He agreed with the Prime Minister that "it was right to oppose the repeal of a Test which shut out Dissenters who would not allow that any establishment was necessary," but Pitt had gone on to employ his arguments indiscriminately against all those who had applied. Fox, however, cited history to prove that "they had been actuated by principles of liberty not inconsistent with the well-being of the State."[31] He used "the authority of that great writer Mr. Locke" to show that the mischiefs in Charles II's reign arose not from Dissenters but from "the governing part of the Church of England." Fox closed by speaking in very high terms of the principles which governed the conduct of Dissenters. They had been persevering and active in their application for redress of injuries in former times; "if they use the same perseverance now, they cannot fail of success. I shall advise them to repeat their applications till the legislature gives them the success they deserve."[32]

Sir William Dolben next asked permission to deny the spirit of moderation which had been attributed to contemporary Dissenters. Beaufoy had disclaimed for them either "levelling principles" or "republican attachments" and denied also any design against the Church of England's endowments which he asserted would be safer once the Dissenters' claims had been met. "Nonsense!" shouted Dolben, and went on to quote passages from Dr. Joseph Priestley to prove how subversive the aims of Dissenters really were.[33] Beaufoy rose to reassert the

---

[30] *Ibid.*, p. 55.
[31] *Ibid.*, p. 56.
[32] *Ibid.*, p. 57.
[33] *Ibid.*, p. 59. Dolben dwelt particularly upon a statement from Priestley's pamphlet on the *Importance of Free Inquiry in Matters of Religion* (London, 1785), in which the radical Dissenter spoke of the activity of

contrary, but his entreaties were to no avail. The motion was lost by 178 votes to 100.

It was obvious from this debate that a substantial majority of the Commons distrusted many of the conclusions that had been drawn from the alleged moderate and antisubversive qualities of contemporary Dissent. The writings of Priestley had been quoted to prove the contrary, and it was certainly most impolitic for that notorious "rational Dissenter" to burst forth into print with a spirited attack upon Pitt, thus confirming all the conservative majority's worst suspicions. Nevertheless, only three days after the debate, in a fifty-two page open letter to the Prime Minister, Priestley expressed his profound disgust at the conduct of one who "had led us to expect a reform in the state of representation in this country and other measures of public utility."[34] He ridiculed Pitt for "employing arguments a century old" which placed expediency above basic human rights, and insisted that "there can be no danger in any alteration which the people can be brought to approve of." Priestley declared that "any present attempts to infuse into them a dread of innovation" would be exposed like all past projects "to keep the people blind to their future interests for the sake of the present interest of certain individuals."[35]

Pitt had alluded to some Dissenters as of a more dangerous complexion than others in consequence of their being enemies to all ecclesiastical establishments, and Priestley responded:

> I avow myself to be one of this class of dissenters, and I glory in it. I have even no doubt but that, as Christianity

---

his co-religionists as "a silent propagation of the truth that will in the end prove efficacious. They are wisely placing, as it were grain by grain, a train of gunpowder to which the match will one day be laid to blow up the fabric of error . . ."

[34] Joseph Priestley, *A Letter to the Right Honourable William Pitt* (London, 1787), p. 53.
[35] *Ibid.*, pp. 8-9.

was promulgated and prevailed in the world without any aid from civil power, it will, when it shall have recovered its pristine purity and its pristine vigour, entirely disengage itself from such an unnatural alliance as it is at present fettered with.... Let the corruptions of Christianity, such as in this country and on the continent of Europe, pass for it, avail themselves of such aid. The Christianity that I profess does not require, but disdains it. It wants no support that you, Sir, as a statesman, can give it, and it will prevail in spite of any obstruction that you can throw in its way.[36]

But Priestley went on to point out that the sovereign, aided by the advice of his ministers, would hardly choose a man like himself to fill any important executive office in the state. As Beaufoy had asserted, the Dissenters' plea was only for eligibility to serve rather than a right to government posts, and so there was no real danger of subversion here.

It had been said, however, that if the Dissenters gained this point, they would aim at something more, and this he acknowledged:

We should ask many things more, because there are things more that we conceive ourselves to be entitled to, and which it will be no injury but an advantage to our country to give us. We are a part of the community which in return for great merit have received great injuries. Part of them, no doubt, are removed; but it does not follow that the remainder are no burden. We feel them to be so and shall take every fair opportunity of endeavouring to relieve ourselves. Let the bench of bishops be fully apprized of this and take their measures accordingly. We have the frankness and magnanimity of which they are destitute and shall not endeavour to take them by surprise....[37]

In this spirit, Priestley concluded his outspoken pamphlet with

---
[36] *Ibid.*, pp. 16–17.
[37] *Ibid.*, pp. 20–21.

a catalogue of "some things which are certainly wanting to a complete toleration in this country and which do not at all affect the established church" — a program which the *Gentleman's Magazine* declared aimed in fact to purge the Establishment of "all New Testament Christianity" and substitute:

> that of the author of *The History of the Corruptions of Christianity,* by letting Unitarians avow their principles . . . by abolishing subscriptions in the *stagnant pools* called universities, by turning the Bishops out of the House of Lords . . . and by abolishing tythes and leaving the clergy as much at the mercy of their congregations as the dissenting ministry are. . . .[38]

As if to confirm the alarm expressed in this caustic review and to justify the government's resolve in no way to depart from the stand taken by North and Pitt in the debate of '87, the Reverend Joseph Berington, a Roman Catholic pamphleteer, stepped into the controversy. In waging their campaign, the Jeffries Committee had asked repeal for Protestant Dissenters only, although they had expressed in their *Appeal to Candour* the pious hope that something might be done for Roman Catholics in the near future. But Berington now insisted that his co-religionists posed far less of a threat to the constitution than did the majority of nonconformists. Roman Catholics could, then, with much less justice be excluded from political rights, for at least they believed in a Trinitarian theology and in the principle of an established church as the foundation of all ordered society, tenets which he alleged could hardly be attributed to the leaders of contemporary Dissent.[39]

Priestley's *Letter to Pitt* was not the only evidence to sup-

---

[38] *Gentleman's Magazine* (May, 1787), p. 423.
[39] Joseph Berington, *Address to the Protestant Dissenters* (London, 1787), p. 12.

port Berington's charges. On April 25, 1787, Dr. Richard Price also provided an admirable illustration of the utterly subversive nature of Dissenting principles when he preached that: "The human mind must soon be emancipated from the chains of Church authority and Church establishments, for the liberality of the times has already loosened their foundations!"[40] Such language could hardly fail to stiffen the resistance of North, Pitt, Burke, Dolben, and all loyal adherents to "our most excellent constitution in Church and State."

Undismayed by their defeat in '87, and by these undercurrents of opposition which followed it, the Jeffries Committee saw in the year 1788, the centenary of the Glorious Revolution, an excellent opportunity to reassert their claim that the work of "that great hero" William III could be brought to complete fruition only by making full citizens of them. From his pulpit at Mill-Hill Chapel in Leeds, the Reverend William Wood admonished his congregation that the liberties which they then enjoyed were "to be defended on the ground of their reasonableness and not of their antiquity"; for "however it may appear to the plodding slaves of long prevailing forms, precedent is not reason and prescription is no bar to the sacred claims of universal justice." In every case the rights of conscience took precedence over the rights of society to punish individuals for "mere religious beliefs." Were each individual permitted to pursue the decisions of his own conscience and the ruling powers solicitous to prevent men from injuring their fellows by overt acts rather than by beliefs only, Wood insisted that all would feel in a state of security and none would be induced to attempt a change by acts of violence."[41]

---

[40] Richard Price, *Sermon on the Evidence of a Future Period of Improvement in the State of Mankind* (London, 1787), p. 27.
[41] William Wood, *Two Sermons Preached . . . on the Celebration of the Hundredth Anniversary of the Happy Revolution* (Leeds, 1788), p. 16.

These same points were also stressed by Dr. William Enfield, the liberal Congregationalist, but his basic hope for a rapid triumph of "reason and Dissenting principles" came from the fact that "in many countries, Catholic as well as Protestant, laudable efforts have been made to convert the errors or improve the wisdom of antiquity":

> In France, which is at present unquestionably one of the most enlightened nations in the world, attempts are now making towards an entire emancipation from despotism, for the event of which all Europe is waiting with impatient expectation. It is the glory of Great Britain that it has perhaps less to do in the important work of political reformation than any other nation in the world. But this is surely a reason not for remaining inactive, but for going on with an accelerated motion towards perfection. This acceleration is as natural in the moral as in the natural world. If our progress be at present retarded by a timid policy which represents all innovations as dangerous, it may be confidently expected that time and further experience will soon correct this mistake and convince those who are intrusted with the administration of public affairs that they cannot execute their trust more faithfully than by listening to and, upon mature deliberation, adopting plans of improvement. In the natural course of human affairs, which is evidently progressive, it must soon come to pass that enlarged views and a liberal spirit will obliterate the maxims of ignorance and bigotry, and that every institution which is manifestly contrary to sound policy and inconsistent with that share of natural or political liberty to which every member of a free state is entitled, will be abolished. . . .[42]

Penal statutes against heresy still remained in force, but they

---

[42] William Enfield, LL.D., *A Sermon on the Centennial Commemoration of the Revolution* (London, 1788), pp. 11–17.

were suspended by "the wisdom and candour of the times," and, asserted Enfield with supreme optimism, "there can be little doubt that very soon these disgraceful relics of intolerance will be cleared away."[43]

Thoroughly dominated by this enthusiastic spirit, Edward Jeffries issued a call for his "Aggregate Committee" to meet at the King's Head Tavern on December 3, 1788. After some debate about how they should pursue a further attempt at repeal, Henry Beaufoy again agreed to introduce the measure "whenever the Committee should think it most likely to succeed."

In order to show that they meant business, the committee then drafted letters "to the Printers of the *Manchester* and *Liverpool Chronicles*," both oppositionist newspapers with wide county circulations, rephrasing the arguments from the *Case of the Protestant Dissenters,* published in 1787, but adding a list of M.P.'s who had voted for the bill in that year. They also appropriated money for two or three thousand copies of these lists to be printed and distributed; and by way of conclusion resolved that:

> . . . it be recommended to the Protestant Dissenters, in town and country, to show a particular and marked attention to the interest of such candidates as they believe to be well affected to civil and religious liberty; but especially to such as, being now in Parliament, have proved themselves friends to the Rights of Protestant Dissenters.[44]

After three months of lobbying it was decided that Beaufoy should again bring the committee's grievances before the Commons, and he did so on May 8, 1789, in a speech which reiterated the arguments he had employed in March of '87. Sir Henry Houghton again seconded the motion and Lord

---
[43] *Ibid.,* p. 18.
[44] Edward Jeffries MS 94. H. 2. (Dr. Williams's Library).

North once more rose to oppose it. The test laws, he said, were acts of self-defense for the Church and not meant as a punishment to any description of persons whatsoever. So far as the objection to employing a *religious* test for a *civil* purpose was concerned, how did this differ in any degree from the use of oaths which Beaufoy accepted as a religious appeal to the Almighty necessary for promoting "the good order of the State?"[45]

Sir James Johnstone replied by summarizing Lord North's contention that the constitution was responsible for the country's civil and religious liberties and that if these principles on which "the present happy arrangement" were based should be changed, the whole fabric of government would be in peril. "If this is to be admitted as a reason for not repealing the Test Act," declared Sir James, "it will apply universally and operate against the repeal of every statute, however absurd and fit to be expunged from the statute book."[46]

William Smith, member for Sudbury and one of the few Dissenters in the House, immediately took up the argument and accused Lord North of uttering "pompous nothings." The Dissenters held, said Smith, that every citizen of the state willing to give requisite proof of his fidelity to the *civil* constitution and government and unconvicted of any crime was "entitled to the participation of every civil right" among which was "to be reckoned the *capacity* of holding offices, though not the *actual possession* of them." To incapacitate, therefore, a whole body of such subjects was "to inflict on them an injury of which they have every right to complain, and to seek redress as a matter not of *favour* but of *justice*!"[47]

---

[45] *The Debate in the House of Commons . . . on the Eighth of May, 1789* (London, 1789), pp. 37–38.
[46] *Ibid.*, pp. 49–50.
[47] *Ibid.*, p. 53.

Fox rose to express disagreement with Mr. Smith's opinion of Lord North's speech. "Far from its being a series of 'pompous nothings' I think the Noble Lord has spoken ably and for the most part reasoned closely and well in support of a cause which yet when brought to the test of argument, even the Noble Lord's abilities can neither defend nor support."[48] Fox then proceeded to lift the whole argument to a higher philosophical plane by insisting that religion ought always to be distinct from civil government; that it was in no manner connected with civil government other than as it tended to promote morality among the people and by so doing was conducive to good order in the state :

No human government has a right to inquire into men's private opinions, to presume that it knows them, or to act on that presumption. Men are the best judges of the consequences of their own opinions and how far they are likely to influence their actions; and it is most unnatural and tyrannical to say 'because you *think* so, you must *act* so. I will collect the evidence of your future conduct, from what I know to be your opinions'. The very reverse of this is the rule of conduct which should be pursued. Men ought to be judged by their actions and not by their thoughts. The one can be fixed and ascertained, the other can only be a matter of guess and speculation. I am so far of this opinion that if any man publishes his political sentiments and says in writing that he dislikes the constitution of this country, and gives it as his judgment that principles in direct contradiction to the Constitution and Government are the principles that ought to be asserted and maintained, I hold that he should not, on this account be disabled from filling any office, civil or military; but if he carries his detestable opinions into practice, the law will then find a

---

[48] *Ibid.*, p. 69.

remedy and punish him for his conduct, grounded on his opinions, as an example to deter others from acting in the same dangerous and absurd manner.[49]

No proposition, said Fox, could be more consonant to common sense, to reason, and to justice than that men were to be tried by their actions and not by their opinions; their actions ought to be waited for and not guessed at, as the probable consequence of the sentiments they were known to entertain and to profess.

If the reverse of this doctrine is ever adopted as a maxim of government, if the actions of men are to be prejudged from their opinions, it will sow the seeds of jealousy and distrust, it will give scope to private malice, it will sharpen men's minds against one another, incite each man to divine the private opinions of his neighbour, to deduce mischievous consequences from them, and thence to prove that he ought to incur disabilities and be fettered with restrictions.[50]

This principle, if true with respect to political ideas, was more peculiarly valid with regard to religious opinions; and from the mischievous precept he had described had flowed "every species of party zeal, every system of political intolernce, every extravagance of religious hate." Fox's argument that the actions of men and not their opinions were the only proper objects of legislation was supported by history save for "one glaring exception, the Papists." But, even if the Roman Catholics of past times "were Papists in the strictest sense of the word by acknowledging a foreign authority paramount to that of the legislature and a title to the Crown superior to that conferred by the voice of the people, and not the loyal Roman Catholics of the present day," still:

---
[49] *Ibid.*, p. 70.
[50] *Ibid.*, pp. 71–72.

I would say that the Legislature ought not to have acted against them till they put in practice some of the dangerous doctrines which they were thought to entertain. Disability and punishment ought to follow, not to anticipate, offence. Those who attempt to justify disabilities imposed on the Dissenters must contend, if they argue fairly on their own ground, not that their religious opinions are inimical to the Established Church, but that their political opinions are inimical to the Constitution. If they fail to prove this, to deprive the Dissenters of any civil or political advantage is a manifest injustice; for it is not sufficient to say to any set of men: 'we apprehend certain dangers from your opinions, we have wisely provided a remedy against them, and you, who feel yourselves aggrieved, calumniated, and proscribed by this remedy must prove that our apprehensions are ill founded.' The *onus probandi* rests on the other side; for whoever demands that any other person be laid under a restriction, it is incumbent on him first to prove that the restriction is necessary to his safety by some overt act, and that the danger he apprehends is not imaginary, but real. . . ."[51]

The Prime Minister replied that he "perfectly agreed" with Fox in "the broad principle" he had laid down that religious opinions of any set of men were "not to be restrained and limited unless they should be found likely to prove the source of civil inconvenience to the State," nor ought the civil magistrate to interfere with them in any other point of view. Nevertheless:

> There has always been admitted to be this solid distinction, that although there is no natural right to interfere with religious opinions, yet when they are such as may produce a civil inconvenience, the Government has a right to guard

---

[51] *Ibid.*, pp. 73–74.

against the probability of the civil inconvenience being produced; nor ought they to wait till, by being carried into action, the inconvenience has actually arisen. It is, therefore, an overstraining of the principle when the Right Honourable Gentleman declares that in no case is it warrantable for a Legislature to interfere with men's religion. . . .[52]

Pitt declared that he was ready to do justice to the Dissenters of former times as he was to those of the present: "It is not on the ground that they *would* do anything to affect the civil government of the country that they have been excluded from holding civil offices, but that, if they had any additional degree of power in their hands they *might*." It would be admitted by all responsible men that the establishment of a settled form of church and of its ministers was necessary to the civil government of the country. Was it then not proper to prevent the emoluments and offices of the government which set up an established church from being distributed among persons who, however respectable they might be, were unfriendly to it?

He concluded by speaking of the "quiet regularity that obtains at present in relation to religious differences," and insisted that:

> If there is anything that can interrupt the harmony and moderation between sects once contending with great virulence and asperity, it is that of awakening a competition and rekindling sparks of ancient animosity which mutual forbearance had almost extinguished.

For these reasons, then, he must deny his consent to the motion and "contend for the principles" he had stated in the debate of '87. Beaufoy's motion was thus lost by 122 votes to 102, at

---

[52] *Ibid.*, p. 90.

least by a much narrower margin than before.[53]

Rather than show discouragement at this second defeat, most liberal Dissenters saw the tides of progress and enlightenment moving relentlessly in their favor. During the summer and autumn of 1789, Englishmen began to suspect that unusual events were taking place across the Channel, and Dissenters fixed their eyes not on the excesses of the mob, but on the complete emancipation of all religious minorities that the French National Assembly declared a basic part of its policy. Tithes, also, were abolished and on November 2 the Assembly proceeded to nationalize all church property. Under the spell of such events, men like Samuel Catlow and David Bradberry wrote open letters to the Jeffries Committee urging a prompt reapplication to Parliament "in the consciousness that we are not craving a *boon,* but demanding a *right.*"[54] The committee needed no such promptings, however, and it soon became common knowledge that they were methodically preparing for a new application to Parliament in 1790.

Such developments both in France and at home could only aggravate all the High Church fears which had contributed so well toward achieving the defeats of 1787 and 1789. Furthermore, when on November 4, the leading "rational Dissenter" Dr. Richard Price delivered a *Discourse on the Love of our Country* to the London "Society for Commemorating the Revolution in Great Britain," he evoked something of a panic among all staunch supporters of the government.

"Our first concern as lovers of our country," declared Price, "must be to enlighten it":

Why are the nations of the world so patient under despot-

---

[53] *Ibid.,* pp. 90–94.
[54] Samuel Catlow, *Address to the Protestant Dissenters* (London, 1789), pp. 13–14, and David Bradberry, *A Letter to Edward Jeffries ,Esq.* (London, 1789), p. 16.

ism? Why do they crouch to tyrants and submit to be treated as if they were a herd of cattle? Is it not because they are kept in darkness and want of knowledge? Enlighten them and you will elevate them. Shew them they are *men* and they will act like *men*. Give them just ideas of civil government and let them know that it is an expedient for gaining protection against injury and defending their rights and it will be impossible for them to submit to governments which, like most of those now in the world, are usurpations on the rights of men and little better than contrivances for enabling the *few* to oppress the *many*. . . . Ignorance is the parent of bigotry, intolerance, and slavery. Inform and instruct mankind and these evils will be excluded . . . Every degree of illumination which we can communicate must do the greatest good. It helps to prepare the minds of men for the recovery of their rights and hastens the overthrow of priestcraft and tyranny.[55]

He went on to criticize "the servile language" used by the London Dissenting ministers in presenting their "late address of thanksgiving on the King's recovery,"[56] and urged them to consider that:

The potentates of this world are sufficiently apt to consider themselves as possessed of an inherent superiority which gives them a right to govern and makes mankind *their own,* and this situation is almost everywhere fostered in them by the creeping sycophants about them and the language of flattery which they are continually hearing. . . . Civil governors are properly the servants of the public, and the king is no more than the first servant of the public, created

---

[55] Richard Price, *A Discourse on the Love of our Country* (London, 1789), pp. 12–15.

[56] On March 24, 1789, the General Body's "address of Unfeigned Congratulations on Your Majesty's Recovery from your late indisposition" had employed the phrase "most sovereign majesty" at least three different times. *Vide Minutes of the General Body,* II, 295.

by it, maintained by it, and responsible to it: and all the homage paid to him is due to him on no other account than his relation to the public. His sacredness is the sacredness of the community, and the term Majesty which is used to apply to him is by no means *his own* majesty, but the majesty of the people."[57]

Price praised the English Revolution of 1688, but held that its work was never completed since there was still a Test Act to restrain "liberty of conscience" and still a parliamentary system that allowed the nation to be politically misrepresented.[58] Nevertheless, these anomalies would soon be eliminated by the pressure of public opinion:

Be encouraged, then, all ye friends of freedom and writers in its defense! The times are suspicious. Your labours have not been in vain. Behold kingdoms, admonished by you, starting from sleep, breaking their fetters, and claiming justice from their oppressors! Behold the light you have struck out after setting America free, reflected in France and there kindled into a blaze that lays despotism in ashes and warms and illuminates Europe![59]

Price's widely distributed *Discourse* immediately set almost every alarmed lover of "the present most excellent constitution in Church and State" to attacking its author and to admonishing Parliament to reject any new application against the Test which Dissenters might prepare. One anonymous pamphleteer pointed an almost hysterical finger at Price as the man "who would wish to blind the judgments of the common people with the specious indefinite notion of unrestrained liberty and would embroil his dear country, tranquil and flourishing and happy as it is, in those miseries which over-

---

[57] Price, *Discourse*, p. 23.
[58] *Vide ibid.*, pp. 39–43 for Price's vigorous attack upon "the inequality of our representation."
[59] *Ibid.*, p. 50.

whelm a neighbouring kingdom."[60]

Similarly, from his rectory at Bemerton, the Reverend William Coxe in an open letter to Price warned that:

> While many parts of Europe are teeming with revolutions it should seem the business of English wisdom to remain in our island on the vantage-ground of the British Constitution, mark the progress of civil discord and endeavour to prevent the conflagration from reaching ourselves. . . . But in opposition to these sound principles of candour and prudence there is not wanting a spirit to prompt the British nation to adopt foreign and unsettled motives and to quit national and established principles; to relinquish present and certain good for distant and uncertain advantages; to confound speculation with practice and theory with experience; to exaggerate the imperfections of our government; to enforce the necessity of amending, or of overturning our civil and religious establishment, and under the semblance of religion and liberty, exciting the people to discontent and division.[61]

Although Coxe prefessed himself "too great a friend to civil and religious liberty" not to wish for repeal of the Test, "if it might be found compatible with the safety of our civil and ecclesiastical establishment," he felt bound to point out that the Dissenters and the repeal committee were acting not generously but partially:

> They make the general good subservient to their particular interests; they make the love of their country to consist in what you so properly reprobate as 'a blind and narrow principle forming men into combinations and the desire of private interest overcoming the public affections.' . . . For

---

[60] *A Review of the Pamphlet entitled "A Discourse on the Love of our Country"* (London, 1790), p. 6.
[61] William Coxe, *A Letter to the Reverend Richard Price* (London, 1790), p. 3.

what does your Committee intend? To exclude every person from being a member of Parliament who does not exactly agree with them on the necessity of repealing the Test Act. But may not a man be a good member of Parliament without supporting that opinion? . . . You object to all tests, and yet you yourselves are going to impose a test upon all members of Parliament; and you act thus narrowly and partially in a point on which the national salvation ultimately depends, namely, the election of proper representatives to serve in Parliament. . . .[62]

These statements were remarkably calm in comparison to the alarmist cries of other pamphleteers who sensed that a "general and vehement bustle" was occurring among Dissenters throughout the kingdom. Indeed, "delegates are hastening together from the East and West, from the North and South for the purpose of subverting the constitution." Let not "the friends of the Church be deceived by their fair speeches," for the Dissenters' real purpose was "to dismantle our fortifications" and "lay all things open as in France" where justice "allowed only seven minutes to prepare for death before one is hanged up by fish-women at a lamp-iron. . . !"[63]

This "general and vehement bustle" which struck such terror into Anglican breasts had begun in earnest in December of 1789. On the fifteenth of that month forty of the most liberal Dissenters in London gathered at the King's Head Tavern, and "resolved that in the present circumstances this meeting is of the opinion that a public meeting of all the Dissenters in London is desirable to be held prior to the expected meeting of Parliament in order to give efficacy to a new application for repeal. . . ."[64] But they deemed themselves "not competent to

---

[62] *Ibid.*, pp. 22–23.
[63] *Observations on the Case of the Protestant Dissenters* (London, 1790).
[64] *Minutes of the Deputies*, II, 489–490. The members of this meeting

call together a public meeting by advertisement of the Dissenters in London," and requested the Protestant Dissenting Deputies to take such action.

When the Deputies met on December 18 to consider this request, they "resolved that it is our opinion that the zeal and unanimity of the Dissenters in and about London for repeal of the Test and Corporation Acts being universally known and acknowledged, a further declaration thereof in a public meeting to be assembled by advertisement is unnecessary."[65] After all, the Jeffries Committee had matters well in hand, and it seemed highly inadvisable, in view of all the ill will that Price's *Discourse* was inspiring, particularly to identify their cause with the most radical dissenting fringe as represented by William Sharp, the freethinker, who had presided over the December 15 meeting.

The General Body of Dissenting Ministers in London reflected this same view in their "extraordinary meeting" at Dr. Williams' Library on December 22, "summoned to consider the measures proper to be adopted to express our concurrence with our brethren in the country" in their determination to reapply for repeal of the Test. After a vote of confidence in the Jeffries Committee, they passed a series of resolutions which left no doubt on what side they, the more conservative of the two Dissenting bodies in London, stood:

---

are listed as follows: Dr. Kippis, Dr. Towers, Mr. Morgan, Mr. Humphries, Mr. Fell, Mr. Hamilton, Mr. R. Heron, Mr. Lee, Mr. H. Smithers, Mr. C. Harris, Mr. B. Stanley, Mr. I. Catham, Mr. I. Cooper, Mr. William Sharp, Chairman, Mr. Richard Sharp, Mr. Saml. Favell, Mr. E. Cowper, Mr. W. Morgan, Mr. I. Weston, Mr. A. Weston, Mr. Vowler, Mr. Warsley, Mr. Davis, Mr. I. Gumoy, Mr. Hawkes, Mr. Wesley, Mr. Waindright, Capel Lofft, Esq., Mr. I. H. Stone, Mr. F. Kemble, Mr. E. Grubb, Jun., Mr. E. Johnston, Mr. B. Tomkins, Mr. A. Rees, Jun., Mr. R. Hills, Mr. Yathard, Mr. Amory, Mr. I. Lepard, Mr. Pearson, Mr. B. Cooper.

[65] *Ibid.*, p. 490.

Resolved : I—*Nem. con,* that the Protestant Dissenters are entitled, equally with their fellow subjects to the complete possession of civil and religious liberty. II—*Nem. con.,* that they have been uniformly distinguished by a zealous attachment to the principles of our Happy Constitution as defined at the Revolution and by a steady and unshaken loyalty to the House of Brunswick at the most dangerous and critical period. III—*Nem. con.,* that the exclusion of them by the Corporation and Test Acts from offices of trust and honour in which they might prove of benefit to the State or enjoy the immunities of faithful citizens is disgraceful to the justice of the nation, the generosity of Britons, and the liberal spirit of the times. IV—*Nem. con.,* that these Acts are not only injurious and oppressive in their civil tendency; but, by enforcing the prostitution of a solemn religious ordinance expose our Christian Faith to the derision of the profligate and the objections of unbelievers. V—*Nem. con.,* that we, therefore, view with pleasure the temperate and manly efforts of our Brethren in different parts of the Kingdom to obtain repeal of these dishonourable and pernicious statutes, and are ready vigorously to concur with them in every wise and practicable measure for bringing about so desirable an end. VI—*With one dissident vote,* that we cannot but add that we hope the time is near at hand when all penal laws for the restriction of men's civil rights and the direction of men's consciences in the business of religion shall be repealed."[66] VII—*Nem. con.,* that these Resolutions . . . be sent for insertion in two of the daily and two of the evening papers."[67]

---

[66] The "one dissident vote" was that of the Reverend John Martin who strenuously objected "to confounding subjects so distinct as civil rights and matters of religion." "We should be content," said Martin, "with the repeal of those statutes which affect the consciences of mankind and not be busy-bodies in other men's affairs, laying ourselves open to charges of avarice for public offices." But Martin was unable to lead an insurgent

With expressions of confidence behind him from both the Lay Deputies and the General Body of Ministers, Jeffries called a meeting of his "Aggregate Committee" for January 13, 1790, at the King's Head Tavern. A resolution was passed to proceed at once to an investigation of "the most effective means to secure repeal." In order to put systematic pressure on all M.P.'s, the committee then drafted a "circular letter to provincial committees," which not only expressed gratification at "having received from all quarters the most unequivocal and unreserved testimonies of approbation and promise of support," but gave some concrete practical advice:

> We take the liberty of suggesting to your committee the necessity of making application to every member of Parliament within your district to give his attendance and support when the motion shall be made in the House of Commons. . . . The zeal in the cause of religious liberty which has so eminently displayed itself in different parts of the Kingdom must now be called into action. . . . We request that a report of the Members of Parliament who have been petitioned be returned to the central committee in London. By this means it will be seen when *every* member has been regularly applied to, and we may be enabled to judge with some degree of precision our prospects of success and regulate our proceedings accordingly . . . Should it be thought by your committee an admirable measure to send delegates from your district to become a part of and cooperate with this Committee, we shall be happy to have

---

movement within the General Body as Henry Mayo had done in 1772. His only vigorous supporter seems to have been the Reverend Henry Peckwell of Heckington in Lincolnshire. *Vide* John Martin, *A Speech on the Repeal of Such Parts of the Test and Corporation Acts as Affect Conscientious Dissenters, intended to have been delivered before the General Body of Dissenting Ministers at the Library in Red Cross Street,* December 22, 1789 (London, 1790), pp. 4–9, 19–20.

[67] *Minutes of the General Body,* II, 300–301.

their assistance and influence, particularly at the moment of our parliamentary application.[68]

The circular letter ended on a triumphant note:

With heartfelt satisfaction we contemplate the union now for the first time effected of the Dissenters of all denominations throughout the Kingdom and see them forming, notwithstanding their difference of opinion upon many points, one great and powerful phalanx for rescuing the right of private judgement from violation. From this new circumstance, assisted as we are by the friends of religious liberty in general and by the increasing influence of liberal principles, we look forward to the event with pleasure. The cause is glorious, the crisis is important, and we have no doubt that the spirit which now pervades the Kingdom must, if properly directed, have its full energy and ultimately be crowned with success.[69]

As Dissenting pressure began to make itself felt in the constituencies, the vast majority of clergy and churchmen rose up in arms. During the months of January and February, in various parts of the kingdom, there were at least two dozen meetings which passed and published strong resolutions against a repeal. At Barnstaple in Devon, "the Mayor, Recorder, Aldermen, Burgesses, and many others at a numerous and respectable meeting of members of the Establishment held at the Guildhall within this town on Wednesday, the 10th day of January, 1790," resolved:

That we are led to suspect from the experience of their past conduct that the motives on which the Dissenters now act are those of private interest and not those of that zeal for the cause of religious liberty of which they boast so much and on which they ground their pretensions, because

---

[68] Edward Jeffries MS 94. H. 4a. (Dr. Williams's Library).
[69] *Ibid.* Attached to the circular letter were lists of those M.P.'s who had supported the Dissenters in 1787 and 1789.

those Acts are not a religious but a political Test; and by their abrogation, the blessings of a full toleration in religious matters (which blessings we conceive that the Protestant Dissenters in this kingdom cannot say that they do not enjoy) would not be enlarged; and a door only would be opened for them to enter into the most powerful and lucrative offices in the state, which might eventually be inconsistent with our own security. . . .[70]

At Southampton on January 11, 1790, another "numerous and respectable meeting" of churchmen resolved that:

The civil power has an undoubted right, from common principles of self-preservation, to commit places of trust and power to such as unite in their attachment to its constitution and are well affected to its ecclesiastical establishment.[71]

The Clergy of the Parish of Leeds, meeting on January 15, professed themselves:

. . . unable but to observe with much concern the apparent eagerness of the whole body of Dissenters to bring this matter again under discussion at the eve of a general election before a parliament which hath already twice, after the fullest hearing, solemnly decided against it.[72]

On February 2, "a Meeting of the Noblemen, Gentlemen and Clergy in the County of Warwick" asserted:

That the Church of England, as by law established, is an essential part of the British Constitution . . . [and] that the right to share the public employments and emoluments of

---

[70] *A Collection of the Resolutions Passed at the Meeting of the Clergy of the Church of England, and of the Counties, Corporations, Cities, and Towns* . . . (London, 1790), p. 24. The concluding item of business was "that these Resolutions be printed in the *General Evening Post,* the *Sherborne Mercury,* and the Exeter papers.

[71] *Ibid.,* p. 26. This meeting provided for the publication of its resolutions in the *General Evening Post,* the *St. James Chronicle,* the *Oracle,* and the Salisbury and Hampshire papers.

[72] *Ibid.,* p. 2.

a state is, like all other rights in a state of society, subject to the control of a supreme power, that is, the Legislature. . . ."[73]

A meeting of "the Clergy of the City of London in a General Court" at Sion College on February 13 resolved:

> That the repeated attempts of the Protestant Dissenters to obtain a Repeal of the Corporation and Test Acts, are a just cause of alarm to every friend of the Established Church and of the Civil Constitution.—That these Acts were professedly made for the preservation of the public peace in Church and State, and the experience of more than a century has shown that they are admirably well calculated for that purpose.—That every Civil Society has a perfect right, inherent in itself, to prescribe the terms on which its members shall be admitted to places of trust and power, and consequently that no individual can have a right inconsistent with that public right. . . ."[74]

Two days later, the Clergy of the Archdeaconry of York, meeting at Wakefield, resolved that:

> Whatever was the behaviour of the Dissenters 'for the space of a whole century,' and particularly in the two critical periods when they affirm that there was not 'a single Protestant Dissenter who joined the hostile banners of a Pretender to the throne or was suspected of an attachment to his cause,' we cannot forget that in the compass of the last century they had nearly effected the ruin of our church and monarchy. . . ."[75]

At Chester, the clergy of that archdeaconry passed similar resolutions on February 15, again asserting the old familiar Warburtonian argument that:

---

[73] *Ibid.*, p. 15. It was resolved that the meeting's minutes should "be published in the London, Birmingham, and other country papers."
[74] *Ibid.*, pp. 3–4.
[75] *Ibid.*, pp. 6–7,

> Every state hath an inherent right to require evidence of the opinions of those whom it shall employ in its offices of trust and power, whether they are friendly or hostile to the constitution which it hath established; and that this right arises not merely from laws which may have been enacted by that state, but from the principle of self-preservation which belongs to communities as well as to individuals, and which is antecedent and superior to all law.[76]

On February 25, a Suffolk County meeting produced the very same resolution "signed by upwards of 1200 Gentlemen, Clergy, and Freeholders."[77]

With monotonous regularity, then, the Establishment upheld the right of the state to select its own instruments in accordance with the dictates of self-preservation. The Dissenters' opponents both in and out of Parliament had based their reasoning on "a supposed alliance between Church and State and the necessity of each to the preservation of the other," but, declared the Dissenting apologist William Parry:

> If the Church of England be an essential part and necessary to the existence of our civil constitution, it is a singular paradox that this civil constitution should have had an origin and continued many centuries before the Church of England had a being, and that during the greater part of her existence she should have been adverse to the true and proper constitution of England.[78]

Moreover, as George Walker pointed out, Parliament did not represent members of the Church of England only, "but all the free sons of Britain."[79] It was instituted not to render justice to Churchmen alone but to all citizens of the kingdom.

---

[76] *Ibid.*, p. 10.
[77] *Ibid.*, p. 23.
[78] William Parry, *Remarks on the Resolutions Passed at a Meeting of the Noblemen, Gentlemen, and Clergy of the County of Warwick on February 2, 1780* (Birmingham, 1790), p. 7.

Away, then, with this reign of privilege in civil matters! Dissenters, contended Walker, were perfectly willing — indeed they desired — that the present friendly relationship between Church and State should continue. Most of them in fact believed in the necessity of some established church or churches in all nations to guarantee the public teaching of Christianity: "It is perfectly natural and desirable for the legislature of a country to prefer one sect of Christianity to another and connect certain ecclesiastical emoluments and honours with the profession of a religious creed," wrote the Reverend Joseph Smith of Liverpool:

> But till the forms of that establishment which exists in this kingdom and the theological tenets it proposes as a test to its members are proved essential to the existence of our civil constitution, we must assert that any test which is only expressive of a religious profession, when applied as a qualification for civil and military offices is not only inconsistent with the principles of freedom, but with the obvious dictates of common sense. . . . A peaceful and respectful behaviour is indeed all that the magnanimity of the Church ought to expect from Dissenters and she ought to have that good opinion of herself as to be above the fear of them.[80]

As an individual man in exercising the freedom of choosing his own religion was not released from the obligation of justice to all his fellow men, so, asserted George Walker, neither was the state when she adopted a state religion at liberty to narrow the debt of equal justice to all her citizens of every description who could answer to the test of civil allegiance.[81] "How," asked

---

[79] George Walker, *The Dissenters' Plea* (Birmingham, 1790), p. 3.

[80] Joseph Smith, *Some Remarks on the Resolutions Passed at a Meeting of the Archdeaconry of Chester on Monday, the 15th of February, 1790* (Liverpool, 1790), p. 9.

[81] George Walker, *op. cit.*, pp. 19–20. He went on to insist that "the extending of this justice is not a favour, but a duty of the governor and

William Parry, "can the good of the whole be promoted by confining all public employments to a part of the community?" Could it ever be expedient for the general good that none should fill offices or trust, or even be eligible for them but members of the Establishment, unless it could be proved that "talents and abilities, honesty and fidelity," were confined to them?[82] Should men, who have "added to their country's strength by their discoveries, and to her 'moral improvement' by their writings and their lives be deprived on account of their religion of any of the usual rights and civil privileges of British subjects?"[83] If it were admitted that peaceful and orderly citizens might be subjected to incapacities and disqualifications merely because their faith did not come up to the public standard or their worship answer the established forms, was it not admitted that men might be made to suffer for their religion only? Would this not also be admitting a principle which would justify the most severe persecution?[84]

---

the right of the governed; and the withholding it in whole or in part is the violation of the fundamental law and condition of the state. We ask no special favours, we maintain our own religion, we contribute to the maintenance of the state's religion, we ask only for those rights which are not committed by the governor as a discretionary estate, but a sacred and inviolable trust."

[82] William Parry, *op. cit.*, p. 21.

[83] The Reverend Charles De Coetlogan, attempting to refute this argument in an alarmist sermon preached before the Lord Mayor and Aldermen of London, denied that it was possible for Dissenters to make an equal contribution to society with those who conformed to the state religion. Indeed, history proved that their admission to the full rights of citizenship "must terminate in the melancholy revolution of government and society itself, as was the case in the last century." *Vide The Test of Truth, Piety, and Allegiance* (London, 1790), p. 22.

[84] Parry, *op. cit.*, p. 19. He went on to ask: "Would not the Act of Uniformity, the rich and ample revenues of the church, and the connection between its interest and that of all the great families of the Kingdom still secure its prosperity and the number of its adherents? Is it impossible that it should stand but upon the ruins of justice and the subversion of the civil rights of Dissenters? Would not the Church enjoy her ritual and all

"Let men be classed in society not according to their speculative opinions," cried the Reverend Joseph Smith, "but according to the level to which their abilities and their virtues will enable them to ascend." Let the operations of reason be unfettered by any sort of restrictions and "no injury ever will or can be sustained by any constitution that is friendly to the happiness of man!"[85] Furthermore, the Reverend Samuel Pearce asserted that his colleagues sought "a repeal of those laws not primarily as oppressive to us as Dissenters only, but as injurious and disgraceful to the nation at large."[86] In other words, by 1790, the appeal was broadening to include all Dissenting groups—even Unitarians and Roman Catholics[87]— for, as Pearce asked: "Doth not the security of the State depend on the number of its wise and faithful and active citizens, whatever be their speculative opinions; and is not the State injured when the number of citizens of this description is diminished?"[88]

---

her emoluments, untouched by any but her own members, although a Dissenter might have a post in the army or a commission in the excise?" Similarly, Capel Lofft, in his *History of the Corporation and Test Acts with an Investigation of their Importance to the Establishment in Church and State* (London, 1790), argued that "according to present appearances, though the establishment of the Church of England, is a human, not a divine, a perishable, not an immortal fabric, yet considering the extent and value of its patronage, and its intimate connection with so many great and opulent families, its devotedness to the government and the reciprocal partiality of the government to it, if it falls after some centuries are passed, it will fall by no concerted plan from without, but by an inordinate exertion of that power in which it glories; a power which is greatly dependent on opinion, and to the maintenance of which, in an age so much enlightened, the greatest prudence and moderation are necessary." p. 5.

[85] *Vide* Joseph Smith, *op. cit.*, p. 34, who defined "the social rights of man" "as those natural rights which may with safety and propriety be admitted into a state of society, and whenever the laws of any country infringe on these rights, they ought to be repealed."

[86] Samuel Pearce, *The Oppressive, Unjust, and Prophane Nature and*

Early in February the Jeffries Committee had "thought it wise to assent to Mr. Beaufoy's suggestion that, since he had failed twice . . . , the bill should be introduced by another . . . and requested the favour of the Rt. Hon. Charles James Fox to bring the motion forward."[89] Despite the publication of numerous resolutions from many sections of the country on the church side of the debate, Fox rose in the Commons on February 15 to give notice that he would shortly move for leave to introduce a bill to repeal the Test. Pitt at once insisted that such an important measure demanded a "call of the House," in order that every member possible could be present for the debate. It was agreed that Fox's motion should be heard on March 2 and that the call should be issued for the day preceding. Consequently, Fox had an audience of some four hundred members of the 1784 Parliament when he rose to present the Dissenters' plea on March 2; a group which, in spite of the imminent general election, was unlikely to be sympathetic toward an issue which was plainly making an increasing appeal to those elements in the country whose "constitutional and patriotic societies" had attempted to play a leading part in politics through agitation for parliamentary reform.

The application now made for repeal of the Test, said Fox, had erroneously been considered as ill-timed, upon the false

---

Tendency of the Corporation and Test Acts exposed in a Sermon (Birmingham, 1790), p. 13.

[87] *Vide* Capel Lofft, *op. cit.*, p. 22, who wrote: "Convinced that Roman Catholics (for the term of Papists as acknowledging a civil supremacy in the Pope paramount to the laws and constitution of the state of which they are members is now obsolete) are capable of sincerely co-operating in the maintenance of the political rights and liberties of this country, I wish all bars of exclusion founded on any difference of religious sentiment to be utterly removed."

[88] Samuel Pearce, *op. cit.*, p. 15.

[89] Edward Jeffries MS 94. H. 4b. (Dr. Williams's Library).

principle, first, that the affairs in France rendered it necessary not to make any alterations in the constitution of Great Britain; and, secondly, that if the revolution abroad had not taken place, the Dissenters would have been less impetuously bent upon their determination to state again the nature of their imaginary grievances to Parliament:

> But the contrary fact is that the situation in France has neither excited the attempts nor raised the hopes of the Dissenters for the accomplishment of their wishes. A similar motion . . . was submitted . . . three years back, when no person could have predicted the singular events which have occurred on the Continent. Granting, however, that any circumstances have arisen subsequently to the second application of the dissenters and almost immediately preceding the present, which may give greater strength to the propriety of their petitions, it naturally follows that such events ought to be considered, in some degree, as operating against the rejection of a claim, which independent of extraneous occurrences, is founded upon justice and civil right.[90]

In other words, there was no historical support for the claim that "French principles" were the basic prop behind the motion under consideration, and the Establishment could not find here all those perils of social and ecclesiastical levelling which she fancied that she saw taking place across the channel.

As to the Church's alarm at the Dissenters' organizing themselves into a pressure group in order to gain support from various M.P.'s, was it not "natural for any body who found themselves aggrieved to join together and act in concert?" Surely there was no group more guilty of forming a political

---

[90] *Two Speeches Delivered in the House of Commons on Tuesday the 2nd by the Right Honourable Charles James Fox* (London, 1790), pp. 34–35.

faction than the Church of England herself; and certainly no illustration of an attempt from Dissenting ranks to influence selection of candidates in the approaching General Election could match the disgraceful action of Samuel Horsley, Bishop of St. David's, who "practically threatened to anathematise every individual of the Clergy of his Diocese who should dare to offend against his own choice. . . ."[91]

Personally, Fox professed himself a believer in establishments and a member of the Church of England; yet he felt that he was speaking not on behalf of one religious denomination, but in the cause of all his fellow believers in the rights of mankind, regardless of their "speculative opinions." He insisted that:

> To exclude any description of men from the participation of the common rights which their fellow-citizens enjoy is violently oppressive. Of what consequence is it to the State whether a man is a Unitarian or a Trinitarian; a believer in transubstantiation or the real presence; an advocate for infant baptism or for adult baptism? To abandon general principles upon the ground of partiality is a procedure which cannot be defended; and, with this idea, I shall venture, without a dread of reasonable contradiction, to

---

[91] *Ibid.*, p. 57. A copy of the letter from Bishop Horsley to the clergy of his diocese is contained in the Edward Jeffries MSS 94. H. 4c, and reads as follows: "Reverend Sir: Sir William Mansell has declared himself a candidate to represent the borough of Carmarthen in the next Parliament. I cannot refrain from declaring that he has my heartiest good wishes. Mr. Phillips, the present Member, has received the thanks of the Dissenters for the part he took in the late attempt to overthrow our Ecclesiastical Constitution by the repeal of the Corporation and Test Acts. By this, it is easy to guess what part he is likely to take in any future attempt for that purpose. I hope I shall not have the mortification to find a single Clergyman in my Diocese who will be so false to his own character and his Duty to the Established Church, as to give his vote to any man who has discovered such principles. . . ." The letter is dated Abergwilly, August 24, 1789.

affirm that even the majority have no right to bind the minority.[92]

After a vigorous attack upon Warburton's theory of alliance, in which he could discover only "religious corruption and political slavery," Fox concluded his three hour speech with a plea "not merely for the system of General Toleration, but for that system the greater object of which is the security of the Universal Rights of Human Nature!"[93] Sir Henry Houghton immediately seconded such sentiments, appealing "not to the generosity of the British Parliament," but demanding the "restoration of a right unjustly withheld."[94]

Again William Pitt replied for the Establishment; again he upheld the interest of the state as the ultimate justification for the status quo. It was not toleration itself which he opposed in the face of the Dissenters' demands:

But the extent of the principles maintained on the present occasion proceed even as far as the admittance of *every* dissenter to a full and complete *equality*. Indeed . . . [Fox's conclusions] throw open a door for the entrance of *some* individuals who might consider it a point of *conscience* to shake our Establishment to its foundations.[95]

If Dissenters were received "into an equality with the Establishment," Pitt contended that they would then quite naturally attempt to secure themselves an exemption from its support, thus threatening "the essentially inseparable union of Church and State." The Dissenters had a right to enjoy their liberty and property, to entertain their own speculative opinions, and

---

[92] *Ibid.*, pp. 18–19.
[93] *Ibid.*, pp. 61–62.
[94] *Vide The Debate in the House of Commons on Tuesday, the 2nd March, 1790, on the Motion of Mr. Fox for a Repeal of the Corporation and Test Acts* (London, 1790), p. 21.
[95] *The Speech of the Right Honourable William Pitt in the Commons on Tuesday, the Second March, 1790* (London, 1790), pp. 9–12.

to educate their children as they saw fit; "but the indispensable necessity of a certain permanent church establishment for the good of the state requires that toleration shall not extend to equality."[96]

After Henry Beaufoy had passionately reiterated many of the points which he had made in the debates of '87 and '89, Edmund Burke rose to deliver a long attack upon the dangerous "abstract principles" advocated by Fox:

Abstract principles my Honourable Friend knows me well enough to know I dislike and have never been able to bear. I detested them when a boy, and I like them no better now that I have silver hairs. Abstract principles are what my clumsy apprehensions cannot grasp; I must have a principle embodied in some manner or other and the conduct held upon it ascertained before I can pretend to judge of its propriety and advantage in practice. But of all abstract principles, abstract principles of natural right (which the Dissenters rely upon as their stronghold) are the most idle because the most useless, and the most dangerous to resort to. They supersede society and brake asunder all those bonds that have formed the happiness of mankind for ages. I should venture to say that if we were to go back abstractedly to original rights, there would be an end to all society. Abstract principles of natural right have been long since given up for the advantage of having what was much better: society, which substitutes wisdom and justice in the room of original right. It annihilated all those natural rights and draws to its mass all the component parts of which these are made up. It takes in all the virtue of the virtuous—all the wisdom of the wise. It gives life, security, and action to every faculty of the soul and secures the possession of every comfort which those proud and boasting

---

[96] *Ibid.*, p. 50.

natural rights impotently hold out, but cannot ascertain. . . ."[97]

After a long panegyric on the advantages of society and established churches, which he declared absolutely necessary for stability, Burke stepped down from his philosophic perch, and attempted to offer his colleagues concrete proof that the Church of England was in actual danger. Not only did he dwell upon the overworked "dangers to the Church" represented by Price and Priestley, but he produced evidence for more insidious dangers proceeding from the Dissenting rank and file. His "first great proof" was the production of a printed catechism written by the Reverend Robert Robinson and circulated with the approbation of the General Meeting of Dissenters at Harlow, "containing no one precept of religion, but consisting of one continued invective against King and Bishops, in which everything is misrepresented, and placed in the worst light, grossly libelling the National Establishment." This catechism, said Burke, was to be put into the hands of Dissenters' children "to teach them to lisp out censures in condemnation of the Church Established, while, possibly, the Dissenting teachers were preaching up robbery and plunder as in France."[98] His other most alarming proof was in the form of a letter from a Mr. Fletcher, the member of a meeting of Dissenting ministers held at Boston in Lincolnshire, who disapproved of his colleagues' subversive tendencies reporting that "they did not care the nip of a straw for the repeal of the Test and Corporation Acts, but that they designed to try for the abolition of Tythes and the Liturgy."[99] Ten years ago Burke confessed that he might have voted for repeal of the Test.

---

[97] *The Debate in the House of Commons . . . 2nd March, 1790. . . .* , pp. 45–46.
[98] *Ibid.*, pp. 48–49.
[99] *Ibid.*, p. 50.

Now, confronted by the principles professed by Dissenters and by the revolutionary upheavals in France with which so many of them seemed to sympathize to the detriment of all ordered society, he could only oppose such a measure.

William Smith, the Dissenter from Sudbury, immediately sprang to his feet to answer Burke's charges and most unwisely hurled a torrent of invective at the distinguished orator. He did not wonder that Burke, "who had attacked a whole nation abroad while in the very act of struggling for their liberties, with the most violent language, calling them an irrational, unprincipled, persecuting, confiscating, plundering, ferocious, bloody, and tyrannical democracy" should "libel a respectable body of men at home who have by no part of their conduct deserved to be treated with so much asperity!"[100] Although Smith vigorously denied ever having heard of the Catechism quoted by Burke and assured his fellow M.P.'s that it was not current among the Dissenters, his vigorous outburst probably served only to confirm the suspicions of the majority that Dissent and subversive principles went hand in hand. At least, Mr. William Wilberforce and Sir William Dolben, who followed him in speaking, both rallied to the support of Burke's view and professed themselves "decidedly against the motion."[101]

When Fox rose to reply to this long and heated debate it was apparent that his measure did not stand a chance of passing. After they had listened to a summary of his earlier arguments, the House divided, 105 for and 294 against repeal; a government majority of 189. Throughout the country there was a great rejoicing at this deliverance from French principles and Long Parliament levellers. "The great senate of the

---

[100] *Ibid.*, pp. 54–55.
[101] *Ibid.*, pp. 56–57. It is interesting to note that William Smith was not returned as member for Sudbury in the General Election of 1790.

nation," declared the *Gentleman's Magazine,* "unawed by any consideration held out to them, have asserted that Independence worthy of the representatives of a free people;" and most of the provincial press echoed these sentiments.[102] The day was fast approaching when Dissenters would be forced to realize that "the spirit of the age," to which they continually appealed, had, in fact, turned against them.

---

[102] *Vide* The *Gentleman's Magazine* for May, 1790, which contains a full account of the debate and the country's reaction to it.

CHAPTER VII

The Principles of Pitt Triumphant

EVEN WITH A government majority of 189 votes against them in the debate on March 2, 1790, the Jeffries Committee's spirit of obstinate optimism died hard. At a *post mortem* meeting held in the King's Head Tavern, London, on April 20, the committee declared that "much good must necessarily arise from a discussion in which some of the dearest rights of mankind are concerned." They professed "no doubt" about "a favourable issue" to their request "at no distant period, when reason and justice shall prevail over prejudice and bigotry, the present difficulties being merely temporary."[1] Jeffries expressed great hope in "the evident general disposition to union and cooperation, founded on motives of liberality and Christian fraternity which has appeared on the present occasion amongst the different denominations of our body; which is the more noticed as some of the Dissenters differ still more in opinion from each other than others of them do from members of the Church of England." In fact, some delegations from different parts of the country had already joined the central committee, and a plan was under way for "the formation of a Standing Committee out of the whole body of Dissenters for the purpose of more vigorously pursuing measures for repeal. . . ."[2]

Meeting again on May 11, the committee conducted a slightly more searching appraisal of the situation, but their

---

[1] Edward Jeffries MS 94. H. 2. (Dr. Williams's Library).
[2] *Ibid.*

confidence remained unshaken. After long discussion, they resolved unanimously that "so clearly founded on the unalterable principles of reason and justice" had their late application been, "we cannot but regard the manner in which it was defeated and the violent spirit that has been raised against us not only as an injury to ourselves, but as a discredit to the character of a free and enlightened nation."[3] The ecclesiastical constitution of the kingdom was far too firmly established to rest upon the Test and Corporation Acts, and Jeffries professed it "astonishing that the public in this enlightened age could have been influenced by such a phantom." Such unjust and ill-founded alarms revived "the unchristian spirit of those bigoted times which disgrace the annals of our country." When the cry of "Church in danger!" had been raised against Dissenters in Sacheverell's time, however, the charges leveled against them were couched in theological jargon; now their heresy rested solely on political grounds. Whereas before they had been decried as "schismatics who would rend the seamless robe of Christ," they were now derided as "republicans and Jacobins."

Acutely conscious of this criticism during their discussions on May 11, the Jeffries Committee met again on the following day to draft *An Address to the People of England* in which they stated unequivocally that :

We cannot but express our surprize and concern that we should so often be reproachfully branded with the name of Republicans. If there be any meaning in this term as malignantly applied to us by our enemies, it must be intended to denote the wish to overturn the present constitution and to establish a republick on the ruins of the monarchial part of our government. But every imputation of this kind we

---

[3] Edward Jeffries MS 94. H. 3a. (Dr. Williams's Library)

absolutely deny. The Dissenters in no sense deserve the appellation of Republicans, but stand in common with all the people of the kingdom in opposition to arbitrary power. None can be more sensible than we are of the excellence of the principles of our free constitution or more zealous for its preservation and continuance. . . .[4]

The Address closed upon a typically unfounded note of optimism:

> Let it suffice to say at present that we are not discouraged by our late defeat, but shall cherish the confidence that when the application for relief from our grievances is renewed, we shall not be censured as obstinately persisting in fruitless attempts. The time will speedily arrive when a generous nation that of late has been misled by false alarms and insidious and bigoted misrepresentations shall return to calmer feelings and more sober reflection. A restoration of our rights must necessarily result from the progress of truth, justice, and sound policy. Great Britain . . . will not permit herself to be exceeded by other countries in the regards which are due to the rights of men and citizens.[5]

Meanwhile, "various delegations of the different denominations of Protestant Dissenters" had been joining the Jeffries Committee and also conferring with the London Deputies on the most feasible procedure for a further application to Parliament. At "an adjourned general meeting of the Deputies at Dr. Williams' Library on Thursday, May 13, 1790," Edward Jeffries reported that:

> The committee of 21, annually appointed at the General Meeting (of the Protestant Dissenting Deputies) had held a conference on the 4th and 5th of the same month with delegates from the country, Dr. Hardy of Northampton

---

[4] *Ibid.*
[5] *Ibid.*

being in the chair, when various resolutions having for their object the formation of a standing committee of the whole body of Dissenters for the purpose of concerting and pursuing measures for obtaining relief from the legislature on the subject of the Test Laws were agreed to at the said conference, *nemine contradicente,* as follows : That it is the opinion of this meeting that an union of Protestant Dissenters is desirable—That it is the opinion of the meeting that a Standing Committee composed of delegates from different parts of the kingdom be appointed to meet in London as soon as convenient for the purpose of concerting and pursuing measures for obtaining relief from the legislature. . . . That the proportion of delegates in the Committee be 21 on the part of the Deputies of the Congregations in and near London, and 42 on the part of the Congregations in the remainder of the kingdom. . . . That it be recommended to the several meetings of Protestant Dissenters in the country to chuse their representative delegates to meet in London on or before the first day of June next . . . and that one-third in number of the above Committee be empowered to call a special meeting of delegates in the country when they shall see it expedient.[6]

On the same day a full general meeting of the Deputies approved the plan and appropriated money for the printing and distribution of the details of representation for each of the counties in England and Wales.[7]

---

[6] Edward Jeffries MS 94. H. 3b. (Dr. Williams's Library).
[7] *Vide ibid.,* for the scheme of county representation which was arranged as follows :

Northumberland	)		Gloucestershire	)		Shropshire	)	
Cumberland	) 3		Monmouthshire	) 2		North Wales	) 2
Westmorland	)						
Durham	)		Somersetshire	)		Sussex	)	
			Wiltshire	) 2		Surrey	) 2
Yorkshire	2					Kent	)	

Favorable replies soon came pouring in from county meetings of Dissenters. Yorkshire was the first to respond, with Northamptonshire and Lancashire close behind. The proceedings of the "General Meeting of Protestant Dissenters of the County of York, held at the Old King's Arms, in Leeds, May 19, 1790," under the chairmanship of Robert Wylde Moult, were typical of the others:

> ... The plan for a general Committee in London, formed by Delegates from the several counties and approved by the London Deputies being read, it was resolved unanimously that John Pemberton Hayward, Esq., and William Buck, Esq., be appointed our representatives in the said committee; and, an *Address to the People of England,* agreed upon by the London Committee and communicated to the secretary by the chairman, being also read, it was resolved unanimously that the *Address* now read be printed at the expense of this district in all the newspapers that are now published in the county of York.[8]

Most Dissenting apologists, following the spirit of the Jeffries Committee, persisted in a basically optimistic vein throughout the year 1790; but their statements grew less hopeful for

		Devonshire	)		
Lancashire	)	Cornwall	) 2	Essex	1
Cheshire	) 2				
		Dorsetshire	)	Hertfordshire	) 1
Nottinghamshire	)	Hampshire	) 2		
Derbyshire	) 2			Bedfordshire	)
		Lincolnshire	)	Buckinghamshire	) 2
Warwickshire	)	Leicestershire	) 2		
Staffordshire	) 2	Rutlandshire	)	Suffolk	)
				Norfolk	) 2
Worcestershire	)	Northamptonshire	1		
Herefordshire	) 2			Cambridge	)
		Oxfordshire	)	Huntingdonshire	) 2
		Berkshire	) 2		
				South Wales	) 4

[8] Edward Jeffries MS 94. H. 3c. (Dr. Williams's Library).

"immediate relief" as the year wore on. Perhaps the pamphlets of the two gifted children of John Aikin, D.D., late theological tutor in the Dissenting academy at Warrington, showed the trend of more thoughtful nonconformist opinion during that year of overwhelming parliamentary defeat. Some men, wrote John Aikin, Jr., shortly after the debate on March 2, might wish "to relinquish a country which distrusts and dishonours its best citizens" and "to seek either in the Transatlantic States or in the neighbouring delightful land of liberty a restoration to those privileges of men on which the noblest of natures set the highest value;"[9] but he urged them to persevere yet a while. Lumping both Pitt and North together with "those low-minded men in all periods who cry out against the improvement of existing institutions," he pronounced that "the genius of the age" was against them.[10] "While men are rational beings," insisted Aikin, "it must be sufficient to appeal to their reason and all prejudice will in a short time give way before it."[11] Let every Dissenter continue, then, to urge his case for "equal citizenship" with real hope of success.

"This is not a contest for power between Churchmen and Dissenters," claimed Aikin's sister, Mrs. Anna Barbauld, "nor is it as Dissenters we wish to enter the lists: we wish to bury every name of distinction in the common appellation of citizen; we wish the name of Dissenter not to be pronounced except in ortheological researches and religious assemblies."[12] Directly challenging the M.P.'s who voted against repeal, she declared:

It is you who force us to make our dissent a prominent feature in our character. It is you who give relief and cause

---

[9] John Aikin, M.D., *The Spirit of the Constitution and that of the Church of England Compared* (London, 1790), Preface, p. iii.
[10] *Ibid.*, p. 3.
[11] *Ibid.*, Preface, p. v.
[12] Anna Laetitia Barbauld, *An Address to the Opposers of the Repeal of the Corporation and Test Acts* (London, 1790), p. 15.

to come out upon the canvas what we modestly wished to have shaded over and thrown into the background. If we are a party, remember it is you who force us to be so."[13] By no unfair or unconstitutional means would Dissenters have sought places of trust, but only "by the open and honourable rivalship of virtuous emulation, by trying to deserve well of our King and country."[14]

Nevertheless, asserted Mrs. Barbauld defiantly:

You will grant us what we ask. The only question is whether you will do it today. Tomorrow you certainly will. You will even intreat us, if need were, to allow you to remove from your country the stigma of illiberality. We appeal to the certain, sure operation of increasing light and knowledge which it is no more in your power to stop than to repel the tide with your naked hand or to wither with your breath the general influence of vegetation. . . . Can ye not discern the signs of the times? The minds of men are in movement from the Borysthenes to the Atlantic. Agitated with new and strong motions, they swell and heave beneath oppression as the seas within the Polar Circle when, at the approach of Spring, they grow impatient to burst their icy chains. . . . The genius of philosophy is walking abroad and with the touch of Ithuriel's spear is trying the establishments of the earth. The various forms of prejudice, superstition, and servility start up in their true shapes, which had long imposed upon the world under the revered semblances of honour, faith, and loyalty. Whatever is loose must be shaken; whatever is corrupt must be lopt away; whatever is not built on the broad basis of public utility must be thrown to the ground. . . . Man as man becomes an object of respect: Tenets are transferred from theory to practice. . . . Systems are analysed into their first

---
[13] *Ibid.*, p. 16.
[14] *Ibid.*, p. 17.

principles, and principles are fairly pursued to their legitimate consequences. The enemies of reformation who palliate what they cannot defend and defer what they dare not refute; who, with Festus, put off to a more convenient season what in the present season is inconvenient, stand aghast, and find they have no power to put back the important hour when nature is labouring with the birth of great events. . . . You see a mighty empire breaking from bondage and exercising the energies of recovered freedom. . . . Nobles, the creature of kings exist no longer; but man, the creature of God, exists there. . . .[15]

"Amidst such mighty operations," Mrs. Barbauld and her co-religionists looked forward to the time when "the name of Dissenter shall no more be heard of than that of Romanist or Episcopalian, when nothing shall be venerable but truth, and nothing valued but utility!"[16]

Clearly the most important political event in the winter of 1790—91 was the printing and circulation of Burke's *Reflections on the Revolution in France*. The governing classes throughout Europe lost no time in adopting its defence of traditional institutions as their own, while the supporters of "innovation" recognized the need for a prompt refutation. Seeing in Burke a "staunch ally of the present powerful ministry which is utterly unfriendly to the rights of mankind," John Aikin, Jr. markedly softened his earlier enthusiastic outbursts. In an *Address to the Dissenters of England*, he observed:

From the *present* you have certainly nothing to expect. But in due course you will obtain justice. . . . The period must at some future time arrive when reformation will no more be called innovation, slavish hierarchies will be destroyed in

---

[15] *Ibid.*, pp. 30–36.
[16] *Ibid.*, p. 40.

the mass of their own abuses, and the dominion of priests will give way to the dominion of reason and conscience."[17]

Other Dissenting apologists refused to succumb to such doubts about the present and did not hesitate to produce direct refutations of the *Reflections*. Joseph Priestley accused Burke of attempting to violate the fundamental nature of man as a rational creature by advocating that "all his thinking and reasoning should be subject to the controul of the state,"[18] and the Scottish lawyer, James Mackintosh, who wrote perhaps the most able philosophical attack upon "the specious theory of Mr. Burke," insisted in the course of his 381 pages that "to spare abuses at such a period as the present is to consecrate them, because the enthusiasm which carries nations to such reforming enterprises [as the ones in France] is short lived; and the opportunity of reform, if once neglected, might be irrecoverably lost."[19]

It was Thomas Paine's *Rights of Man,* however, which evoked the most alarm, not primarily because it attacked Burke and his fellow defenders of the status quo, but because it held the institution of monarchy itself up to ridicule. As if this were not enough to provoke excitement, Paine proceeded to undertake a bitter criticism of the Hanoverian dynasty in England:

> If government be what Mr. Burke describes it, 'a contrivance of human wisdom,' I might ask him if wisdom was at such a low ebb in England that it was necessary to import

---

[17] John Aikin, M.D., *An Address to the Dissenters of England* (London, 1790), p. 31.

[18] Joseph Priestley, *Letters to the Right Honourable Edmund Burke* (Birmingham, 1791) in *Works of Priestley.* J. T. Rutt (ed.) (London, 1823), XXII, p. 185.

[19] *Vide* James Mackintosh, *Vindiciae Gallicae* (4th ed.; London, 1792), p. 109.

it from Holland and Hanover? . . . If a country does not understand its own affairs, how is a foreigner to understand them, who knows neither its laws, its manners, nor its language?"[20]

As a result, reviewers at once began to dwell upon "the evils arising from such inflammatory publications" and to urge strict police measures against "writers of this class who are more fit to plan treasons, stratagems, and spoils than to suggest useful remarks with respect to the government of a free people."[21]

During the course of this bitter pamphleteering, members of the new Standing Committee of Protestant Dissenters in England and Wales had not been idle. The old Jeffries Committee had resolved that "when the new committee shall be formed we shall consider our appointment as suspended,"[22] and had accordingly disappeared as a body by the beginning of 1791. It is not clear from any existing records in Dr. Williams' Library, the Guildhall, or the British Museum whether the meeting of forty-two delegates from the counties and twenty-one from the Deputies actually took place in London according to schedule on June 1, 1790; but it is clear from the correspondence of Theophilus Lindsey that the new committee, under the chairmanship of Michael Dodson, the London barrister and member of Lindsey's Essex Street Chapel, had met to discuss politics early in 1791.

It was not until the last week in February that Dodson's committee took any definite action. This centered upon the

---

[20] Thomas Paine, *The Rights of Man, being an Answer to Mr. Burke's attack on the French Revolution* (5th ed.; London, 1791), pp. 138–139.
[21] *The Critical Review*, March, 1791, p. 341.
[22] Edward Jeffries MS, 94. H. 3b. (Dr. Williams's Library).

application of a committee of "Protesting Catholic Dissenters" for further relief from the penal code and brought to specific articulation the earlier general expressions of goodwill manifested toward Roman Catholics by the Jeffries Committee. Lindsey described what happened as follows:

> On Friday last, the Standing Committee of the Dissenters in England and Wales, resident in London, held a meeting in which they came to a resolution to address the Catholics now petitioning Parliament that although they themselves had been disappointed, they most cordially wished them success in their present application and should truly rejoice in their obtaining it. This resolution was communicated to the Catholics by their Chairman, and produced an answer, which I saw today, from their body assembled, thanking the Dissenters for their kindness to them and for their very seasonable encouragement; implying as if they had rather expected opposition from that quarter. . . . It is expected that there will be a good debate in the House upon the subject today. Some say that the Minister will try to put a stop to the business, forseeing that it will involve him in difficulties respecting the Dissenters. . . .[23]

Far from attempting to hinder the measure, however, the Minister did just the opposite, the bill passed the Commons without a division, and in the House of Lords the only alteration made was one which had been requested by the Vicars Apostolic. The oath required by the original bill, drafted in the name of "Protesting Catholic Dissenters" and condemning the spiritual power of the Pope over English Catholics in harsh terms, was too strong for the Catholic bishops, and another somewhat simpler form of oath, almost identical with that in the Irish Relief Act of 1774, was substituted. With this change,

---

[23] Lindsey to Tayleur, March 1, 1791, in Theophilus Lindsey, *Letters,* ed. H. McLachlan (Manchester, 1920), p. 66.

the bill, repealing the old statutes against "popish recusants" and removing various disabilities including the payment of a double land tax, passed unanimously through both Houses.[24] Expressing pleasure at this action, Theophilus Lindsey had particular commendation for Fox, whom he had heard speak in favor of the bill on the night when it was first introduced into the Commons:

> How much to be esteemed is Mr. Fox! Upon the Catholic Dissenters' Bill last night, among other excellent things, he declared his intention of bringing in a bill on better and more extensive principles for the relief of Protestant as well as Catholic Dissenters if the Ministry would not undertake it.[25]

But circumstances during the summer and autumn of '91 were hardly favorable for the introduction of any relief measure on behalf of Protestant Dissenters. The excitement which had been roused by hostile resolutions of the clergy and bodies of Anglican laymen meeting in various parts of the country could not be silenced by their mere parliamentary victory on March 2, 1790; and continued Dissenting activity in the direction of a further attempt at repeal, now confirmed by Fox, when coupled with news of increasingly more radical occurrences across the Channel, kept the alarmists at white heat. Then all eyes turned to Birmingham where these mounting tensions finally exploded on Joseph Priestley's doorstep.

That notorious preacher-scientist himself provided a realistic

---

[24] This astonishing spectacle of Pitt in the Commons and the prelates in the Lords finding themselves for once in agreement with Fox, the Whigs, and the Protestant Dissenters can be explained only by events across the Channel rather than by any change of heart toward the principle of a broader toleration for disaffected religious groups. Seeing the spoliation of the Church of France by the Jacobins, the Ministry were prepared to build a buttress for her support in days when they thought religion and civilization in Europe were in danger of collapse.

[25] Lindsey to Tayleur, April 7, 1791, *Ibid.*, p. 67.

picture of the reaction in Binringham to continental affairs when he wrote to Theophilus Lindsey at the end of June:

> Our anxiety during the King of France's escape and our joy on his capture cannot be described. . . . The High Church Party are mortified in the extreme. . . . But a majority, I fear, of Englishmen are in their sentiments, so that we are far indeed behind the French. In spite of all we can write or do, an attachment to high maxims of government gains ground here, and the love of liberty is on the decline.[26]

Nevertheless the Revolutionary Society at Birmingham, of which Priestley was the most prominent member, proceeded to advertise their intention of meeting on July 14 to commemorate the taking of the Bastille; and, a few days before the projected gathering a most seditious and inflamatory handbill, which was afterwards disclaimed by the Society, began to circulate. It exhorted the people of Birmingham to:

> Remember that on the 14th of July, the Bastille, that "High Altar and Castle of Despotism," fell! Remember the enthusiasm, peculiar to the cause of liberty, with which it was attacked! . . . But is it possible to forget that your own parliament is venal?—your minister hypocritical?—your clergy legal oppressors?—the reigning family extravagant? —the crown of a certain great personage becoming every day too weighty for the head that wears it?—too weighty for people who *gave* it?—your taxes partial and excessive? —your representation a cruel insult upon the sacred rights of property, religion, and freedom? . . .[27]

Then, on the evening before the meeting, certain people, supposedly in the interest of Priestley, chalked in large letters

---

[26] Joseph Priestley, *Works*, II, 114.
[27] *Vide* John Waddington, *Congregational History, 1700–1800* (London, 1876), pp. 652 ff. for this handbill and a good selection of local documents on the Birmingham Riots.

on most Church of England doors throughout the city: "This useless Barn to be let or sold!"[28] The result was a popular uprising in the name of "Church and King" which reproduced on a smaller scale nearly all the features of the Gordon Riots in London. Within four days the houses of prominent Dissenters and "republicans," including Priestley's house and library and the two principal Dissenting meeting houses, were burned to the ground.[29] On July 16, George III himself intervened with a letter to Secretary Dundas urging that troops be provided at once to restore order. But the king did not hesitate to reveal his personal attitude toward Priestley and his fellow "rational dissenters":

> The sending orders for three troops of the 15th regiment of dragoons to march towards Birmingham to restore order, if the civil magistrates have not been able, is incumbent on Government, though I cannot but feel better pleased that Priestley is the sufferer for the doctrines he and his party have instilled, and that people see them in their true light. . . .[30]

Public opinion shared his majesty's view, and meeting houses in Norwich, London, and Oxford also went up in flames as beacon fires to warn and rouse all loyal Englishmen against the subversive unpatriotic "French principles" of Dr. Priestley and Thomas Paine. If the Gordon Riots had demonstrated that John Bull was against any concessions to popery, their successors ten years later were a warning that neither would he stomach Protestant Dissenters or even Whig gentry dallying with the dangerous doctrines of a foreign revolution.

If most Dissenters were not now able to read the signs of

---

[28] *Ibid.*, p. 654.
[29] *Vide The Gentleman's Magazine* (August, 1791), for an account of the riots, and pp. 752–54 for the editor's hostile reaction to Priestley and his "fellow levellers."
[30] Waddington, *op. cit.*, p. 654.

the times, another telling illustration was quickly provided for their edification. Early in 1791 Lindsey, Dodson, Priestley, Tayleur and their associates had founded a Unitarian Society for promoting Christian Knowledge which lost no time in formulating plans for a repeal of the penal code against "Blasphemers of the Trinity." In a letter to Tayleur, written in mid-February of 1792, Lindsey indicated the progress of this movement:

> Tomorrow there is to be a general meeting of the members of our Unitarian Society to consider a petition to Parliament for the repeal of the laws against Anti-trinitarians. Mr. Dodson, Dr. Priestley, and another person were last Thursday appointed to draw up a petition to be offered to the meeting, and the former of these has drawn up a very proper one. Whether it is to be presented or no this Session is undetermined. Mr. Fox has very obligingly offered his services and advised this mode of application. There is a printed paper which Dr. Priestley had seen from some High Church men inviting all that wish well to the establishment to unite against the efforts that are making against it by Socinians, Republicans, Deists, etc. . . .[31]

Despite the vigorous High Church hostility which Lindsey himself recorded here, the indefatigable Unitarian pushed on and by mid-March was personally responsible for the collection of four hundred signatures "to be added to the 1600 with which Mr. Fox had first announced the petition"[32] — almost double the number he had succeeded in collecting during the anti-subscriptionist agitation of 1771. Finally, true to his pledge during the debate on the Roman Catholic Relief Bill of '91 that, if the government did not soon introduce measures for the further relief of Protestant Dissenters, he would do so

---

[31] Lindsey to Tayleur, February 15, 1792, *op. cit.*, p. 70.
[32] Lindsey to Tayleur, March 26, 1792, *Ibid.*, p. 71.

himself, Fox moved for permission to bring in a bill for repeal of the anti-Trinitarian penal code.

In opposing Fox's motion, the Prime Minister argued on the basis of prudence in the face of the ferment which the French Revolution had produced. No practical evil had resulted or was likely to result from these laws to any description of men. It was always wise to treat old laws relating to religion with extreme caution, and it would be "especially foolish at this time to give encouragement to avowed enemies of the Constitution." The great body of English people, he was convinced, were firmly attached to the Constitution under which they lived; but an "active section" were animated by different principles, and if the measure of Fox were carried, these men would "most certainly represent it as a first step to the gradual abolition of all the establishments and fundamental principles of the Constitution."[33]

So spoke Pitt, but it was Burke who inveighed most strongly against the motion. With all the oratorical powers at his command, he denounced Unitarians as the allies of Jacobins and the disciples of Thomas Paine. He contended that they were "associated for the express purpose of proselytism," aiming "to collect a multitude sufficient by force and violence to overturn the Church" and that this was "concurrent with a design to subvert the State." With hysterical vehemence he begged the House not to wait "till the conspirators, met to commemorate the 14th July, shall seize on the Tower of London and the magazines it contains, murder the governor and the mayor of London, seize upon the King's person, drive out the House of Lords, occupy your gallery, and thence, as from an high tribunal dictate to you!"[34] It was

---

[33] Cobbett, *Parliamentary History* (London, 1808), XXIV 1399–1400.
[34] *Ibid.*, pp. 1393–1395.

hardly surprising that when the House divided Fox's motion was defeated by 142 votes to 63, a government majority of 79. Well might the Dissenters' Standing Committee, meeting at the King's Head Tavern on May 30, 1792, under the chairmanship of Michael Dodson, declare their conviction "that the case of the Protestant Dissenters respecting the Test Laws is not likely to gain an impartial attention during the present session of Parliament."[35]

Prompted by the same emotions which Burke had expressed in the debate on May 11, before the close of 1792 a vigorous association was established at the Crown and Anchor Tavern in the Strand for the avowed purpose of "preserving Liberty and Property against Republicans and Levellers," but whose real object according to the Reverend Joseph Towers was "the suppression of freedom of conversation and freedom of the press."[36] Within a few months, under inspiration of the war with France, Crown and Anchor Associations grew up in many country areas, where they were "the first to raise the cry of sedition against anyone who dared to criticize the Government."[37] Small wonder that the Reverend John Pope, as he traveled about preaching to various Dissenting congregations during the year 1792—93 was moved to lament in almost every sermon about "the prevalence of party rage and bigotry" and to decry "a union of religious and political prejudice which has restored the enormities of the year '15."[38] He could find no sounder counsel to offer than that of "moderation." They must "cultivate a quiet spirit" during the current national emergency. Under no circumstances should "Dis-

---

[35] Michael Dodson MS 94. H. 5. (Dr. Williams's Library).
[36] *Vide* Joseph Towers, *Thoughts on National Insanity* (London, 1797), pp. 12–14.
[37] *Ibid.,* p. 25.
[38] John Pope, *Two Sermons Preached to Protestant Dissenters in the County of Lancaster* (London, 1793), pp. 40–41.

senters who are made to feel the sting of persecution in the present upheavals in their turn adopt the methods of their persecutors." Rather, "virtue and reason will prove their triumph in the long run"[39]; for, like John Aikin, Jr., Pope was no longer prepared to forecast anything like immediate success.

Indeed, the basically conservative General Body of Protestant Dissenting Ministers in London needed no such admonitions. Alarmed at the charges of Jacobinism which were daily being leveled indiscriminately in the press at all Dissenters, they held "an extraordinary meeting . . . to take into consideration the propriety of expressing at the present juncture of public affairs our attachment to the Constitution of these Kingdoms." After some discussion, to which "eight of our brethren from the country" were admitted, the following resolutions were adopted:

That it is our duty at the present juncture to declare in the most explicit manner: That we hold and ever have held in the highest respect and veneration that excellent form of government by King, Lords, and Commons which hath obtained from time immemorial in this country, the blessings of which were confirmed and enlarged at the glorious era of the Revolution of 1688, and which possesses those invaluable principles that are essential to its prosperity and improvement: That we are firmly attached to his present Majesty and to the succession of the Crown of his Kingdoms in his family, as by law established: That we abhor all seditious practices tending to subvert this our excellent Constitution; and that we will exert ourselves to the utmost of our power to promote peace and reverence of the Laws and peace and good order in society.[40]

---

[39] *Ibid.*, p. 43.
[40] *Minutes of the General Body*, II, 312–313.

Motions were unanimously carried at the end of the meeting for publication of these resolutions in the daily and evening papers, and for the appropriation of money to finance the printing of two thousand copies for distribution among Dissenters of the Three Denominations.

It can hardly be doubted that large numbers of Dissenters were succumbing to the spirit of reticence which pervaded the London Ministers. Certainly after war had broken out between England and the French Revolutionary Republic in February of 1793, many Dissenting ministers and propertied laymen agreed with the noted Presbyterian theologian, Dr. William Laurence Brown, when he preached that:

> It is the evident duty of every Christian, of every man who wishes well to his species, is impressed with a due sense of right and wrong, and has learned to make any tolerable estimate of the sources of human happiness to abhor the opinions and conduct of the fanatical sect I have just described [i.e., the Jacobins] and to oppose them to the utmost of his power ... for they seek to destroy the grand foundations of morality by withdrawing God from the universe.
> ... It is evidently the duty of every good citizen to strengthen the hands of government by yielding a willing and ready obedience to his lawful superiors. ... The contest is between order and confusion, between humanity and cruelty, between justice and violence, between religion and impiety, between heaven and hell! ... The French Revolutionists mean to establish an equality of external condition which is absolutely incompatible with civil society.
> ... Indeed, in the present alarming crisis which affects not one country or nation only, but all Europe, the question is not whether this or that other political party shall prevail, whether the constitution already existing ought to remain untouched or some reforms ought to be introduced into it;

but whether or not the present order of things, the present establishments, laws, manners, usages and religion shall at once be swept away and give place to visionary schemes of political perfection which have hitherto produced nothing but every species of wickedness and calamity to the community where they have been introduced and uncontrolled dominion to the obscure contrivers and directors of them."[41]

Before the year 1793 was out it had become clear that not only voluntary organizations like the Crown and Anchor Societies were prepared to ferret out subversive activities, but the Government itself had begun to show its teeth. Writing to his friend Tayleur on December 2, 1793, Lindsey could deal in detail with three particularly glaring examples of political persecution. The first had centered upon Thomas Muir, a Glasgow graduate and a member of the Faculty of Advocates at Edinburgh who had taken part in the promotion of a society for obtaining parliamentary reform. Accused of exciting a spirit of disloyalty and sedition, of recommending Paine's *Rights of Man,* and of distributing subversive literature, he was sentenced on August 31 to the brutal penalty of fourteen years' transportation.

Muir's case was followed by judgment against the pious Thomas Fysche Palmer, a former Fellow of Queens' College, Cambridge, who had been converted to Unitarianism by the writings of Priestley and Lindsey and became minister to a Unitarian congregation in Dundee. On September 12 he was sentenced to seven years' transportation to Botany Bay for being involved in the publication of an address to the people of Scotland complaining of extravagant war taxation and demanding universal suffrage and short parliaments.

Then, the Reverend William Winterbottom, a Baptist

---

[41] William Laurence Brown, D.D., *The Spirit of the Times Considered* (London, 1793), pp. 23–24.

minister at Plymouth, was sentenced on November 27 to four years' imprisonment and a £500 fine for preaching a democratic view of kingship and discussing the political aspect of the prevailing national crisis in a sence derogatory to Pitt's Government. Winterbottom was made to serve his full sentence; and, in March of 1794, Muir and Palmer, together with two others, Skirving and Margarot, convicted of similar activities, were sent in chains on convict hulks to Botany Bay, the legality of their sentences having been unsuccessfully disputed in both Houses of Parliament.[42]

After dealing with these fierce persecutions, Theophilus Lindsey, with singular political insight, lamented:

> If there was but a prospect of Mr. Fox's coming into power, who would certainly bring better principles with him and require them to be acted upon! But the day at present is far distant. I presume you know that there has lately been a sort of negotiation of the Ministers with the Duke of Portland. . . . Three Cabinet Ministers and patronage without end was offered, and without reserve, only Mr. Fox was to be excluded, for that the King could not bear him. It did not go on, however, as the Duke did not choose to submit to the last condition. But as he and other Whig Lords are much under Burke's direction, one can be surprised at nothing.[43]

And how right Lindsey was; for, in July of 1794, Pitt was able to face Britain and the world with the spectacle of

---

[42] *Vide The New Annual Register for 1793*, Principal Occurrences section, pp. 45–46, which records that on December 1, Muir and Palmer "arrived in the River from Leith. . . . Orders were sent down for delivering them into the custody of the contractor for the hulks at Woolwich. . . . They are in irons among the convicts and were ordered yesterday to assist them in the common labour." An account of the failure of their appeals and their transportation to Botany Bay is contained in the 1794 issue.

[43] Lindsey to Tayleur, December 2, 1793, *op. cit.*, p. 90.

a full coalition achieved with the Duke of Portland.

Thus strengthened, during the month of November the Government had no difficulty in passing two very severe bills on Treasonable Practices and Seditious Meetings; and these were used most effectively in breaking up "subversive groups" like the London Society for Constitutional Information and the London Corresponding Society which had continued to agitate publicly for universal suffrage and annual parliaments. "So presumptuous a young man as Mr. Pitt," exclaimed Lindsey, "has never before been placed at the helm in this country!" By "his want of wisdom," he was bringing Great Britain "to the very brink of ruin." Yet "the fascination for him" seemed to grow stronger day by day and might well persist "until he has completed our fate."[44]

In an earlier letter, Lindsey had expressed concern that "the war with France is likely to continue"; for it would "prevent the nation from cooling and returning to a better temper." A long war could only serve "to lay the unavoidable evils and burdens that must result from it at the door of Dissenters of all sorts" and prevent any hope of their relief from "persecuting laws" for many years to come.[45] More than this, by 1800 Pitt had not only succeeded in carrying through "Combination Acts" against all trade unionists, whom he viewed as Jacobinical revolutionaries, but he actually prepared and was determined to press a measure abridging the Toleration Act, restricting the right of "indiscriminate" preaching, and empowering the local justices to refuse licences for new "conventicles." Only the forceful entreaties of his old friend William Wilberforce prevented introduction of the bill to a parliament where it would in all probability have received a

---

[44] Lindsey to John Rowe, *ibid.*, p. 91.
[45] Lindsey to W. Turner, Jun., *ibid.*, p. 89.

hearty welcome and swift enactment.[46] Lindsey lived, then, to see his most extreme fears come to pass. On November 8, 1808, the day of his death, war was still raging with France and there seemed better prospects for further test legislation and penal measures against Dissenters than for repeal of the existing restrictions.

By the middle seventeen-nineties it had thus become obvious to every Dissenter, no matter how enthusiastically hopeful he may have been at the beginning of the decade, that further agitation could achieve nothing but government suppression. At last the scales of naïve optimism fell from his eyes and he saw that "the enlightened sentiments of refined liberality" had never really governed any nation, nor did they seem likely to do so in the future under inspiration of the bloody mob violence pursued in their name across the Channel. He must be contented to lower his gaze from the Olympian heights of pure and undefiled human rights and to traffic in the market place of every day affairs, confining himself to the rôle of a second-class citizen. Surrendering to the inevitable, Michael Dodson's Standing Committee published an account of discriminatory legislation against Dissenters as its final act, and disbanded in 1796.[47] Another generation would have to pass before a similar group could fight repeal of the Test and Corporation Acts through to success.

So it was that by the end of the eighteenth century the theory and practice of religious toleration in England had come a long way from Milton's plea for "Christian libertie" in

---

[46] Wilberforce, Robert and Samuel, *The Life of William Wilberforce* (London, 1838), II, 360–362.

[47] *Vide An Abstract of the Proceedings of the Deputies and Committee Appointed for Supporting the Civil Rights of Protestant Dissenters* (London, 1796).

matters of conscience and from the High Church position that if Trinitarian nonconformists must be suffered to exist, official permission for them to engage in any corporate activity other than public worship behind unlocked doors was unthinkable. Although the idea of toleration as expressed by Locke and tenaciously upheld by a few liberal Churchmen from the time of Bishop Burnet to Archdeacon Paley's day, as well as by most Dissenters, was too liberal and comprehensive to secure statutory enactment, the limited indulgence granted in 1689 and confirmed in 1718 proved lasting. If it was not extended during the eighteenth century, neither was it restricted; indeed, it came to enjoy the surprising experience of apotheosis. Bishop Warburton and the Church of England, supported by the writings of Barlow, Proast, and Stebbing, had reached the conclusion by 1736 that by the Law of Nature every man possessed the right of worshiping God according to his own conscience, but that an established church and an attendant test law were also based upon the great and unerring maxims of the laws of nature and of nations. They were able to achieve this reasoning on the basis of "civil utility" in the conviction that the principles of Truth and Utility had met together in a union as happy as unexpected; and, after the publication of Warburton's *Alliance between Church and State,* all parties felt that "necessity of state" alone could justify the interference of government in matters of religion.

After the decade of the seventeen-thirties all arguments about religious toleration had thus been reduced to the basic question of the rights of the individual against the rights of the state. With monotonous regularity, statesmen from the time of Walpole to that of Pitt, and divines from Bishop Sherlock's day to Dean Tucker's, defended Warburton's thesis that the laws of self-preservation demanded a state church which must be protected by allowing only those who could subscribe to its doctrines to serve in civil offices of consequence. It was to assert their belief that nonconformists could render loyal service to the civil constitution of their country without the necessity of subscribing to established articles of religion that Dissenters of the three major denominations in London set up central agencies in their Ministers and Lay Deputies through whom they could approach the government and state their case for repeal of the Test and Corporation Acts. Falling short of that goal, they used the organizational experience thus gained to defend what few legal privileges the Act of 1689 had granted them and finally secured pronouncement from the Lord Chief Justice in 1767 that nonconformity was no longer a crime in the laws of England.

Meanwhile, liberal Churchmen themselves were growing restive under the requirement of subscription to "medieval articles of religion," and the clerical petition movement, together with widespread discontent over the policies of George III, roused Dissenters to petition for relief of their ministers, tutors, and schoolmasters from the burden of subscription to the Thirty-Nine Articles. By the time the government condescended to grant this in 1779, however, it was no longer enough to satisfy most Dissenters and passed by almost unnoticed amid the stirring political events of the day. Indeed, by 1787 the Three Denominations were no longer content to approach the government for the favor of a repeal of the Test, but began to demand it as a political right for all Protestants. True, they continued to employ basically the same vocabulary used during the seventeen-thirties, arguing for a "legal capacity" to serve in civil offices on the basis of individual merit, rather than any inherent "natural right" to such positions; and disestablishment became no more a real issue than it had ever been. The significant change was that, under inspiration of the American and French Revolutions, by 1790 most articulate Dissenters had clearly outgrown the restricted toleration advocated by Locke and now insisted that the very term of "toleration" itself was too narrow a description for so fundamental a human right as religious freedom. They had thus come to embrace "all honest men," whether Protestants, Roman Catholics, Jews, or Atheists, on condition of their civil allegiance only.

Fortified by bloody mob violence across the Channel and by the increasingly radical tone adopted by "republicans and levellers" under the inspiration of Tom Paine, Pitt's government turned a deaf ear to the Dissenters' pleas for repeal of the penal code against nonconformists. Pitt, like Walpole before him, insisted that such enactments, far from causing harm, were the great bulwark of order in the state. Most of them were unenforced and a man like Theophilus Lindsey might continue to preach Unitarian sermons so long as he did not directly attack the government. Once he began to threaten the established order, however, the laws were there with which to punish him. Just because the sword of Damocles had not fallen was no reason why it should not continue to be kept suspended.

Public opinion stood solidly behind the Prime Minister. In the course of the century Jews, Papists, and all denominations of Protestant Dissenters had in turn felt the fury of a theologically-minded proletariat, and the actions of the man in the street — even in "the most enlightened of ages" — had never indicated any inclination to be governed by the principles of "free and candid reason." Under threat of invasion, it became evident to John Bull that the disciples of Tom Paine or of Priestley and Price, Deists and Dissenters, Roman Catholics, members of constitutional clubs or corresponding societies, and trade unionists were all one and the same thing — traitors to their country, offenders against civilization, and enemies of true religion. Events had conspired in times of great peril for the state to produce a general attitude that all nonconformists must content themselves at best with second-class citizenship for a long time to come.

Was, then, all the feverish lobbying, all the pamphleteering, all the agitation in the name of "candour" and the rights of man completely in vain? Surely it was not. In the course of their vigorous efforts to attain full citizenship before the law Dissenters had mastered basic techniques of propaganda and political organization which were to stand them in good stead during the late eighteen-twenties. But far more significant than this was their concept of a new type of citizenship based on the principle of every man's right to serve his community and his country according to his best abilities. Before suspending their meetings, Michael Dodson and his committee insisted that their idea of citizenship would be vindicated by the future; the principles of William Pitt could triumph only for one last season because they belonged wholly to the past. "Laws," declared Dodson, "which aggrandize one body of citizens at the expense of another and penal statutes on subjects of religion by which man arrogates to himself the prerogatives of his creator and effects to say to the human intellect: 'Hitherto thou shalt go, but no farther,' must inevitably fall when peace is restored to the world and calmer counsels prevail."[48] As Mrs. Barbauld had insisted, the day would come when it would "no longer be required of the candidate for civil employment what he believes on theological subjects, but what are his abilities for the service of his country."[49] When this day did arrive, it would

---

[48] Michael Dodson, MS, 94. H. 5. (Dr. Williams's Library).
[49] *Vide* Anna Laetitia Barbauld, *op. cit.*, p. 29.

find Dissenters well prepared to share the status of full citizenship with a responsibility which could redound only to their country's advantage.

Bibliography

MANUSCRIPT SOURCES (all to be found in Dr. Williams's Library, London, unless otherwise indicated).

Philip Doddridge, *Correspondence,* Vols. I–IX (in the Library of New College, London).

Michael Dodson MSS

Evans MS

Edward Jeffries MSS

Minute Books of the Protestant Dissenting Deputies (in the Guildhall Library, London).

Minute Books of the General Body of Ministers of the Three Denominations in and about the Cities of London and Westminster.

Fysche Palmer MSS

Benjamin Stinton MS

PRINTED MANUSCRIPT MATERIALS

Burnet, Gilbert, *Harleian MSS,* ed. by H. C. Foxcroft (Oxford, 1902).

Doddridge, Philip, *Correspondence and Diary,* ed. by J. D. Humphreys (London, 1829).

Egmont, John Percival, First Earl, *Diary,* Historical MSS Commission (London, 1920).

George III, *Correspondence with Lord North from 1768 to 1783,* ed. by W. B. Donne (London, 1867).

Complete Correspondence from 1760 to December 1783, ed. by Sir John Fortesque, 6 vols. (London, 1927–28).

Lindsey, Theophilus, *Letters,* ed. by H. McLachlan (Manchester, 1920).

Neville, Sylas, *Diary, 1767–1788*, ed. by B. Cozens-Hardy (Oxford, 1950).
Ryder, Dudley, *Diary, 1715–1716*, ed. by W. Matthews (London, 1939).

NEWSPAPERS AND PERIODICALS

The Annual Register (1758–1800)
The Critical Review (1756–1800)
The Gentleman's Magazine (1731–1800)
The Liverpool Chronicle (1760–1800)
The London Magazine (1743–1800)
The Manchester Chronicle (1780–1800)
The Monthly Review (1749–1800)
The New Annual Register (1780–1800)
The Occasional Paper (1716–1720)
The Old Whig (1721–1741)
The St. James Chronicle (1768–1800)
The Whitehall Evening Post (1770–1800)

CONTEMPORARY BOOKS AND PAMPHLETS

Abernethy, John, *Reasons for Repeal of the Sacramental Test* (Dublin, 1732).
—— *Scarce and Valuable Tracts and Sermons* (London, 1751).
Abingdon, Willoughby Bertie, Fourth Earl, *Thoughts on a Letter of Edmund Burke, Esq.* (London, 1777).
An Account of the Dissenters and their Management with regard to the Test and Corporation Acts (London, 1732).
Adams, William, *An Answer to Dr. Rotherham's Apology for the Athanasian Creed* (London, 1773).
Addison, Joseph, *Evidence of the Christian Religion* (London, 1730).
An Address to the Dissenting Laity in Relation to the Test Acts (London, 1736).
An Address to the Gentlemen who are deputed from the

several Congregations of Protestant Dissenters . . . (London, 1733).

Advice from a Bishop in a Series of Letters to a Young Clergyman (London, 1759).

Aikin, John, *An Address to the Dissenters of England* (London, 1790).

The Spirit of the Constitution and that of the Church of England Compared (London, 1790).

Antinarkia, or an Inquiry into the true Acceptation or Idea of Religious Liberty as set forth in the Scriptures (London, 1774).

An Apology for the Church of England (London, 1732).

An Apology for the Reverend Mr. Thomas Bradbury (London, 1719).

Apostolical Conformity stated and asserted in a Dialogue between a Conformist and a Dissenter (London, 1703).

An Appeal to Candour, Magnanimity, and Justice . . . (London, 1787).

An Appeal from the Protestant Association to the People of Great Britain (London, 1780).

An Appeal to Reason . . . (Devizes, 1774).

The Argument with Dissenters about Subscription and Repeal . . . (London, 1735).

Astell, Mary [pseud. Tom Single], *Moderation Truly Stated* (London, 1703).

Atkinson, Benjamin, *Catholic Principles, or St. Paul's* . . . *Practice Recommended* (London, 1730).

Baguley, William, *The Lord Chancellor's Proceedings about the Chappel in Gt. Queens Street* (London, 1709).

Balguy, John, *Silvius' Defence of a Dialogue between a Papist and a Protestant in Answer to the Revd. Mr. Stebbing* (London, 1720).

Silvius' Letter to the Reverend Dr. Sherlock (London, 1719).

Balguy, Thomas, *A Sermon Preached at Lambeth Chapel* (London, 1769).

Barbauld, Anna Laetitia, *An Address to the Opposers of the Repeal of the Corporation and Test Acts* (London, 1790).

Barlow, Thomas, *Several Miscellaneous and Weighty Cases of Conscience* (London, 1692).

Baron, Peter, *A Sermon Preached at Exeter* (London, 1742).

Baron, Richard (ed.), *The Pillars of Priestcraft and Orthodoxy Shaken*, new ed., 4 Vols. (London, 1768).

Barrington, John Shute, Viscount, *An Answer to Some Queries* (London, 1732).

A Dissuasive from Jacobitism (London, 1713).

Letter from a Layman (London, 1714).

Essay upon the Interest of England (London, 1701).

The Interest of England Considered . . . with Some Thoughts on Occasional Conformity (London, 1703).

The Rights of Protestant Dissenters (London, 1704).

Beauclerk, James, *A Martyrdom Sermon Preached before the Rt. Hon. Lords Spiritual and Temporal* (London, 1752).

Beaufoy, Henry, *The Substance of a Speech delivered in the House of Commons upon the 28th of March, 1787* (London, 1787).

A Speech delivered in the House of Commons upon the 8th of May, 1789 (London, 1789).

Beilby, Samuel, *A Sermon on Religious Toleration* (London, 1790).

Belsham, Thomas, *Memoirs of Theophilus Lindsey* (London, 1812).

Belsham, William, *Essays Philosophical and Moral, Historical and Literary*, 2nd ed., 2 Vols. (London, 1799).

Bennett, Benjamin, *Irenicum, or a Review of Some Late Controversies . . .* (London, 1722).

Bennett, Thomas, *A Defence of the Discourse of Schism* (Cambridge, 1703).

A Discourse of Schism (Cambridge, 1702).

Benson, George, *A Collection of Tracts* (London, 1753).

The Reasonableness of Christianity as Derived from the Scriptures (London, 1743).

Berington, Joseph, *An Address to the Protestant Dissenters* (London, 1786).

The Rights of Dissenters . . . in Relation . . . to English Catholics (Birmingham, 1789).

Blackburne, Francis (ed.), *A Collection of Letters and Essays in Favour of Public Liberty*, 3 Vols. (London, 1774).

Four Discourses (Newcastle-upon-Tyne, 1775).

Memoirs of Thomas Hollis, 2 Vols. (London, 1780).

Proposals for an Application to Parliament for Relief in Subscription . . . (London, 1771).

Reflections on the Fate of a Petition for Relief . . . (London, 1772).

A Sermon Preached on Christmas Day, 1753 (London, 1754).

Blackstone, Sir William, *Commentaries on the Laws of England* (London, 1769), Vol. IV.

A Reply to Dr. Priestley's Remarks on the Fourth Volume of the Commentaries . . . (London, 1769).

Blair, Patrick, *Thoughts on Nature and Religion* (Cork, 1774).

Blennerhaysett, Thomas, *A Sermon Preach'd at Patching in Sussex* (London, 1715).

Botwell, John, *A Sermon preach'd to prove the Dissenters . . . ought to Conform to the Church of England* (London, 1711).

Bourn, Benjamin, *A Sure Guide to Hell* (London, 1750).

Bourn, Samuel, *An Answer to the Remarks of an Unknown Clergyman . . .* (London, 1749).

A Vindication of the Principles and Practices of Protestant Dissenters (London, 1747).

Bradberry, David, *A Letter to Edward Jeffries, Esq.,* (London, 1789).

Bradbury, Thomas, *An Answer to the Reproaches Cast on those Dissenting Ministers who subscribed their Belief of the Eternal Trinity* (London, 1719).
    The Ass or the Serpent (London, 1712).
    Establishment of the Kingdom in the Hand of Solomon (London, 1716).
    The Lawfulness of Resisting Tyrants (London, 1713).
    Twenty-Eight Sermons concerning Offences (London, 1720).
Bristow, William, *Cursory Reflections on the . . . Expediency of Repealing the Test and Corporation Acts* (London, 1790).
Britannicus (Pseud.), *Friendly Admonitions to the Inhabitants of Great Britain* (London, 1758).
Brown, John, *An Estimate of the Manners and Principles of the Times* (London, 1757).
    Thoughts on Civil Liberty, on Licentiousness and Faction (London, 1765).
Brown, William Lawrence, *An Essay on the Folly of Scepticism . . .* (London, 1788).
    The Spirit of the Times Considered (London, 1793).
Browne, Simon, *A Fit Rebuke to . . . Mr. Woolston's Fifth Discourse . . .* (London, 1732).
    Some Remarks upon a Late Pamphlet . . . (London, 1716).
Buckridge, William, *A Letter . . . in which Occasional Conformists are Proved Guilty of Schism and Hypocrisy* (London, 1704).
Burdett, Charles, *A Sermon Preach'd before . . . the Deputy-Governor of . . . the Levant Company* (London, 1724).
Burke, Edmund, *An Appeal from the New to the Old Whigs* (London, 1791).
    On Oeconomical Reform (London, 1780).
    Reflections on the Revolution in France (London, 1790).
    Speech at the Guildhall in Bristol (London, 1780).

Thoughts on the Cause of the Present Discontents (London, 1770).

Two Letters on the Proposal for a Peace with the Regicide Directory of France (London, 1796).

Burnet, Gilbert, *A Charge to the Clergy . . . of Salisbury* (London, 1704).

A History of My Own Time, 6 Vols. (Oxford, 1823 ed.).

An Enquiry into the Measures of Submission to the Supream Authority (London, 1689).

Calamy, Edmund, *Comfort and Counsel to Protestant Dissenters* (London, 1712).

A Defence of Moderate Nonconformity (London, 1703).

An Historical Account of My Own Life, 2 Vols. J. T. Rutt ed. (London, 1830).

Repeal of the Act against Occasional Conformity Considr'd (London, 1717).

Candid Thoughts on the Late Application . . . to Parliament (London, 1772).

The Case of Dissenters and Others in Office with Respect to the Laws now in Force (London, 1712).

The Case of English Catholic Dissenters (London, 1789).

The Case of Moderation and Occasional Communion (London, 1705).

The Case of Toleration Recognized (London, 1702).

Chandler, Samuel, *The Case of Subscription . . . Calmly and Impartially Review'd* (London, 1748).

The Dispute Better Adjusted (London, 1732).

The History of Persecution (London, 1736).

The Notes of the Church Considered (London, 1735).

A Vindication of the Christian Religion (London, 1725).

The Character of Ecclesiastics (London, 1763).

A Charge to Englishmen (London, 1768).

Christian Liberty Asserted in Opposition to Protestant Popery . . . (London, 1719).

Christianity without Persecution (London, 1719).
Chubb, Thomas, *Three Tracts* (London, 1727).
  Two Enquiries (London, 1717).
The Church of England Man's Memorial; or the History of Comprehension and Toleration (London, 1718).
The Church of England Vindicated (London, 1739).
The Claims of Church Authority Considered and the Rights of Private Judgment Defended (London, 1749).
The Clergyman's Petition for Repeal of the Sacramental Test (London, 1736).
Cobbett, William, *Parliamentary History*, Vols. VI, IX, XIV, XVII, XX, XXIX (London, 1808–1810).
Cockman, Thomas, *Two Sermons* (Oxford, 1732).
Cocks, Sir Richard, *The Church of England Secur'd . . .* (London, 1722).
Cokayne, William, *A Sermon Preached before the Rt. Hon. the Lord Mayor . . .* (London, 1750).
Colebrooke, Sir George, *A Letter to a Nobleman* (London, 1790).
A Collection of the Resolutions Passed at Meetings of the Clergy of the Church of England . . . (London, 1790).
Collins, Charles, *Howell and Hoadly* (London, 1717).
Considerations upon War and Religion (London, 1761).
Conybeare, John, *The Case of Subscription to Articles of Religion Consider'd* (Oxford, 1725).
Cooper, Thomas, *A Letter to the Rt. Hon. Edmund Burke* (London, 1790).
  A Reply to Mr. Burke's Invective (London, 1792).
A Country Curate's Observations (London, 1790).
Courtney, John, *Philosophical Reflections on the Late Revolution in France and the Conduct of Dissenters in England* (London, 1790).
Coxe, William, *A Letter to the Revd. Richard Price* (London, 1790).

Cursory Animadversions upon the Free and Candid Disquisitions (London, 1753).

Dalrymple, Alexander, *Letter to a Friend on the Test Act* (London, 1790).

The Danger of a Rash and Unreasonable Application (London, 1732).

The Danger of Repealing the Test Act (London, 1790).

The Dangerous Consequences of Repealing the Sacramental Test at this Time (London, 1732).

Davis, Benjamin, *Human Liberty Philosophically Consider'd* (Canterbury, 1733).

Dawson, Benjamin, *A Free and Candid Disquisition on Religious Establishments* (London, 1770).

The Debate in the House of Commons on Mr. Beaufoy's Motion for Repeal of Such Parts of the Test and Corporation Acts as Affect the Protestant Dissenters, on Friday, the Eighth of May, 1789 (London, 1789).

Debate on the Repeal of the Test and Corporation Act in the House of Commons, March 28th, 1787 (London, 1787).

The Debate in the House of Commons on the Repeal of the Test and Corporation Acts March 2nd, 1790 (London, 1790).

De Coetlogan, Charles Edward, *The Test of Truth, Piety, and Allegiance* (London, 1790).

A Defence of the Act of Parliament . . . for Relief of Roman Catholics (London, 1780).

A Defence of the Private Academies (London, 1714).

A Defence of the Lord Bishop of St. David's (London, 1729).

Defoe, Daniel, *The Case of Dissenters* (London, 1703).

The Coffee-House Preachers (London, 1706).

Enquiry into Occasional Conformity (London, 1697).

An Essay towards Real Moderation (London, 1716).

A Letter to the Dissenters (London, 1713).

More Short Ways with Dissenters (London, 1704).

A New Test of the Church of England's Loyalty (London, 1702).

Party Tyranny (London, 1705).

Sincerity of the Dissenters Vindicated (London, 1705).

A Tour through the Whole Island of Great Britain, 4 Vols. (London, 1738).

Delaune, William, *Martyrdom Sermon Preach'd before the House of Commons* (London, 1703).

Derham, William, *Physio-Theology or a Demonstration of the Being and Attributes of God from his Works of Creation* (London, 1713, 12th ed. 1754).

Disney, John, *An Arranged Catalogue . . . of Publications . . . relating to the Enlargement of Toleration . . .* (London, 1790).

A Letter to the Most Reverend Lord Archbishop of Canterbury on the Present Opposition to any Further Reformation (London, 1774).

The Works and Memoirs of Dr. John Jebb, 3 Vols. (London, 1787).

Dissenters No Schismatics (London, 1714).

A Dissuasive from Party and Religious Animosities (London, 1736).

Doddridge, Philip, *The Absurdity and Iniquity of Persecution for Conscience Sake* (London, 1736).

A Course of Lectures . . . in Pneumatology, Ethics, and Divinity (London, 1763).

Free Thoughts on the Most Probable Means of Reviving the Dissenting Interest (London, 1730).

Dodwell, Henry, *Occasional Communion* (London, 1705).

Christianity Not Founded on Argument (London, 1743).

Douglas, John, *Martyrdom Sermon . . . before the House of Lords* (London, 1790).

The Downfall of Bigotry (London, 1739).

Drummond, George William, *On the Necessity of an Established Order in the Church* (London, 1790).

Duncan, John, *An Address to the Rational Advocates for the Church of England* (London, 1769).

Durnford, Charles, and East, Edward Hyde, *Reports of Cases Argued and Determined in the Court of King's Bench* (London, 1787–1790), 4 Vols.

Dyer, George, *Memoirs of the Life and Writings of Robert Robinson* (London, 1796).

Earle, Jabez, *A Sermon Preach'd at Hanover Street* (London, 1725).

Edwards, Thomas, *The Indispensible Duty of Contending for the Faith* (Cambridge, 1766).

Two Dissertations (Cambridge, 1766).

Eccles, Samuel, *National Sins the Cause of National Judgments* (London, 1750).

Eden, Robert, *The Connexion of Publick and Private Happiness* (London, 1743).

Ellys, Anthony, *A Plea for the Sacramental Test* (London, 1736).

Enfield, William, *An Essay towards the History of Liverpool* (London, 1774).

Funeral Sermon for the Reverend John Aikin (Warrington, 1781).

A Sermon on the Centennial Commemoration of the Revolution (London, 1788).

England, John, *The Perplexity of Protestant Dissenters Consider'd* (London, 1712).

Englefield, Sir Henry Charles, *A Letter . . . with Observations on Anti-Roman Catholic Penal Laws* (London, 1790).

An Enquiry concerning Superstition (London, 1730).

Episcopal Opinions on the Test and Corporation Acts, delivered in the House of Peers in December, 1718 (London, 1790).

An Equal Capacity in the Subjects of Great Britain for Civil Employment the Best Security to the Government and the Protestant Religion (London, 1717).

An Essay on the Origin, Character, and Views of Protestant Dissenters (London, 1790).

Evans, Caleb, *Funeral Sermon for the Reverend John Newton* (London, 1790).

Sermon to the Bristol Education Society (London, 1775).

Evans, Theophilus, *A History of Modern Enthusiasm* (London, 1752).

Fawcett, Benjamin, *The Encouraging Prospect that Religious Liberty will be Enlarged* (Shrewsbury, 1773).

A Few Strictures on the Confessional (London, 1775).

Fleetwood, William, *An Answer to the Bishop of Bangor* (London, 1719).

Reasons against the Bill now pending in the House of Commons (London, 1719).

Fleming, Caleb, *An Answer to the 'Dispute Adjusted'* (London, 1732).

An Apology for Protestant Dissent (London, 1755).

The Claims of the Church of England Seriously Examined (London, 1764).

Comment on Warburton's 'Alliance' (London, 1748).

The Devout Laugh (London, 1750).

Religion not in the Magistrate's Province (London, 1773).

Remarks on Mr. Thomas Chubb's 'Vindication' (London, 1739).

Foster, James, *An Answer to Dr. Stebbing's Second Letter on the Subject of Heresy* (London, 1736).

Foster, Nathaniel, *The Establishment of the Church of England Defended upon the Principles of Religious Liberty* (London, 1770).

Fothergill, Thomas, *The Qualifications and Advantages of Religious Trust in Times of Danger* (Oxford, 1757).

The Foundations of Religious Liberty Explained (London, 1755).

Fownes, Joseph, *An Enquiry into the Principles of Religious Toleration*, 2nd ed. (Shrewsbury, 1773).

Fox, Charles, James, *A Letter to the Worthy and Independent Electors of Westminster* (London, 1793).

Two Speeches Delivered in the House of Commons on Tuesday, the 2nd of March, 1790 (London, 1790).

Free Thoughts upon the Book of Common Prayer (London, 1771).

Frost, Richard, *Funeral Sermon for Philip Doddridge* (London, 1752).

Furneaux, Philip, *An Essay on Toleration* (London, 1773).

Letters to the Honourable Mr. Justice Blackstone (London, 1770).

Gardner, William, *The Principles of Religion Recommended* (London, 1726).

Geddes, Alexander, *Letter to the Archbishops and Bishops of England* (London, 1790).

Gibbons, Thomas, *Objections against the Application to the Legislature for Relief for Protestant Dissenting Ministers* (London, 1773).

Gibson, Edmund, *The Dispute Adjusted* (London, 1732).

Three Pastoral Letters (London, 1732).

Gordon, Thomas, *The Character of an Independent Whig*, 2d ed. (London, 1719).

A Sermon Preached before the Learned Society of Lincoln's Inn (London, 1733).

Gough, John, *A History of the People Called Quakers*, 4 Vols. (Dublin, 1790).

Gough, Strickland, *An Enquiry into the Causes of the Decay of the Dissenting Interest* (London, 1730).

Grafton, Henry Augustus, Third Duke, *Autobiography and*

Political Correspondence, ed. by Sir W. Anson (London, 1898).

Graham, William, *A Sermon Preached at Kingston upon Hull* (London, 1759).

Grascome, Samuel, *The Mask of Moderation pull'd off the Foul Face of Occasional Conformity* (London, 1719).

Gray, James, *Reasons for Abrogating the Corporation and Test Acts* (London, 1718).

Gray, Zachary, *The Schismatics Delineated* (London, 1739).

Grey, Richard, *The Miserable and Distracted State of Religion in England upon the Downfall of the Church Establishment* (London, 1736).

Grosvenor, Benjamin, *Cruelty in Religion No Service to God* (London, 1725).

An Essay on Bigotry (London, 1718).

An Essay on the Christian Name (London, 1720).

Persecution and Cruelty in . . . the Romish Church (London, 1735).

A Sermon Preach'd at Crosby Square (London, 1710).

Grove, Henry, *Sermons and Tracts* (London, 1740).

The Wisdom of God the First Spring of Action in Deity (London, 1734).

Haggitt, George, *Observations suggested by Mr. Lofft's History of the Test Act* (London, 1790).

Hales, Stephen, *The Wisdom and Goodness of God in the Formation of Man* (London, 1751).

Half an Hour's Conversation between a Churchman and a Dissenter (London, 1790).

Hall, Robert, *An Apology for the Freedom of the Press and for General Liberty* (London, 1793).

Hallett, Joseph, *Fate and Force* (London, 1732).

Hare, Francis, *Church Authority Vindicated* (London, 1720).

Harries, Solomon, *Practical Influence of Christianity on Believing Minds* (London, 1783).

Harris, William, *Lukewarmness in Religion Represented and Reproved* (London, 1732).

— *Brief Remarks upon 'The Dispute Adjusted'* (London, 1733).

Herne, Thomas, *An Essay on Imposing and Subscribing Articles of Religion* (London, 1719).

— *Preface to Dr. Samuel Werenfels' 'Three Discourses'* (London, 1718).

Heywood, Samuel, *High Church Politics* (London, 1792).

Hinger, William, *Treatise against Occasional Conformity* (London, 1704).

Hints Respectfully Addressed to Members of the House of Commons on the Subject of the Test Laws (London, 1790).

Hoadly, Benjamin, *An Answer to Dr. Hare's Sermon* (London, 1720).

— *The Common Rights of Subjects Defended* (London, 1719).

— *Objections against the Repeal of the Corporation and Test Acts* (London, 1739).

— *Sermons*, 2 Vols. (London, 1754).

Hobhouse, Sir Benjamin, *Thoughts to Dissenters who accept Corporate Offices* (London, 1791).

— *A Treatise on Heresy* (London, 1792).

Hobson, John, *An Appeal to Common Sense* (London, 1790).

Hodge, John, *A Sermon Preached at Little St. Helen's* (London, 1751).

Holden, Samuel, *An Answer to a Letter to Samuel Holden, Esq.* (London, 1732).

Hole, Matthew, *An Antidote against the Poison of Some Late Pamphlets* (Oxford, 1717).

Holliday, John, *The Life of William Late Earl of Mansfield* (London, 1797).

Hood, Robert, *Fourteen Sermons* (London, 1782).

Sermon on the Nature of Christ's Kingdom (London, 1781).
Hooke, John, *Catholicism without Popery* (London, 1704).
Horbery, Matthew, *Animadversions upon a Late Pamphlet* (London, 1735).
Horne, George, *Considerations on the Projected Reformation of the Church of England* (London, 1772).
Horsley, Samuel, *Review of the 'Case of the Protestant Dissenters'* (London, 1790).
An Impartial Account of the Late Transactions of Dissenters (London, 1734).
An Inquiry into the Propriety of Applying to Parliament . . . (London, 1732).
The Interest of England in Relation to Protestant Dissenters (London, 1714).
Jack and Martin, a Poetical Dialogue on the Proposed Repeal (London, 1790).
Jebb, John, *A Letter to Sir William Meredith . . .* (London, 1772).
—— *Letters on the Subject of Subscription . . .* (London, 1772).
Jenyns, Soame, *Free Enquiry into the Nature and Origin of Evil* (London, 1757).
—— *View of the Internal Evidence of the Christian Religion* (London, 1776).
Jesse, William, *Remonstrance Addressed to the Protestant Association* (London, 1780).
Johnson, Samuel, *The False Alarm* (London, 1770).
—— *The Patriot* (London, 1774).
—— *Taxation No Tyranny* (London, 1775).
Junius, *Letters*, Woodfall's ed. (London, 1812).
Keate, William, *A Free Examination of Dr. Price's and Dr. Priestley's Sermons* (London, 1790).

Kippis, Andrew, *A Vindication of the Protestant Dissenting Ministers* (London, 1773).
Knowles, Thomas, *A Dialogue between Hoadly and Sherlock on the Corporation and Test Acts* (London, 1790).
Law, Edmund, *Considerations on the State of the World with Regard to the Theory of Religion* (London, 1745).
Leslie, Charles, *The Wolf Stript of his Shepherd's Cloathing in answer to* ... '*Moderation a Virtue*' ... (London, 1704).
 Principles of Dissenters concerning Toleration and Occasional Conformity (London, 1705).
A Letter to the Protestant Dissenters of All Denominations (London, 1733).
A Letter to the Public Meeting of Friends to the Repeal ... (London, 1790).
A Letter to the Reverend the Dean of Chichester (London, 1716).
A Letter from the Reverend Sir Harry Trelawney (London, 1780).
A Letter to the Reverend John Martin (London, 1790).
A Letter to the Rt. Hon. the Lord Mayor on the Sacramental Qualification ... (London, 1790).
A Letter to the Right Honourable Lord North (London, 1772).
A Letter written by a County Clergyman (London, 1771).
Liberty the Support of Truth and the Natural Property of Mankind (London, 1732).
Lindsey, Theophilus, *Apology on Resigning the Vicarage of Catterick* (London, 1774).
 An Historical View of the State of the Unitarian Doctrine and Worship (London, 1783).
Lobb, Samuel, *Sermon on Benevolence* (London, 1746).
Lobb, Theophilus, *Discourse of Ministerial Education* (London, 1712).
Locke, John, *Works*, 6 Vols. (London, 1823 ed.)

Lofft, Capel, *An History of the Corporation and Test Acts* (London, 1790).
    Observations on a Dialogue on the Actual State of Parliament (London, 1783).
A Look to the Last Century, or the Dissenters weighed in their Own Scales (London, 1790).
Low, Andrew, *A Letter from Scotland* (London, 1708).
Lowman, Moses, *The Danger of the Church Considr'd* (London, 1716).
    Principles of an Occasional Conformist Stated and Defended (London, 1718).
Mackintosh, James, *Vindiciae Galliae* (London, 1791).
Madan, Spencer, *Letter to Dr. Priestley* (London, 1790).
    Principal Claims of the Dissenters Considered (London, 1790).
Mandeville, Bernard, *Free Thoughts on Religion, the Church, and National Happiness* (London, 1729).
Manning, Robert, *The Shortest Way to End Disputes about Religion* (Brussels, 1716).
Martin, John, *A Speech on the Repeal of the Test . . .* (London, 1790).
Mauduit, Israel, *The Case of the Dissenting Ministers* (London, 1772).
Mayo, Henry, *Remarks on the Postscript to 'The Case of the Dissenting Ministers'* (London, 1772).
Mayonnet, John, *The Nature and Grounds of Religious Liberty* (London, 1736).
Milton, John, *A Treatise of Civil Power in Ecclesiastical Causes* (London, 1790 ed.).
Monoux, Louis, *A Sermon Preached at Bishop Stortford . . .* (London, 1751).
Morton, Charles, *An Argument on the Merits of the Test Act* (London, 1717).
Mudge, Zachariah, *Liberty* (London, 1731).

Murrey, Robert, *Liberty without Licentiousness* (London, 1721).
A Narrative of the Case of the Reverend Mr. John Jackson (London, 1736).
A Narrative of the Proceedings of the Protestant Dissenters (London, 1734).
Neal, Daniel, *A Letter to the Reverend Dr. Travis Hare* (London, 1720).
Newton, Thomas, *The Sentiments of a Moderate Man concerning Toleration* (London, 1779).
—— *A Speech Designed for the House of Lords* (London, 1772).
North, Frederick, Lord, *Speeches delivered in the House of Commons against Repeal of the Test* . . . (London, 1790).
Nott, John, *Very Familiar Letters addressed to Dr. Priestley* (London, 1790).
An Objection Drawn from the Act of Union against a Review of the Liturgy . . . (London, 1770).
Observations on the 'Case of the Protestant Dissenters' (London, 1787).
Observations on the Conduct of Protestant Dissenters (London, 1790).
Observations on Dr. Price Revolution Sermon (London, 1790).
Observations on the Present Dispute Concerning the Repeal of the Corporation and Test Acts (London, 1733).
Observations on the Present State of the Dissenting Interest (London, 1731).
Observations Suggested by . . . *Mr. Lofft's 'History'* (Bury St. Edmunds, 1790).
Orpheus, Priest of Nature and Prophet of Infidelity (London, 1781).
Orton, Job, *Memoirs of Philip Doddridge* (London, 1766).
Owen, Charles, *The Dissenters' Claim of Right to Civil Office* (London, 1717).

Owen, Edward, *The Dissenters' Claims Considered* (London, 1790).
Owen, James, *Moderation a Virtue* (London, 1703; 2d ed. 1712).
Owen, John, *Indulgence and Toleration Considered* (London, 1667).
The Pacific Temper of the Priesthood (London, 1795).
Paine, Thomas, *The Rights of Man* (London, 1791).
    The Rights of Man, Part II (London, 1792).
    The Age of Reason (London, 1794).
    The Age of Reason, Part II (London, 1795).
    Letter to Mr. Secretary Dundas (London, 1792).
Paley, William, *Considerations on the Propriety of Requiring a Subscription to Articles of Faith* (London, 1774).
    Principles of Moral and Political Philosophy (London, 1785).
Palmer, John, *Free Thoughts on the Inconsistency of Conforming to any Religious Test as a Condition of Toleration* (London, 1779).
Palmer, Samuel, *A Defence of the Dissenters' Education in their Private Academies* (London, 1703).
Parker, William, *The Grounds of Submission to Government* (Oxford, 1752).
    A Sermon Preached before the Honourable House of Commons (London, 1757).
Parry, William, *Remarks on the Resolutions Passed at a Meeting . . . of the County of Warwick . . .* (Birmingham, 1790).
    Thoughts on . . . Penal Statutes (London, 1791).
Pearce, Samuel, *The Oppressive, Unjust, and Prophane Nature and Tendency of the Corporation and Test Acts* (Birmingham, 1790).
Pecard, Peter, *Visitation Sermon* (Cambridge, 1772).
Peckwell, Henry, *The Account of an Appeal from a Summary*

Conviction on the Conventicle Act to the Hon. Court of King's Bench (London, 1787).

Peirce, James, *Christ's Kingdom Advanced by Peace* (London, 1723).

 Dissenters' Reasons for Opposing Persecution (London, 1718).

 Interests of the Whigs with relation to the Test Act (London, 1718).

 Reflections on Sherlock's 'Vindication' (London, 1718).

Percival, John, Second Earl Egmont, *A Full and Fair Discussion of the Pretensions of the Dissenters* (London, 1790).

Petit, Peter, *Natural Occasions of Terror considered as International Warnings of Providence* (London, 1756).

Petre, Robert Edward, Lord, *A Letter to the Rt. Revd. Dr. Horsley* (London, 1790).

Pickering, Roger, *Reflections on Sentimental Differences in Points of Faith* (London, 1752).

Pickering, Thomas, *A Sermon Preach'd before the Rt. Hon. the Lord Mayor . . .* (London, 1750).

Pitt, William, *A Speech in the House of Commons on Tuesday the Second of March, 1790* (London, 1790).

Political Logic Displayed, or a Key to the 'Thoughts on Civil Liberty, Licentiousness, and Faction' (London, 1765).

Pope, John, *Two Sermons* (London, 1792).

Potter, John, *A Charge to the Clergy of the Diocese of Oxford* (London,

 A Defence of the Late Charge deliver'd to the Clergy of the Diocese of Oxford (London,

A Presb'n Getting on Horseback, or the Dissenters Run Mad in Politics (London, 1717).

The Present Dispute between the Dissenters and the Church of England (London, 1733).

The Present Exigencies of Government Consider'd (London, 1719).

Price, Richard, *Additional Observations on the Nature and Value of Civil Liberty and the War in America* (London, 1777).
    A Discourse on the Love of our Country (London, 1789).
    Sermon on the Evidence of a Future Period of Improvement in the State of Mankind (London, 1787).

Priestley, Joseph, *An Essay on the First Principles of Government* (London, 1768).
    A History of the Corruptions of Christianity (London, 1782).
    On the Importance of Free Enquiry in Matters of Religion (London, 1785).
    A Letter of Advice to those Dissenters who Conduct the Application to Parliament . . . (London, 1773).
    A Letter to Dr. Blackstone (St. James' Chronicle, London, 10 October, 1769).
    Letters to the Right Honourable Edmund Burke (Birmingham, 1791).
    A Letter to the Right Honourable William Pitt (London, 1787).
    The Present State of Liberty in Great Britain and Her Colonies (London, 1769).
    Remarks on Some Paragraphs in the Fourth Volume of Dr. Blackstone's 'Commentaries' (London, 1769).
    A View of the Principles and Conduct of the Protestant Dissenters . . . (London, 1769).
    Works, J. T. Rutt, ed. (London, 1823).

Proast, Jonas, *The Argument of the Letter concerning Toleration briefly Considr'd and Answer'd* (Oxford, 1690).

Pye, Benjamin, *Five Letters on Several Subjects Religious and Historical* (London, 1769).

Pyle, Thomas, *An Answer to Mr. Stebbing's Remarks concerning Religious Sincerity and Church Authority* (London, 1719).

Queries concerning the Reasonableness of Repealing the Corporation and Test Acts as Far as they Relate to the Protestant Dissenters (London, 1732).

The Question Fairly Stated whether Now is not the Time to do Justice to the Friends of the Government . . . (London, 1717).

Radcliffe, Ebenezer, *A Sermon Preached to a Congregation of Protestant Dissenters at Crutched Friars* (London, 1772).

Two Letters addressed to the Right Reverend Prelates who a Second Time Rejected the Dissenters' Bill (London, 1773).

The Real Seeker (London, 1769).

Reasons for Applying to Parliament . . . (London, 1732).

Reasons for Enabling Protestant Dissenters to Bear Public Offices (London, 1717).

Reasons Offered against Pushing for Repeal . . . (London, 1732).

Reasons Offered for Unanimously Pushing for Repeal . . . (London, 1732).

Reasons Why the Bill in Parliament for the Relief of Dissenting Ministers, Tutors, and Schoolmasters should Pass in the Present Form (London, 1779).

Rees, Abraham, *Two Sermons Preached at Cambridge on Occasion of the Death of the Reverend Robert Robinson* (London, 1790).

Reflections upon Mr. Bradbury's Late Libel Intitled 'The Ass and the Serpent' (London, 1713).

Reflections upon the Corporation and Test Acts (London, 1732).

Remarks on Dr. Sherlock's Answer to Mr. Sykes (London, 1718).

Remarks on the Letter [by Daniel Defoe] to the Dissenters (London, 1714).

Removal of the Sacramental Test (London, 1717).

A Reply to the Dean of Chichester's 'Vindication' (London, 1718).

Resolutions of the Society of Protestant Dissenting Ministers Meeting at the New York Coffee House (London, 1773).

A Review of the Pamphlet entitled A Discourse on the Love of our Country (London, 1790).

Reynolds, George, *An Historical Essay upon the Government of the Church of England* (London, 1743).

Reynolds, Thomas, *A Discourse Preach'd on the Fifth of November* (London, 1712).

A Discourse Preach'd at Little St. Helen's (London, 1714).

Richardson, John, *Christian Liberty and Love Represented and Earnestly Recommended* (London, 1752).

The Right of the Committee considered . . . (London, 1734).

Rights of Discussion, or a Vindication of Dissenters of Every Denomination . . . (London, 1799).

The Rights and Liberties of Subjects Vindicated (London, 1732).

Robinson, Robert, *Arcana, or the Principles of the Late Petitioners to Parliament for Relief in the Matter of Subscription* (Cambridge, 1774).

A Discourse on Sacramental Tests (London, 1788).

The General Doctrine of Toleration applied to the Particular Case of Free Communion (London, 1781).

A Plan of Lectures on the Principles of Nonconformity, 6th ed. (Nottingham, 1797).

Robles, Matthew, *Bigotry, Superstition, and Hypocrisy worse than Atheism* (London, 1742).

Roe, Samuel, *Enthusiasm Detected and Defeated* (London, 1768).

A Serious Important Letter to the Right Reverend Learned Bishops and Clergy of the Church of England (Cambridge, 1768).

Another Pertinent and Curious Letter humbly offered to

the Public in Favour of a Revisal and Amendment of our Liturgy (Cambridge, 1768).

Sacheverell, Henry, *Answer to the Articles of Impeachment exhibited against him by the Honourable House of Commons* (London, 1710).
   The Perils of False Brethren both in Church and State (London, 1709).
   The Rights of the Church of England Asserted and Proved (London, 1705).

Sayer, Edward, *Observations on Dr. Price's Revolution Sermon* (London, 1790).

Scott, John, *The Constitution Defended* (London, 1770).

A Scourge for the Dissenters, or Nonconformity Unmasked (London, 1790).

Seagrave, Robert, *An Answer to the Reverend Dr. Trapp's Four Sermons against Mr. Whitefield* (London, 1739).
   Observations upon the Conduct of the Clergy in Relation to the Thirty-Nine Articles (London, 1738).
   The Principles of Liberty (London, 1755).
   The True Protestant (London, 1751).

Sewell, Sir Thomas, *The Case of the Dissenters as it Stands upon the Corporation and Test Acts with Regard to Corporation Offices* (London, 1739).

Sharp, Granville, *Declaration of the People's Natural Right to a Share in the Legislature* (London, 1774).

Sharp, Richard, *A Letter . . . to the Friends of Repeal* (London, 1790).

Sharp, William, *The Protestant, or the Doctrine of Universal Liberty Asserted* (London, 1766).

Shepherd, Richard, *The Requisition of Subscription to Thirty-Nine Articles and Liturgy of the Church of England not Inconsistent with Christian Liberty* (London, 1771).

Sherlock, Thomas, *The History of the Test Act* (London, 1732).

A Vindication of the Corporation and Test Acts (London, 1718).
A Short Examination of the Reasons for Repeal (London, 1790).
A Short View of Popery (London, 1767).
A Short Way with Prophaneness and Impiety (London, 1730).
Shylock, R. (Pseud.), *The Rabbi's Lamentation upon the Repeal of the Jew Act* (London, 1768).
Silvester, Tipping, *A Critical Dissertation . . . wherein Mr. Foster's Notion of Heresy is Considered and Confuted* (London, 1735).
Smith, Jeremiah, *The Magistrate and the Christian . . . being Memoirs of the Life and character of Sir Thomas Abney* (London, 1722).
Smith, Joseph, *Some Remarks on the Resolutions which were formed at the Meeting of the Archdeaconry of Chester* (London, 1790).
Smyth, George, *The Proper Regulation of Religious Zeal* (London, 1729).
South, R., *Comprehension and Toleration Considered* (London, 1716).
Stebbing, Henry, *An Appeal to the Word of God for the Terms of Christian Salvation* (London, 1720).
    An Essay concerning Civil Government as it stands Related to Religion (London, 1724).
    A True State of the Controversy with Mr. Foster on the Subject of Heresy (London, 1736).
Steele, Richard, *A Letter to a Member of Parliament concerning the Bill for Preventing the Growth of Schism* (London, 1714).
Stennett, Samuel, *Considerations on the Propriety of Protestant Dissenting Ministers acceding to a Declaration of their Belief in the Holy Scriptures* (London, 1779).
Sturges, John, *Considerations on the Present State of the*

Church Establishment (London, 1779).

Reflections on the Principles and Institutions of Popery (Winchester, 1799).

A Summary of the Penal Laws relating to Nonjurors, Papists, Popish Recusants, and Nonconformists (London, 1716).

A Summary View of the Laws relating to Subscription (London, 1771).

Swift, Joanthan, *Advantages Proposed by Repealing the Sacramental Test Impartially Considered* (Dublin, 1732).

Tracts on Repeal (London, 1790).

Sykes, Arthur Ashley, *The Corporation and Test Acts shewn to be of No Importance to the Church of England* (London, 1736).

The Reasonableness of Applying for Repeal or Explanation of the Corporation and Test Acts (London, 1736).

Synge, Edward, *The Case of Toleration consider'd with respect both to Religion and Civil Government* (Dublin, 1725) (London, 1726).

Taylor, John, *The Glory of any House erected for Public Worship and the True Principles . . . of Protestant Dissenters* (London, 1756).

Temple, Anthony, *Visitation Sermon* (London, 1766).

Test against Test, or a Review of Measures proposed in Resolutions of the Dissenters to remove all Tests by imposing one of their own . . . (London, 1790).

Thomas, Benjamin, *A Letter to Shute, Lord Bishop of Llandaff* (London, 1774).

The Political and Religious Conduct of Dissenters Vindicated (Marlborough, 1777).

Thoughts on the Corporation and Test Acts (London, 1732).

Tillotson, John, *A Sermon Preach'd . . . at Cripple Gate* (London, 1709 ed.).

Tindal, Matthew, *The Defection Considered and the Designs*

of those who divided the Friends of the Government set in a True Light (London, 1717).

Toland, John, *The State Anatomy of Great Britain* (London, 1717).

——— *The Second Part of the State Anatomy . . .* (London, 1717).

Toulmin, Joshua, *Letters to the Bishops on the Application for Repeal* (London, 1789).

——— *Letters to the Rev. John Sturges in Answer to his 'Considerations on the Present State of the Church Establishment'* (London, 1782).

——— *Two Letters on the Late Application to Parliament* (London, 1774).

Towers, Joseph, *A Dialogue between Two Gentlemen concerning the Late Application to Parliament for Relief in the Matter of Suscription* (London, 1772).

——— *On Juries in Trials for Libels* (London, 1784).

——— *A Letter to the Reverend Mr. John Wesley* (London, 1771).

——— *A Letter to the Reverend Dr. Nowell* (London, 1772).

——— *A Letter to Dr. Samuel Johnson* (London, 1775).

——— *Observations on Public Liberty, Patriotism, Ministerial Despotism, and National Grievances* (London, 1769).

——— *Thoughts on National Insanity* (London, 1797).

——— *Tracts on Political and Other Subjects*, 3 Vols. (London, 1796).

——— *A Vindication of the Political Principles of Mr. Locke* (London, 1782).

Towgood, Micaijah, *The Dissenters' Apology* (London, 1739).

Trenchard, John and Gordon, Thomas, *Cato's Letters*, 4 Vols. (London, 1724).

Trist, Jeremiah, *Historical Memoirs of Religious Dissension* (London, 1790).

A True Churchman's Reasons for Repealing the Corporation and Test Acts (London, 1732).

Tucker, Josiah, *An Apology for the Present Church of England as by Law Established* (Gloucester, 1772).

Four Letters on Important National Subjects . . . (London, 1783).

Letters to the Rev. Dr. Kippis . . . (London, 1773).

A Treatise concerning Civil Government (London, 1781).

Tunstall, James, *A Sermon Preached before the Honourable House of Commons* (London, 1746).

Usher, James, *A Free Examination of the Common Methods employed to prevent the Growth of Popery* (London, 1767).

Vaughan, Benjamin, *A Collection of Testimonies in Favour of Religious Liberty* (London, 1790).

Venn, Richard, *A Sermon Preached before the Right Honourable the Lord Mayor* . . . (London, 1737).

A Vindication of the Protestant Dissenters . . . (London, 1734).

A Vindication of the Test Act (London, 1736).

Wakefield, Gilbert, *Address to the Inhabitants of Nottingham* (London, 1789).

Cursory Reflections . . . *on Repeal* . . . (London, 1790).

Defence . . . *delivered in the Court of King's Bench* (London, 1799).

An Examination of the 'Age of Reason' by Thomas Paine (London, 1794).

A Reply to the Letter of Edmund Burke, Esq. . . . (London, 1794).

A Reply to Thomas Paine's Second Part of the 'Age of Reason' (London, 1795).

The Spirit of Christianity and the Spirit of the Times Compared (London, 1794).

Walker, George, *The Dissenters Plea* (Birmingham, 1790).

Sermons, 2 Vols. (London, 1790).

Warburton, William, *The Alliance between Church and State* (London, 1736).

Wallis, William, *A Sermon Preach'd at the Guildford Assizes* (London, 1730).

Walpole, Horace, *Memoirs of the Last Ten Years of the Reign of George the Second*, 2d ed. 3 Vols. (London, 1847).

Wansey, Henry, *A Letter to the Bishop of Salisbury* (London, 1798).

Waterland, Daniel, *The Case of Anti-Subscription Considered and Several Pleas and Excuses for it Particularly Examined and Confuted* (Cambridge, 1721).

The Religious Education of Children ... (London, 1723).

Watson, John, *Moderation, or a Candid Disposition toward those that Differ from us Recommended* (London, 1751).

Watson, Richard, *An Apology for the Bible* (London, 1796).

An Apology for Christianity (London, 1776).

A Charge to the Clergy of Llandaff (London, 1792).

A Letter addressed to the Archbishop of Canterbury (London, 1783).

The Principles of Revolution Vindicated (London, 1776).

Webster, James, *An Essay upon Toleration* (London, 1703).

Webster, William, *The Church of England Vindicated* (London, 1735).

Wesley, John, *A Calm Address to the Inhabitants of England* (London, 1777).

A Defence of the Protestant Association (London, 1780).

A Preservative Against Unsettled Notions in Religion (London, 1770).

Free Thoughts on the Present State of Public Affairs (London, 1771).

Wesley, Samuel, *A Reply to Mr. Palmer's Vindication of the Dissenters* (London, 1707).

Weston, Edward, *A Letter to the Right Reverend the Lord Bishop of London* (London, 1756).

Some Reflections upon the Question Relating to the Naturalization of Jews . . . (London, 1754).

Wilberforce, William, *A Practical View of the Prevailing System of Professed Christians . . . Contrasted with Real Christianity* (London, 1797).

Williams, Daniel, *An Enquiry into the Present Duty of Protestant Dissenters* (London, 1712).

Williams, David, *Essays on Public Worship, Patriotism and Projects of Reformation* (London, 1773).

A Letter to the Body of Protestant Dissenters and to Protestant Dissenting Ministers of all Denominations (London, 1777).

Williams, Edward, *An Account of the Rotheram Independent Academy* (London, 1797).

Williams, John, *A Serious and Earnest Address to Gentlemen . . . who opposed the Late Application* . . . (London, 1773).

Williams, Joseph, *The Principle Causes of Some Late Divisions in Dissenting Congregations* . . . (London, 1740).

Williams, William, *A Letter to the Right Reverend the Lord Bishop of Bangor* (London, 1720).

Wilton, Samuel, *An Apology for the Renewal of an Application to Parliament by the Protestant Dissenting Ministers* (London, 1773).

A Review of Some of the Articles of the Church of England to which a Subscription is Required (London, 1774).

Witherspoon, John, *Ecclesiastical Characteristics* (Glasgow, 1753).

A Serious Apology for the 'Ecclesiastical Characteristics' (Edinburgh, 1763).

Wood, John, *Institutes of Ecclesiastical and Civil Polity* (London, 1773).

Wood, William, *Two Sermons Preached at Mill-Hill Chapel* (Leeds, 1788).

Worthington, Hugh, *A Sermon . . . delivered . . . to the Supporters of a New Academical Institution among Protestant Dissenters* (London, 1789).
Wright, Samuel, *The Character of a Protestant* (London, 1716).
    The Church in Perils . . . or the Danger of the Church from her Pretended Friends but Secret Enemies . . . (London, 1733).
    A Sermon Preach'd on the Fifth of November (London, 1719).
    Two Sermons Preach'd at Black Fryars (London, 1712).
Wyvill, Christopher, *A Defence of Dr. Price and the Reformers of England* (London, 1793).
    Political Papers, 6 Vols. (London, 1794–1806).
    A Sermon Preached . . . at Kelvedon (London, 1772).
    Thoughts on our Articles of Religion with respect to their Utility to the State (London, 1771).

SECONDARY AUTHORITIES

Abbey, C. J., and Overton, J. H., *The English Church in the Eighteenth Century*, 2 Vols., rev. ed. (London, 1887).
Addison, W. G., *Religious Equality in Modern England, 1714–1914* (London, 1944).
Amherst, J. W., *A History of Catholic Emancipation*, 2 Vols. (London, 1886).
Andrews, Alexander, *The History of British Journalism*, 2 Vols. (London, 1859).
Bainton, R. H., *The Travail of Religious Liberty* (Philadelphia, 1951).
Bates, M. Searle, *Religious Liberty, an Inquiry* (New York and London, 1945).
Bebb, E. D., *Nonconformity and Social and Economic Life* (London, 1935).

Becker, Carl L., *The Heavenly City of the Eighteenth Century Philosophers* (New Haven, 1932).

Beckett, J. C., *Protestant Dissent in Ireland, 1687–1780* (London, 1948).

Bevan, J. O., *The Birth and Growth of Toleration* (London, 1909).

Bogue, David, *A History of the Dissenters from the Revolution to the Year 1808,* 2d ed. by James Bennett (London, 1833).

Book, Benjamin, *The History of Religious Liberty,* Vol. II (London, 1820).

Bourne, H. R. Fox, *The Life of John Locke,* 2 Vols. (London, 1876).

Braithwaite, W. C., *The Second Period of Quakerism* (London, 1919).

Burn, Richard, *The Ecclesiastical Law,* 9th ed., 4 Vols. (London, 1842).

Burton, E. H., *The Life and Times of Bishop Challoner,* 2 Vols. (London, 1909).

Cardwell, Edward, *Synodalia: a Collection of Articles, Canons, and Proceedings of Convocation in the Province of Canterbury from the Year 1547 to the Year 1717,* 2 Vols. (Oxford, 1842).

Clark, H. W., *A History of English Nonconformity,* 2 Vols. (London, 1913).

Cobban, Alfred, *Edmund Burke and the Revolt against the Eighteenth Century* (London, 1929).

Colligan, J. H., *The Arian Movement in England* (Manchester, 1913).

Eighteenth Century Nonconformity (London, 1915).

Coomer, Duncan, *English Dissent under the Early Hanoverians* (London, 1946).

Costin, W. C., and Watson, J. S., *The Law and Working of the Constitution: Documents 1660–1914,* Vol. I (London, 1952).

Coxe, William, *Memoirs of the Administration of the Right Honourable Henry Pelham,* 2 Vols. (London, 1829).
  Memoirs of the Life and Administration of Sir Robert Walpole, 4 Vols. (London, 1816).
Cragg, G. R., *From Puritanism to the Age of Reason* (Cambridge, 1950).
Cranfield, G. A., *The Development of the Provincial Newspaper, 1700-1760* (Unpublished Cambridge Ph.D., 1952).
Dale, R. W., *A History of English Congregationalism,* 2nd ed. (London, 1907).
Davies, Arthur P., *Isaac Watts* (London, 1948).
Dicey, A. V., *Introduction to the Study of the Law of the Constitution* (London, 1946 ed).
Dodge, Guy H., *The Political Theory of the Huguenots of the Dispersion* (New York, 1947).
Drysdale, A. H., *A History of the Presbyterians in England* (London, 1889).
Evans, Arthur W., *Warburton and the Warburtonians* (London, 1932).
Every, George, *The High Church Party, 1688-1718* (London, 1956).
Figgis, J. N., *Churches in the Modern State* (London, 1914).
  "Political Thought in the Sixteenth Century," *The Cambridge Modern History,* Vol. III (Cambridge, 1904), pp. 736-769.
Fitzmaurice, Lord, *Life of William Earl of Shelburne,* 2 Vols. (London, 1912).
Gee, Henry, and Hardy, John, *Documents Illustrative of English Church History* (London, 1896).
Gill, Conrad, *A History of Birmingham,* Vol. I. (Oxford, 1952).
Grant, James, *The Newspaper Press,* 3 Vols. (London, 1871).
Griffiths, Olive M., *Religion and Learning* (Cambridge, 1935).
Gwatkin, H. M., *Church and State in England to the Death of Queen Anne* (London, 1917).

"Religious Toleration in England," *The Cambridge Modern History*, Vol. V (Cambridge, 1908), pp. 324–337.

Halley, Robert, *Lancashire, its Puritanism and Nonconformity* (Manchester, 1869).

Hans, Nicholas, *New Trends in Education in the Eighteenth Century* (London, 1951).

Hanson, Laurence, *Government and the Press, 1695–1763* (London, 1936).

Hardwick, Charles, *A History of the Articles of Religion of the Church of England* (Cambridge, 1851).

Hazard, Paul, *European Thought in the Eighteenth Century* J. Lewis May trans. (London, 1954).

Hearnshaw, F. J. C., ed., *The Social and Political Ideas of Some English Thinkers of the Augustan Age* (London, 1928).

Henderson, A. J., *London and the National Government* (Durham, N.C., 1945).

Hertling, Georg Freiherrn von, *John Locke und die Schule von Cambridge* (Freiburg im Breisgau, 1892).

Hodgson, Robert, *The Life of Bishop Porteus* (London, 1811).

Holdsworth, W. A., *A History of English Law*, Vol. X (London, 1938).

Hore, A. H., *The Church in England from William III to Victoria*, 2 Vols. (London, 1886).

Hunt, John, *Religious Thought in England from the Reformation to the End of the Last Century*, Vol. III (London, 1873).

Hunt, N. C., *A Consideration of the Relationship between some Religious and Economic Organisations and the Government, especially from 1730 to 1742* (Unpublished Cambridge Ph.D., 1951).

Sir Robert Walpole, Samuel Holden, and the Dissenting Deputies (London, 1957).

Jeremy, Walter D., *The Presbyterian Fund and Dr. Daniel Williams's Trust* (London, 1885).
Jones, M. G., *The Charity School Movement* (Cambridge, 1938).
Jones, R. M., *The Later Period of Quakerism* (London, 1921).
Jordan, W. K., *The Development of Religious Toleration in England from the Reformation to the Restoration*, 4 Vols. (Cambridge, Mass., 1932–1940).
Keir, D. L., *The Constitutional History of Modern Britain*, 3rd ed. (London, 1946).
Kendrick, Sir Thomas, *The Lisbon Earthquake* (London, 1956).
King, Lord Peter, *The Life of John Locke*, 2 Vols. (London, 1830).
Lathbury, Thomas, *A History of the Convocation of the Church of England* (London, 1853).
Lecky, W. E. H., *A History of England in the Eighteenth Century*, 7 Vols. (London, 1892 ed.).
Lincoln, Anthony, *Some Political and Social Ideas of English Dissent, 1763–1800* (Cambridge, 1936).
Lockitt, C. H., *The Relations of French and English Society, 1763–1793* (London, 1920).
Lyon, Thomas, *The Theory of Religious Liberty in England, 1603–1639* (Cambridge, 1937).
Macaulay, T. B., *The History of England from the Accession of James II*, 6 Vols. (New York, 1866 ed.).
Maccoby, Simon, *English Radicalism, 1762–1785* (London, 1955).
English Radicalism, 1785–1832 (London, 1955).
Mackinnon, James, *A History of Modern Liberty*, Vol. IV (London, 1941).
McLachlan, Herbert, *English Education under the Test Acts* (Manchester, 1931).

The Religious Opinions of Milton, Locke, and Newton (Manchester, 1941).

The Unitarian Movement in the Religious Life of England (London, 1934).

MacLean, Kenneth, *John Locke and English Literature of the Eighteenth Century* (New Haven, 1936).

Maitland, F. W., *The Constitutional History of England* (Cambridge, 1918).

Manning, B. L., *Essays in Orthodox Dissent* (London, 1939).

The Protestant Dissenting Deputies (Cambridge, 1952).

Middelton, J. W., *An Ecclesiastical Memoir of the Reign of George the Third* (London, 1822).

Mossner, E. C., *Bishop Butler and the Age of Reason* (New York, 1936).

Murch, Jerome, *Presbyterian and General Baptist Churches in the West of England* (London, 1835).

Namier, Sir Lewis, *England in the Age of the American Revolution* (London, 1930).

The Structure of Politics at the Accession of George III, 2d ed. (London, 1957).

Overton, J. H. and Relton, Frederick, *The English Church from the Accession of George I to the End of the Eighteenth Century* (London, 1906).

Parker, Irene, *The Dissenting Academies* (Cambridge, 1914).

Parkin, Charles, *The Moral Basis of Burke's Political Thought* (Cambridge, 1956).

Pattison, Mark, "Tendencies of Religious Thought in England, 1688–1750," in *Essays* ed. by Henry Nettleship, Vol. II (Oxford, 1889).

Plumb, J. H., *Chatham* (London, 1953).

The First Four Georges (London, 1956).

Sir Robert Walpole (London, 1956).

Pollock, Frederick, "The Theory of Persecution" in *Essays on Jurisprudence and Ethics* (London, 1882), pp. 144–175.

Rees, Thomas, *A Sketch of the History of the Regium Donum* (London, 1834).
Robbins, Caroline, *The Eighteenth-Century Commonwealthman* (Cambridge, Mass., 1959).
Roth, Cecil, *A History of the Jews in England*, 2d ed. (Oxford, 1949).
Rowden, A. W., *The Primates of the Four Georges* (London, 1916).
Ruffini, Francesco, *Religious Liberty*, J. P. Heyes trans. (London, 1912).
Russell Smith, H. F., *Religious Liberty in the Reigns of Charles II and James II* (Cambridge, 1911).
St. John, Wallace, *The Contest for Liberty of Conscience in England* (Chicago, 1900).
Schaff, Philip, *The Progress of Religious Freedom as shown in the History of Toleration Acts* (New York, 1889).
—— *The Toleration Act of 1689* (London, 1888).
Scudi, Abbie T., *The Sacheverell Affair* (New York, 1939).
Seaton, A. A., *The Theory of Toleration under the Later Stuarts* (Cambridge, 1911).
Seymour, A. C. H., *The Life and Times of Silena, Countess of Huntingdon*, 2 Vols. (London, 1844).
Skeats, Herbert S., *A History of the Free Churches of England from A.D. 1688 to A.D. 1851*, 2d ed. (London, 1869).
A Sketch of the History and Proceedings of the Deputies (London, 1813).
Smith, J. W. Ashley, *The Birth of Modern Education* (London, 1954).
Smyth, Charles, "Archbishop Herring and the '45," *The Church Quarterly Review* (London, April–June, 1946), pp. 30–47.
Stephen, Leslie, *A History of English Thought in the Eighteenth Century*, 2 Vols. (New York, 1902 ed.).

"Poisonous Opinions," in *An Agnostic's Apology and Other Essays* (London, 1893).

Stoughton, John, *Religion in England under Queen Anne and the Georges,* 2 Vols. (London, 1878).

Stromberg, Roland N., *Religious Liberalism in Eighteenth-Century England* (London, 1954).

Sykes, Norman, *Church and State in England in the Eighteenth Century* (Cambridge, 1934).

"The Duke of Newcastle as Ecclesiastical Minister," *The English Historical Review* (January, 1942).

Edmund Gibson (Oxford, 1926).

From Sheldon to Secker (Cambridge, 1959).

William Wake, 2 Vols. (Cambridge, 1957).

Tayler, John J., *A Retrospect of the Religious Life of England* (London, 1876).

Thomas, Roger, "The Non-Subscription Controversy amongst Dissenters in 1719," *The Journal of Ecclesiastical History,* Vol. IV., pp. 162–186 (London, 1953).

Thomas, Roland, *Richard Price, Philosopher and Apostle of Liberty* (London, 1924).

Trevelyan, G. M., *England under Queen Anne,* 3 Vols. (London, 1934).

Urwick, William, *Nonconformity in Cheshire* (London, 1864).

Waddington, John, *Congregational History, 1700–1800* (London, 1876).

Webb, Sidney and Beatrice, *The Manor and the Borough,* 2 Vols. (London, 1908).

Whitney, W. T., *The Baptists of London* (London, 1928).

Willey, Basil, *The Seventeenth Century Background* (London, 1953 ed.).

The Eighteenth Century Background (London, 1953 ed.).

Williams, Basil, *The Whig Supremacy* (Oxford, 1939).

Wilson, Walter, *The History and Antiquities of Dissenting*

Meeting Houses in London, Westminster, and Southwark, 4 Vols. (London, 1808).

Wright, Thomas, *A Caricature History of the Georges* (London, 1904 ed.).

ACKNOWLEDGMENTS

The author wishes to express his appreciation to the following publishers and owners of copyrights for permission to print quotations or summaries from sections of their materials:

Cambridge University Press for Anthony Lincoln, *Some Political and Social Ideas of English Dissent* (1938). B. L. Manning, *The Protestant Dissenting Deputies* (1952). H. F. Russell Smith, *Religious Liberty under Charles II and James II* (1911). Norman Sykes, *Church and State in England in the Eighteenth Century* (1934). *From Sheldon to Secker* (1959). *William Wake*, 2 Vols. (1957).

Basil Cozens-Hardy for *The Diary of Sylas Neville, 1767–1788* (Oxford, 1950).

The Friends of Dr. Williams's Library for N. C. Hunt's lecture on *Sir Robert Walpole, Samuel Holden, and the Dissenting Deputies* (Oxford University Press, 1957).

George Allen and Unwin for Simon Maccoby, *English Radicalism, 1762–1785* (1955).

Manchester University Press for Herbert McLachlan, *The Letters of Theophilus Lindsey* (1920).

Methuen and Company for William Matthews, ed., *The Diary of Dudley Ryder, 1715–1716* (1939).

Oxford University Press for Cecil Roth, *A History of the Jews in England* (1948, 2 ed.).

Routledge and Kegan Paul for Nicholas Hans, *New Trends in Education in the Eighteenth Century* (1951).

The Westminster Press (Philadelphia) for R. H. Bainton, *The Travail of Religious Liberty* (1951).

The Trustees of Dr. Williams's Library, London, for the use of manuscripts related to this study.

INDEX

Abernethy, John, 78–79
Abney, Sir Thomas, 66–67
Abney, Thomas Jr. 68
Act of Union, 151, 154, 156, 159, 169, 205
Adair, James, 201n
Aikin, John, D.D., 277
Aikin, John, M.D., 277, 279–280, 289
American Revolution, 130, 194, 197, 203, 207, 215, 218, 251, 297
Amory, Dr. T., 173
Amory, W., 254n
Anne, Queen, 60, 63
Annet, Peter, 130
Arianism, 128–129
Arlington, Henry Bennet, Earl, 17
Arminianism, 58, 129
Arundel, Lord, 204n
Athanasian Creed, 114, 117
Atterbury, Francis, Bishop, 67
Avery, Benjamin, 93–94, 96

Bagot, Sir William, M.P., 177, 186–187
Bainton, Professor R. H., 34
Balguy, John, 45
Balguy, Thomas, Archdeacon, 144–145
Bangorian Controversy, 44–46
Baptists, 18, 22, 72, 76, 104
Barbauld, Anna Laetitia, 277–279, 298
Barklay, James, 130
Barlow, Thomas, Bishop, 16, 25, 28–32, 40, 56, 295
Barnard, Sir John, M.P., 121
Barnardiston, Nathaniel, 227n
Barnstaple, meeting to oppose repeal, 257–258

Barrington, J. S., Viscount, 67, 72, 73n, 77n, 79–80
Barrington, Shute, Bishop, 179, 183, 196, 198
Barron, Richard, 133n, 135n,, 136
Bates, Dr. William, 58
Baxter, Richard, 18
Beauchamp, Lord, 235–236
Beauclerk, James, Bishop, 109n
Beaufoy, Henry, M.P., 227n, 232–233, 234, 237–238, 243–244, 264, 268
Bennet, Joseph, 57
Benson, George, 110–111
Benson, Robert, 234n
Berington, Joseph, 240–241
Birmingham, Lunar Society, 131
  Revolutionary Society, 284–285
  Riots, 283–285
Blackburne, Francis, Archdeacon, 120, 137–139, 148–149, 168, 171, 205
Blackstone, Sir William, 160–169
Boddington, Benjamin, 223n
Boddington, Thomas, 223n
Bond, John, 223n
Boston, Lincolnshire, Meeting of Dissenters, 269
Boulton, Matthew, 131
Bourn, Benjamin, 122
Bourn, Samuel, 111
Boyle, Robert, 28n
Bradberry, David, 249
Bradbury, Thomas, 77n, 79–80n
Bradney, John, 223n
Bridges, George, 130
Brown, John, 123n, 198n
Brown, William Laurence, 290–291

Buck, William, 276
Buckingham, Lord, 17
Burke, Edmund, 151n, 154–156, 157, 159, 161, 171, 176–177, 186–187, 205, 212, 241, 268–270, 279–280, 292
Burnet, Gilbert, Bishop, 21, 24–25, 295
Bute, John Stuart, Third Earl, 132–133
Butler, John, Bishop, 181
Butler, Joseph, Bishop, 45, 172

Calamy, Edmund, 20, 34, 57–58, 66n, 77n
Calamy, Edmund III, 257n
Calvin, John, 28, 33
Calvinism, 16–17, 33–34, 128
Calvinist Dissenters, 183–188
Camden, Charles Pratt, Lord, 189
Catham, I., 254n
Catholic Relief Act of 1778, 204–207, 210–213
Catholic Relief Act of 1791, 282–283, 286
Catlow, Samuel, 249
Chambers, Robert, 187–188
Chandler, Samuel, 85, 89, 94, 96, 113–116
Charles I, 108, 177
Charles II, 17–19, 71
Chatham, William Pitt, First Lord, 132, 179
Chester, meeting of clergy to oppose repeal, 259–260
Chubb, Thomas, 130
Clare, Lord Robert, 176
Clerical petition movement, 138–160, 186, 296
Clifford, Thomas, 17
Cockayne, William, 108
Comprehension project, 18–19, 21–22
Conder, Dr. John, 173
Confessional, 138, 144–145
Convocation of Canterbury, 60

Cooke, Richard, 223n
Cooper, Benjamin, 254n
Cooper, I., 254n
Cornwallis, Archbishop, 151n, 201
Coronation Oath, 151, 154, 159, 169
Corporation Act:
 Provisions, 71–72
 Amendment of 1719, 74–75
 Attempts at Repeal:
  1736, 80–93;
  1739, 94–97;
  1787, 223–238;
  1789, 243–249;
  1790, 264–271
Coventry, the Hon. Henry, 17
Cowper, E., 254n
Coxe, William, 252–253
Cromwell, Oliver, 121
Crown and Anchor Societies, 288–289, 291

Darwin, Erasmus, 131
Davis, S., 254n
Dawson, Benjamin, 147–148
De Coetlogan, Charles, 262n
Defoe, Daniel, 73n, 76
Disney, John, 160, 168, 200–201
Dissenters' Relief Bill of 1779, 207–209
Dissenting Academies, 58–64, 126–129
Doddridge, Philip, 128–129
Dodson, Michael, 175, 227n, 281–282, 286, 288, 294–298
Dolben, Sir William, M.P., 175–177, 179, 237, 241, 270
Dormer, Lord, 235n
Dowdswell, William, 157
Dowson, John, 223n
Duncan, John, 143
Dunning, John, M.P., 154, 204
Dyson, Jeremiah, M.P., 174, 186, 194

Erskine, James, 206n

INDEX 343

Eccles, Samuel, 122
Eden, Robert, 106–107
Edwards, Thomas, 139–141
Edwin, Sir Humphrey, 66
Egmont, John Percival, First Earl, 84
Enfield, Dr. William, 241–242
Esdaile, Sir James, 227n
Essex Street Chapel, 158, 281
Evans, Allen, 100–101
Evanson, Edward, 158, 160, 168
Exeter Academy, 128

Favell, Samuel, 254n
Fawcett, Benjamin, 199
Feathers Tavern Association, 149–150, 186
Fell, Israel, 75n
Findern Academy, 128
Five Mile Act, 59
Fleming, Caleb, 85–86, 89, 109–110, 134–135, 150n
Foster, Michael, 68, 101n
Foster, Nathaniel, 146–147
Fownes, Joseph, 169–170, 190
Fox, Charles James, 156–157, 159, 167–168, 171, 212, 222n, 237, 245–247, 264–268, 270, 283n, 286–287, 292
Frankland, Richard, 59
Franklin, Benjamin, 131
French, James Bogle, 223n
French Revolution, 197, 229, 241, 249, 251, 253, 265, 270, 283–284, 287–288, 290, 297
Fryer, Sir John, 67
Fuller, William, 223n
Furneaux, Philip, 131, 164–168, 171–173, 190–191, 207

Galton, Samuel, 131
Gascoigne, Sir Crisp, 121
General Body of Dissenting Ministers, 80, 171–175, 177–179, 182–184, 189, 221, 254–256, 289–290

General Election of:
1734, 88;
1741, 97;
1772, 178;
1780, 212–213;
1784, 222;
1790, 264, 270n
George I, 67, 69, 73, 77n
George II, 111
George III, 131, 133n, 135n, 151n, 178–179, 189n, 285, 296
Germaine, Sir George, M.P., 125n, 151
Gibbons, Dr. Thomas, 173
Gibson, Edmund, Bishop, 76, 84–85, 90, 95
Gideon, Samson, 121
Gooch, Sir Thomas, Bishop, 113–114
Gordon, Lord George, 205–206, 210
Gordon Riots, 212, 285
Gordon, Thomas, 136
Grafton, Henry, Third Duke, 150–151n
Graham, William, 116
Green, John, Bishop, 189n
Grey, Richard, 90
Grosvenor, Benjamin, 135
Grosvenor, Robert, 99–100
Grove, Henry, 128
Grubb, Edward, 254n
Gumoy, I., 254n
Gwatkin, H. M., 17–18

Hackney Academy, 127
Hales, Stephen, 124
Halifax, George Savile, Marquis, 17, 20
Hall, Samuel, 234n
Hamilton, W., 254n
Hans, Nicholas, 127n, 129–130
Harley, Robert, 62–63
Harlow, General Meeting of Dissenters, 269
Harris, C., 254n

Harris, Dr., Secretary to the General Body, 173n
Harris, William, 86, 89
Harrison v. Evans, 7, 160
Hawkes, M., 254n
Hayward, John Pemberton, 276
Heathcoat, Alderman, 92–93
Henley, John, 130
Henry VIII, 17
Heron, R., 254n
Herring, Thomas, Archbishop, 98, 114–115
Heywood, Samuel, 227n
Hill, Noah, 207n
Hills, R., 254n
Hinchcliffe, John, Bishop, 204
Hoadly, Benjamin, Bishop, 44–46, 94–95, 172
Hodge, John, 112
Holden, Samuel, 81–82, 87–89, 93, 101
Hollis, Thomas Brand, 221n
Hollis, Timothy, 227n
Hopkins, Benjamin Bond, M.P., 223
Horsley, Samuel, Bishop, 266
Houghton, Sir Henry ("Harry"), M.P., 156, 174, 175, 177, 178, 185, 207, 227n
Howard, John, 272
Howe, John, 58
Humphries, M., 254n
Hunt, Dr. N. C., 73, 81
Huntingdon, Selina, Countess, 151n
Hutchings, Richard, 185n

Indemnity Acts, 73–74, 228
Independents, 18, 22, 72, 76, 104
The Independent Whig, 136
Indulgence and toleration compared, 19n
Irish Act of 1774, 203, 282; 1779, 225
Irish Presbyterians, 77–78

Jacobins, 287, 289, 290, 293
Jacobite Rebellion of 1715, 69
James II, 17, 19, 20, 21
Jebb, John, 131, 140–142, 160, 168, 171, 212, 222n
Jeffries, Dr., 173
Jeffries, Edward and the Jeffries Committee, 223n, 224, 227–232, 240–241, 243, 249, 252–253, 254, 256, 264, 272–276, 281, 283
Jenkinson, Charles, M.P., 129
Jennings, John, 129
Jennings, Nathaniel, 207n
Jenyns, Soame, 124, 125n
Jew Bill, 120–122
Johnson, James, 223n
Johnson, Dr. Samuel, 162n, 163n
Johnston, E., 254n
Johnstone, Sir James, M.P., 235, 244
Jones, John, 116–118
Jordan, Professor W. K., 17
Joseph II, Emperor, 229

Kemble, F., 254n
Kemp v. Wickes, 99
Kendal Academy, 128
Kibworth Academy, 145
The King v. Samuel Hall, 234n
Kippis, Andrew, 131, 173, 191–192, 207–209, 211, 221–223, 254n

Langford, John, 185n
Lauderdale, John Maitland, Earl, 17
Law, Edmund, Bishop, 150n
Lawson, Sir Wilfred, M.P., 91
Lecky, W. E. H., 124
Lee, John, M.P., 227n, 254n
Leeds, Edward, 68
Leeds, meeting of clergy to oppose repeal, 258
Leopard, I., 254n
Lincoln, Anthony, 16, 25
Lindsey, Theophilus, 131, 149–151, 157–160, 168, 171, 281–283, 284, 286, 291–293, 297

Lisbon Earthquake, 122–124
Litchfield and Coventry, Ecclesiastical Court, 60
Liverpool Chronicle, 126, 243
Liverpool Debating Club, 129
Lobb, Samuel, 107
Locke John, 16, 24, 33, 35–44, 48–51, 54–56, 134, 167, 170n, 172, 177, 190–192, 198, 213–218, 226, 237, 295
Lofft, Capel, 254n, 264n
London Journal, 126
London, meeting of clergy to oppose repeal, 259
London, Sheriffs' Cases, 94, 100
London Society for Constitutional Information, 293
Louis XIV, 66
Louis XVI, 284
Lowdell, Stephen, 223–224n
Lowman, Moses, 135
Lunar Society of Birmingham, 131
Luther, Martin, 28
Lutheranism, 16–17
Lyttelton, Lord George, 179, 189

Maccoby, Simon, 132
Mackintosh, James, 280
Maitland, John, 227n
Manchester Chronicle, 243
Manning, B. L., 81, 98
Mansell, Sir Philip, 266n
Mansfield, Lord Chief Justice, 160, 162, 167–168, 188–189, 194, 234n
Mansion House Fund, 94, 100
Margarot, W., 292
Martin, James, M.P., 227n
Martin, John, 255–256n
Martyrdom sermons, 109n
Mawbey, Sir Joseph, 212
Mayo, Dr. Henry, 173n, 179n, 182, 256n

Meredith, Sir William, M.P., 151, 156, 158–159
Methodists, 151n, 210–211
Middlesex Election, 162n
Mile End Academy, 128n
Milner, Dr. John, 210
Milton, John, 16, 24–29, 32, 40, 56, 294
Móntague, Frederick, M.P., 176, 207
Moore, John, 128
Morgan, W., 254n
Moult, Robert Wylde, 276
Mount, William, 227n
Muir, Thomas, 291–292

Neville, Sylas, 133n, 135n, 150n
Newcastle, Thomas Pelham-Holles, Duke, 98, 115
Newdigate, Sir Roger, M.P., 151–152, 156, 159, 175, 177, 185–186
Newton, Thomas, Bishop, 179–181
Nicholson, William, Bishop, 71
Nonjouror schism, 22
Norfolk, Bernard Howard, Twelfth Duke, 204n
Northampton Academy, 127
Northampton Mercury, 126
North Briton, 133
North, Lord Frederick, 151n, 154, 156–157, 159, 169, 171, 188, 208–209, 212, 222n, 223, 225, 241, 244, 277
Norwich Mercury, 126
Nottingham, Daniel Finch, Second Earl, 21, 65, 69
Nullum tempus axiom, 156–157

Occasional conformity, 64–68
Occasional Paper, 135–136
Oldfield, Dr. Joshua, 59–60
Onslow, George, M.P., 157, 174, 176, 194
Oswald, M., 173n, 179n, 184

Owen, John, 16, 25, 32–35, 40, 56, 94

Packington, Sir John, M.P., 60
Page, Francis, M.P., 186–187
Paice, Joseph, 224n
Paine, Thomas, 280–281, 287, 291, 297
Paley, William, Archdeacon, 201–202, 219, 295
Palmer, John, 183n
Palmer, Thomas Fysche, 291–292
Parker, Irene, 127n
Parker, William, 108–109
Parry, William, 261–262
Pearce, Samuel, 263
Pearson, M., 254n
Peckwell, Henry, 256n
Pelham, Henry, 120
Petre, Lord, 203
Phipps, Constantine, M.P., 176
Pickard, Edward, 171–174, 177–178, 181–184, 189, 207
Pickering, Roger, 108
Pickering, Thomas, 109–110
Pitt, Thomas, M.P., 151, 154, 156
Pitt, William, 221–223, 235–237, 238–239, 241, 247–248, 264, 267–268, 277, 283n, 287, 292–293, 295–298
Plumb, Dr. J. H., 126
Plummer, William, M.P., 90–92
Polwarth, Lord, 92–93
Pope, John, 288–289
Pope, M., 173
Porteous, Beilby, Bishop, 150–151n, 158n
Porteous, William, 206n
Portland, William Bentinck, Third Duke, 292–293
Presbyterians, 18, 21, 72, 77
Price, Richard, 110n, 131–132, 173, 200, 211, 215, 222, 241, 249–254, 269, 297

Priestley, Joseph, 101n, 131–132, 161–165, 170n, 179, 195–198, 202n, 211, 217, 222, 237–240, 269, 280, 286, 291, 297
Proast, Jonas, 28, 42–44, 56, 295
Protestant Association, 210–211
Protestant Dissenting Deputies, 81–82, 87–89, 93–102, 178, 221, 254, 256–257
Pye, Benjamin, 143

Quadruple Alliance, 70
Quakers, 23, 75, 76n, 221
Quebec Act, 138, 230

Radcliffe, Ebenezer, 182
Rathmell Academy, 59
Raymond, John, 224n
Rebellion of 1715, 69
Rebellion of 1745, 125
Reder, William, 130
Rees, Dr. Abraham, 207n
Rees, Abraham Jr., 254n
Registry Act of 1784, 221–222
Regium Donum, 77n, 195
Revolution of 1688, 241–242, 251
Reynolds, George, Archdeacon, 105–106
Reynolds, Thomas, 57, 62n
Richardson, John, 110
Richmond, Lord Charles, 179, 188
Rickards, Thomas, 227n
Robin Hood Society, 129–131
Robinson, Robert, 192, 269
Robles, Matthew, 104–105
Rockingham, Charles Wentworth, Marquis, 204
Rogers, Thomas, 143
Roe, Samuel, 143
Roman Catholics, 23, 76, 84, 170n, 203–207, 210–211, 229, 246–247, 263, 264n, 282–283
Rousseau, J. J., 200n
Ryder, Dudley, 68–69

INDEX

Sacheverell, Henry, 23, 61, 120, 153, 169, 273
St. John, Henry, 62, 67
Salters' Hall controversy, 77n, 103
Sancroft, William, Archbishop, 20–21
Savage, Dr., 173
Savile, Sir George, M.P., 159, 174, 204, 207
Schism Act, 62–64
Scott, John of Amwell, 162n
Scottish reaction to the Roman Catholic Relief Act of 1778, 205–206
Seagrave, Robert, 94–95, 118–119
Secker, Thomas, Archbishop, 137, 138n
Seditious Meetings Act, 293
Seldon, William, 203
Seymour, Henry, M.P., 156–157
Shaftesbury, Anthony Ashley Cooper, First Earl, 17
Sharp, John, Archbishop, 60
Sharp, William, 170n, 254
Shelburne, Lord, 131, 179, 189, 204
Shepherd, Richard, 145
Sherlock, Thomas, Bishop, 82–83, 114, 231, 295
Shore, Samuel Jr., 227n
Sinclair, Sir John, 227n
Skinner, John, M.P., 157
Skirving, M., 292
Smith, James, 224n
Smith, Joseph, 261–262
Smith, Samuel, 227n, 235
Smith, William, M.P., 227n, 244, 245, 270
Smithers, H., 254
Somers, Sir John, 58, 61
Southampton, meeting to oppose repeal, 258
Spanish Succession, War of, 61–62, 70
Stanhope, James, Earl, 67, 69–70

Stanley, B., 254n
Stanley, Hans, M.P., 152–153
Stebbing, Henry, 16, 25, 28, 42, 44–46, 56, 144, 145–147, 295
Steele, Sir Richard, 62n
Stennett, Dr. Samuel, 173
Stillingfleet, Edward, Archbishop, 18
Stone, I. H., 254n
Sturges, John, 201–202, 218
Subscription to the Thirty-Nine Articles, 139–156
Suffolk County, meeting to oppose repeal, 260
Sunderland, Charles, 64
Swift, Jonathan, 72n
Sykes, Arthur Ashley, 90

Tunstall, James, 107–108
Taunton Academy, 128
Tayleur, William, 286, 291
Taylor, Jeremy, 15n
Taylor, Dr. John, 112–113, 116, 127–129
Temple, Anthony, 142
Test Act:
    Provisions, 72
    Attempts at Repeal:
        1736, 80–93;
        1739, 94–97;
        1787, 233–238;
        1789, 243–249;
        1790, 264–267
Thirty-Nine Articles, 23, 58, 114, 116–120, 139–156, 177, 296
Thomas, Benjamin, 198–199
Thomas, John, Bishop, 108
Thomson, David, 73, 74n
Thornton, Henry, M.P., 227n
Thornton, Robert, M.P., 227n
Thornton, Samuel, M.P., 227n
Throckmorton, Sir John, 203
Tillotson, John, Archbishop, 18
Toleration Act, 22, 98, 100, 107, 160–167

Toleration and indulgence compared, 19n
Toller, M., 173n
Tomkins, B., 254n
Toulmin, Joshua, 110n, 131, 199, 211, 218–219, 222
Towers, John, 224n
Towers, Joseph, 131, 161–162n, 163n, 182, 211, 213, 216–220, 254n, 288
Towgood, Matthew, 224n
Townshend, Charles, Second Viscount, 64
Townshend, Thomas, M.P., 186
Treasonable Practices Act, 293
Trenchard, John, 136
Tucker, Josiah, Dean, 168–169, 201–202, 213–218, 295
Turner, William, 58

Unitarian Society, 286–287
University Subscription, 159, 160

Vaughn, Benjamin, 227n
Vowler, M., 254n

Waindright, M., 254n
Wake, William, Archbishop, 21, 70–71
Wakefield, Gilbert, 131
Walker, George, 261–262
Wallin, M., 173
Walpole, Sir Robert, 71, 78, 81–82, 88–89, 91–93, 96, 295, 297
Warburton, William, Bishop, 16, 25, 28, 42, 52–56, 109n, 137, 144, 146, 160, 167, 170n,, 259, 260, 267, 295
Warrington Academy, 127–128
Warsley, M., 254n
Warwickshire, meeting to oppose repeal, 258–259
Watson, James, 227n

Watson, John, 117–118
Watt, James, 131
Watts, Isaac, 102–104
Webb, James, 207n
Webb, Sidney and Beatrice, 75
Wedderburn, Alexander, 156
Wedgewood, Josiah, 131
Wesley, John, 163n, 210, 211n
Wesley, M., 254n
West, James, 227n
Weston, A., 254n
Weston, Edward, 122–123
Weston, I., 254n
White, John, 103–104
Whitmore, Thomas, M.P., 227n
Whitefield, George, 94
Wilberforce, William, 270, 293
Wilkes, John, 126, 133, 162n, 202n
William III, 59–60, 66, 241
Williams, Daniel, 72, 73n
Williams, David, 193–195, 198
Wilson, Walter, 113
Wilson, William, 224n
Wilton, Samuel, 188–189n, 199, 207
Winter, Captain James, 87–88
Winterbottom, William, 291–292
Wollaston, Francis, 151n, 158n
Wood, John, 202
Wood, William, 241
Wray, Sir Cecil, 222n
Wright, Samuel, 135
Wyvill, Christopher, 147–148, 212, 216n, 222n

Yathard, M., 254n
Yerbury, John, 224n
York, Archiepiscopal Court, 59
Yorkshire, General Meeting of Protestant Dissenters, 276
Yorkshire, meeting of clergy to oppose repeal, 259